THE WORLD AT PLAY IN BOCCACCIO'S
Decameron

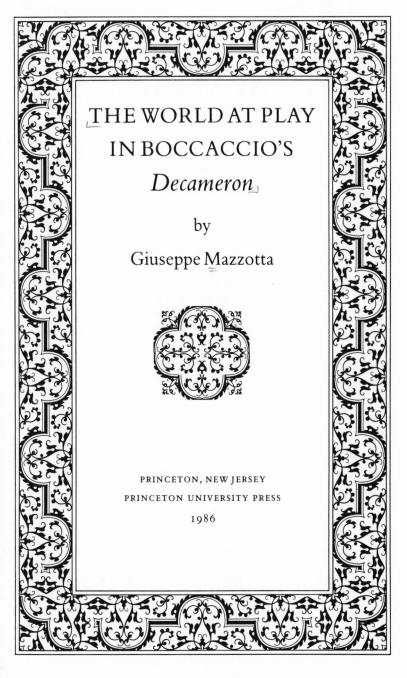

THE WORLD AT PLAY
IN BOCCACCIO'S
Decameron

by

Giuseppe Mazzotta

PRINCETON, NEW JERSEY

PRINCETON UNIVERSITY PRESS

1986

LIBRARY OF CONGRESS CATALOGING IN PUBLICATION
DATA WILL BE FOUND ON THE LAST PRINTED PAGE OF THIS BOOK

ISBN 0-691-06677-9

THIS BOOK HAS BEEN COMPOSED IN LINOTRON BEMBO

CLOTHBOUND EDITIONS OF PRINCETON UNIVERSITY
PRESS BOOKS ARE PRINTED ON ACID-FREE
PAPER, AND BINDING MATERIALS
ARE CHOSEN FOR STRENGTH
AND DURABILITY

★

PRINTED IN THE UNITED STATES
OF AMERICA BY PRINCETON UNIVERSITY PRESS
PRINCETON, NEW JERSEY

For
Rosanna, for Antony,
and for Paula

Time is a child playing, moving counters on a game-board: the kingdom belongs to a child.
                                        HERACLITUS

For to declare it once and for all, man plays only when he is in the full sense of the word a man, and he is only wholly man when he is playing. This proposition . . . will assume great and deep significance; it will, I promise you, support the whole fabric of aesthetic art, and the still more difficult art of living.   J.C.F. SCHILLER

For the Logos on high plays stirring the whole cosmos back and forth, as he wills, into shapes of every kind.   GREGORY (OF) NAZIANZUS

" 'I was daily his delight, always making play before him.' PROV. 8:30"
      AS QUOTED BY ST. THOMAS AQUINAS,
                              Expositio super Boethium

CONTENTS

ACKNOWLEDGMENTS

It is always difficult to pinpoint the origin of a book. But to me
this book is certainly tied to the unforgettable period in which
I learned and taught at Cornell University. And so it becomes
easy, as I look back, to recognize the seeds of its various chapters in the many happy hours I spent there talking about exile,
basketball, the soul, love, movies, politics, with friends and
colleagues. A special place in my mind is occupied by the constant memory of Eugenio Donato. I still grieve as I remember
how often we tired the sun with our talking and sent him
down the sky. In the same breath I mention John Freccero,
who, among other things, spoke to me about margins one
Sunday afternoon in Rome; Bob Kaske, in whose living room,
while watching the World Series, I began thinking seriously,
(how else?) about play; David Grossvogel, Ralph Johnson, Pi-
ero Pucci, Pete Wetherbee, Roberto Gonzalez, Richard Klein,
Albert Ascoli, Enrico Santi, Mihai Spariosu, Robbie Harri-
son, Tony Caputi. They, who well know Boccaccio's art of
conversation and conviviality, will come to see, I hope, some
flickers of their own light in this work.

 The extraordinary help of two other friends, Tom Hill and
Phil Lewis, must be especially acknowledged. They alone read
the manuscript in its entirety and, from their different perspectives, improved the quality of my writing. I also owe a special
thanks to Charlotte Rosen, who helped me find the title of the
book; to the two anonymous readers from Princeton University Press who read with great care; to Kristen Olsen who
typed an early draft. But the research would not have been
completed without an ACLS fellowship that enabled me in
1978–79 to live and work in Rome and the fellowship awarded
by the Society for the Humanities at Cornell during the aca-

demic year 1980–81. Finally, I acknowledge permission to reprint, with some changes, three chapters. The bulk of chapter 2, "The Marginality of Literature" first appeared as "The *Decameron*: The Marginality of Literature," *The University of Toronto Quarterly*, 42 (1972), pp. 64–81; chapter 4 is a partial rewriting of "The *Decameron*: The Literal and the Allegorical," *Italian Quarterly*, 18 (1975), pp. 53–73; chapter 7 is a slight revision of "Games of Laughter in the *Decameron*," *Romanic Review*, 49 (1978), pp. 115–131.

BIBLIOGRAPHIC NOTE

All quotations from the *Decameron*, unless otherwise stated, are taken from *Tutte le opere di Giovanni Boccaccio*, vol. IV, *Decameron*, ed. Vittore Branca (Milan, 1976). I have used Roman and Arabic numerals in the body of my text to indicate respectively the day and the novella to be discussed. For the sake of clarity I have given the page number, which always refers to Branca's edition, for each quotation. The translations from the *Decameron* are mine. I have, however, kept steadily before my eyes the translations by G. H. McWilliam (New York: Penguin Books, 1972); the recent one by Mark Musa and Peter Bondanella (New York: New American Library, 1982), and G. Boccaccio, *Decameron. The John Payne Translation*, rev. Charles S. Singleton (Berkeley: University of California Press, 1982).

A few special editions and translations of other texts are mentioned so frequently that I have chosen to cite them in abbreviated form throughout, to avoid constant repetition of bibliographic data. These are:

The Art of Courtly Love, trans. Parry :
> Andreas Capellanus, *The Art of Courtly Love*, trans. Parry (New York, Norton & Co., 1969)

Boccaccio on Poetry, trans. Osgood :
> *Boccaccio on Poetry*, trans. Charles G. Osgood (Indianapolis-New York, The Bobbs-Merrill Co., 1956)

Isidore of Seville, *Etym.* :
> Isidore of Seville, *Etymologiarum sive originum libri xx*, ed. W. M. Lindsay (Oxford: Clarenden, 1966)

PL : *Patrologia Latina*, ed. J. P. Migne (Paris: 1844–64), with later printings.

Le Roman de la Rose, ed. Langlois :
> Jean de Meun, *Le Roman de la Rose*, ed. Ernest Langlois, 5 vols. (Paris: Champion, 1914–22)

The Romance of the Rose, trans. Dahlberg :
> *The Romance of the Rose*, trans. Charles Dahlberg (Princeton: Princeton University Press, 1971)

Complete bibliographic data is given for all other references upon first mention in each chapter.

PREFACE

The *Decameron* has long been acknowledged as a classic, but, as is so often the case in literary history, such a distinction, undisputed for this text, carries with it a clear drawback. The chief liability of a classic is, paradoxically, at one with its canonization. It is as if the special aura that surrounds a classic engenders the tendency to treat it as untouchable, to make it the object of perfunctory critical pieties which in fact desiccate the text's imaginative powers.

It would not be entirely accurate to claim that such has been the fate of the *Decameron*. Recent critical thought has managed on several occasions to respond to the textual subtleties and energy of Boccaccio's prose, but the bulk of the scholarship consists in partial, isolated accounts of sundry thematic motifs or clusters of tales or in perspectives which rarely move beyond the overt, surface significations of the text.

The present study, which is certainly not the first of its kind, suggests a mode of reading within which the lavish heterogeneity of the narrative can begin to be interpreted. What this mode of reading is can be quickly told. It is primarily an analysis of the metaphoric patterns and the way metaphors shed light on one another; more generally, each chapter retrieves a particular intellectual tradition which the *Decameron* evokes—medical texts, for instance, and Boccaccio's sense of the crisis of scientific discourse, the vocabulary and values of courtly love, legal lore, etc.—in order to define the cultural frame of reference for the narrative. But each chapter returns to the question of the role literature plays in Boccaccio's concerns. It cannot come as a surprise to hear that for Boccaccio literature and the resources of imagination and desire, which are the matter of literature, shape every experience in the *Decameron*.

As such it can claim a unique role in assessing the myths of the world. But literature also exceeds the reductive, cramped confines of literalism and thematic formulations. In the steady oscillation between surface literal values and the play of the imagination lies the at once delightful and unsettling power of the *Decameron*.

THE WORLD AT PLAY IN BOCCACCIO'S
Decameron

INTRODUCTION

From the time when just a few of its stories were circulating and there was no inkling of its overall narrative design, the *Decameron* has been viewed as something of a scandal in the canon of Italian and European letters. In the wake of its publication there was, to be sure, an extraordinary flowering in the genre of storytelling, and the names of Giovanni Fiorentino, Sercambi, Sacchetti and Masuccio legitimately belong to the prose tradition Boccaccio established. But the generous acknowledgments and imitations that came from these quarters markedly differ from the patronizing reception accorded to the *Decameron* by the more conspicuous intellectuals of Italian Humanism.

The rigor of their scholarly standards did not make allowance for stories they saw simply as "domestic trifles," and they never hid either their preference for Boccaccio the humanist or their astonishment at his encyclopedic erudition that would find its way into works such as the *Genealogy of the Gentile Gods*. One reasonably suspects a palpable condescension even in Petrarch's decision to translate the novella of Griselda into Latin. The gesture was primarily meant, no doubt, as a friendly recognition of Boccaccio's treatment of a grave matter, but the compliment was bound to appear double-edged. For it also amounted to suggesting the desirability of transplanting the tale into the tested, settled soil of Latin, presumably because Petrarch felt Latin to be adequate to the solemn cadence of the narrative, possibly because he thought it promised a more durable fame and certainly that it would fend off the noise and crowd of the marketplace.

Petrarch, at least in this respect, did not see very far. A reversal took place in the Renaissance, and, ironically, the *De-*

cameron, like Petrarch's own *Canzoniere*, became the repository of stylistic resources, the model for a supple language that
would fuel the debates among the Renaissance rhetoricians. It
is not in their writings, however, that one can hope to find the
awareness of the *Decameron*'s imaginative powers. The evidence of its substantial impact on literary history is available in
the works of a Castiglione, a Bembo or an Ariosto, but au-
thoritative, if lapidary, acknowledgments of its status as a classic occurred outside Italy. Leaving aside the case of Chaucer,
one could mention Montaigne, who, with sure instinct, in-
scribed the eccentricities of Rabelais' laughter in the tradition
of the *Decameron*, or Tirso de Molina, who called the Cervantes of the *Novelas ejemplares* the "Castilian Boccaccio."

It should probably be stressed that the geographic "outside"
perspective does not necessarily entail an inherent cognitive
privilege, nor should it be taken in too narrow a literal sense.
It is, above all, a metaphor, and as such it does bring out what
has been the drift of these preceding paragraphs, flagrantly
structured, as they are, in terms of an antithetical opposition
between writers who think from "within" the patterns of the
imagination and scholars who view literary texts only as reflections of cultural history. That the scheme is simplified and
not all that reliable is suggested by having Petrarch lined up
with the scholars. The opposition is of interest, nonetheless,
because it dramatizes what, in effect, were Boccaccio's own
ambivalences toward the *Decameron*, his shift from a passionate defense of the novelle, recorded within the text, to his narrative posture that the stories are nothing more than innocuous
pieces of entertainment for ladies, to the equally passionate re-
jection, in the letter to Mainardo Cavalcanti, of the book's
dangerous morality.

Boccaccio's ambivalences, all too well known to historians,
have never received a careful textual analysis. In the nineteenth
century, for instance, the ambivalences were viewed as symptoms of a historical shift from medieval spirituality, identified,
predictably enough, with Dante, to the vision of a secular mo-
dernity that the *Decameron* is said to embody. From Foscolo to

Schlegel (and Branca's account of the literary criticism of this period is exemplary),[1] the shift was taken to be a sign of decadence and the *Decameron* was viewed as the objective parable of the eclipse of traditonal moral values. This perspective is not altogether shared by De Sanctis, who is rightly credited with setting the future analyses of the *Decameron* on a solid ideological footing. In truth his judgments decisively leave behind the attitudes of the eighteenth-century rhetoricians, who would cull phrases from the collection or even marvel at the inimitable—and all too imitated—cadences of Boccaccio's prose in the conviction that its meaning was an irrelevant proposition. For De Sanctis there are no transcendent values or ideal significations in the *novelle*: their only morality is the morality of art, and their novelty, as it were, lies in the pursuit of realism—a handy, if to us vague, category that seeks to define Boccaccio's affirmations of a world bounded by the horizons of place and time, a world experienced as man's world.

This line of critical thought extends to our own days in the direction of sociological studies, which somewhat sharpen De Sanctis' understanding of the *Decameron* as a mimesis of reality and make it, perhaps more accurately, the mirror of the rising mercantile interests. It also extends in the direction of an ideological assertion whereby the *Decameron* comes to be read in terms of a militant polemic in favor of Naturalism. It could be said that the still rampant insistence that the *Decameron* tells the story of a relaxed amusement, comparable to the Humanists' *otium*, of an esthetic escape into a pleasant landscape, legitimately belongs to the same De Sanctis matrix as much as the other two positions just described.

This array of traditional reactions that the *Decameron* has steadily elicited in no way accounts for the remarkable vigor

[1] Vittore Branca, *Linee di una storia della critica al "Decameron"* (Milan: Società Anonima Editrice Dante Alighieri, 1939), esp. pp. 38–46. Branca's bibliographical work is supplemented in the general reviews by Franca Ageno in *Giornale storico della letteratura italiana*, 135 (1958), pp. 116–126 and A. E. Quaglio in the same journal, 137 (1960), pp. 409–438 and 142 (1965), pp. 581–613. For the recent bibliography, see the regular appendix in *Studi sul Boccaccio*.

and inventiveness that a number of recent individual studies have displayed. It does suggest, however, that De Sanctis' esthetic theories still cast their light on the contemporary critical debate: even some refined works, explicitly written in the last few years with the aim of arguing for the morality of Boccaccio's art and of reversing De Sanctis' assessment, remain caught within his ideology of literary history. For, like De Sanctis, whose esthetic criteria call for organic literary structures which would release a unified sense, they, too, want to find in the *Decameron* a univocal, abstract meaning, variously identifiable as the celebration of intelligence, social morality, realism, etc.

This sketch of the boundaries within which the criticism of the *Decameron* has been consistently articulated should not be taken as the familiar scholarly ploy of rejecting the misconceptions held by one's predecessors in order to justify as necessary one's own work. On the contrary, far from being discarded as aberrant, the various readings are recognized as responding to genuine concerns of Boccaccio's text. What is possibly objectionable in some particular critical procedures is their tendency to move from episodic and partial analyses to generalized conclusions, often at the risk of bypassing the specific formal structure—the overt narrative disjunctions, fragmentary viewpoints, overlapping narrators, shifty symbolic patterns, which one would expect to be the delight of contemporary semioticians and which demonstrably punctuate the textual unfolding of the *Decameron*. The conventional tendency to privilege a theme and make it the significant substance of the collection has as its inevitable consequence the reduction of the metaphoric obliquities, the contradictory voices and, in brief, the inflections of Boccaccio's esthetic imagination to a literal and "realistic" surface.

There is no doubt that the *Decameron*'s frame of reference is the natural, real world, but Boccaccio's vision of its value is much more troubled than critics have thought. What essentially lies at the core of this troubled vision is his awareness of the distance separating facts from values, the recognition of the instability of our common assumptions, as well as of the crisis investing moral and intellectual systems. But Boccaccio, who seems to have such a disenchanted, such a reassuring and well-adjusted gaze on the stage on which his characters play out their passions, is much too lucid not to explore how the real, the material solidity of the world and its exact identities, is the locus of the play of appearances and of steady imaginative displacements. One of the claims to be made in this book is that the *Decameron*, without ever leaving the world of reality and, actually, by sinking into it more deeply than has been acknowledged, launches us into the realm of the imagination where we confront the traps of delusion characters construct for others and, consequently, for themselves.

The main metaphor through which Boccaccio reflects on the imagination and also organizes his text is the metaphor of play. The plague is the experience that triggers the activity of play and their connection is explored in chapter 1, but play stands at the center of the *Decameron*. The move, in purely cultural terms, is of some moment. For traditionally, as any reader of Huizinga's *Homo ludens* may remember, play is viewed as an activity which is secondary to the "serious" pursuits of life.[2] One may even remember, to mention a view-

[2] A fundamental overview of the play element is Johan Huizinga, *Homo Ludens: A Study of the Play Element in Culture*, trans. R.F.C. Hull (Boston: Beacon Press, 1955). See also the remarks on esthetics, religious and social formalizations in his *The Waning of the Middle Ages* (Garden City: Doubleday and Co., 1954). Other general or specific studies on play that I have found useful are: R. B. Braithwaite, *Theory of Games as a Tool for the Moral Philosopher* (Cambridge: Cambridge University Press, 1963); Friedrich J. J. Buytendijk, *Wesen und Sinn des Spiels* (Berlin: K. Wolff Verlag, 1933); Roger Callois, *Man, Play and Games*, trans. Meyer Barash (New York: The Free Press of Glencoe, 1961); Joseph Campbell, *The Masks of God*, 4 vols. (New York: Viking Press, 1959–68); Clement of Alexandria, *Selections from the Protreptikos*, trans. T. Merton (New York: New Directions, 1962); Jacques Derrida, "Structure, Sign and Play in the Discourse of the Human Sciences," in *The Languages of Criticism and the Sciences of Man: The Structuralist Controversy*, eds. Richard Macksey and Eugenio Donato (Baltimore: The Johns Hopkins Press, 1970), p. 247–272; Jacques Ehrmann, "Homo Ludens Revisited," *Yale French Studies* 41 (1968), pp. 31–57; Eugen Fink, *Spiel als Weltsymbol* (Stuttgart: W. Kohl-

point which is exemplary in its own way, John of Salisbury's severe pronouncements against actors, mimics, buffoons, jesters and jugglers in the *Policraticus* (I, 8). They are all emblems of the frivolity that John believes holds sway in his own age, because they give, as he refers to their practices, "the solace of some pleasure" to idle lives. John of Salisbury's earnest dismissal of frivolity and idleness is turned around by Boccaccio, who, as he foregrounds play, retrieves the value of worldliness and its frivolous pleasures as the imaginative category through which he can challenge, as chapter 2 shows, the spirit of seriousness that weighs on the world.

John of Salisbury's strictures, no doubt, depend on the perception of play's potential subversiveness of his moral

---

nammer, 1960), available in French translation as *Le Jeu comme symbole du monde*, trans. H. Hildebrand and A. Lindenberg (Paris: Editions de Minuit, 1960); Sigmund Freud, *Beyond the Pleasure Principle* (New York: Bantam Books, 1967); Thomas M. Greene, "*Il Cortegiano* and the Choice of a Game," *Renaissance Quarterly*, 32 (1979), pp. 173–186; Romano Guardini, *The Spirit of Liturgy*, trans. Ada Lane (New York: Sheed and Ward, 1935); Hermann Hesse *Magister Ludi*, trans. M. Savill (New York: Ungar Publishing Co., 1965); David L. Miller, *Gods and Games: Toward a Theology of Play* (New York and Cleveland: The World Publishing Co., 1970); Joseph Pieper, *Leisure: The Basis of Culture*, trans. A. Dru (New York: New American Library, 1963); Hugo Rahner, *Man at Play*, trans. Brian Battershaw and Edward Quinn (New York: Herder and Herder, 1967); Rainer Maria Rilke, *Duino Elegies*, trans. C. F. MacIntyre (Berkeley: University of California Press, 1965); J.C.F. Schiller, *On the Esthetic Education of Man*, trans. R. Snell (London: Routledge and Kegan Paul, 1954); Mihai Spariosu, *Literature, Mimesis and Play: Essays in Literary Theory* (Tubingen: Gunter Narr Verlag, 1982); Ludwig Wittgenstein, *Philosophical Investigations*, trans. G.E.M. Anscombe (Oxford: Blackwell; New York: The Macmillan Co., 1953). Although the question of play in its complex ramifications has not been extensively treated in the scholarship on the *Decameron*, there are some specific contributions that touch on some aspects of the metaphorics of play: Giovanni Getto, "Le novelle dello scambio di illusione e realtà," in *Vita di forme e forme di vita nel Decameron* (Turin: Casa Editrice G. B. Petrini, 1958), pp. 164–187; Mario Baratto, *Realtà e stile nel Decameron* (Vicenza: Pozza, 1970), pp. 238–269; Carlo Muscetta, *Giovanni Boccaccio* (Bari: Laterza, 1972), esp. pp. 296–304; Joy H. Potter, "Boccaccio as Illusionist: The Play of Frames in the *Decameron*," *Humanities Association Review*, 26 (1975), pp. 327–345, now expanded in her *Five Frames of the Decameron* (Princeton: Princeton University Press, 1982), pp. 120–151.

schemes. That play can be a dangerous activity is best exemplified in a text that I believe lies behind the lengthy ceremonies preceding the tournament in Boccaccio's *Teseida*, namely book v of the *Aeneid*. This narrative section tells of the Trojans who on the shores of Sicily are holding their games on the anniversary of Anchises' death. The memorial is meant to prepare Aeneas' descent to Hades and his encounter with his father's shade. Yet the book's focus is on the women who, while their men are busy playing and displaying their enduring prowess, burn the ships. The sudden outbreak of violence in the middle of the ritual games decisively conveys Vergil's insight on the illusiveness of repose. At the same time, it also conveys the women's powerful response to the lure of play: the past is the horror of the ravage of Troy; the future, which for Aeneas holds the golden myths of new heroics, is to the women a dark promise and its fulfillment an ever receding illusion. By burning the ships the women yield to the seductiveness of that occasional repose and, implicitly, disavow as intolerable their subjection to the buffets of fate.

If the events of book v of the *Aeneid* suggest how divided Vergil is about both the inevitable ordeals of history and the feasibility of a bucolic order imaged by the games, in the *Decameron* the world of play is a necessary choice. It is the strategy of survival, a manner of dealing with the task of living for the *brigata*, the company of young men and women who retreat to a garden. One might add that for Boccaccio the first fascination of the world of play—which is the realm of the imagination—is that it is begun by man, and the text insists that play is an experience of enjoyment and imaginative freedom as well as a system governed by precise rules the storytellers impose on themselves—rules which, paradoxically, even make provisions for Dioneo's infractions. Since the storytellers view the world *sub specie ludi*, the *Decameron* is a repertory of the rhetorical forms and traditions of play—play as a therapy for love diseases and the plague, games of *alea*, the raw comedy of the *fabliaux*, games of chess and dice, spectacles, joustings, tricks, disguises, dance, music, references to mimicry, gambling, etc.

This insistence on play does not mean that Boccaccio's text

is detached from the moorings to the world of reality and "seriousness," nor does it mean that play is a sort of magic wand that merely puts us into direct contact with the spontaneous pleasures one imagines may take place in a utopian landscape. The pastoral landscape in the *Decameron* is the perspective from which the storytellers, as the very assumption of stability in the pattern of nature falls apart because of the plague, reflect on and recollect the real world. There is a rationality to the play in which the storytellers are engaged, and their dances, music and songs—repeatedly recorded in both introductory and conclusive statements framing each day—are the emblem of this rationality. But their rational, controlled pastimes pale in comparison to the freedom of their imaginations. The stories they tell, which are the text we read, variously evoke the world of serious utilitarian pursuits or feats of sexuality only to end up showing characters bewitched by their own fantasies or, more generally, that the world of rationality is inseparable from that of the imagination.

It is Boccaccio's radical insight, however, that the play of the imagination cannot be simply hedged within the boundaries of rational reality. Chapter 7, for instance, discusses characters such as Calandrino and Simone, conventionally dismissed as fools, the butt of everybody's laughter, who long to reach the realm outside of everyday experience. It is through them, through their beliefs, that the dreams of utopia may be realized, or through the merchants' schemes of power that we catch a glimpse of the ambiguities of the imagination. The imagination is always forced by the men of reason within recognizable forms of sensible living or it is dismissed by them as mere nonsense; at the same time, the imagination always exceeds the ordinary, rigid determinations of commonsense reality. The possibilities of the imagination, its fleeting shadows and dazzling fabrications, are probed throughout this book. But Boccaccio does not abandon himself to a web of dreams and fictions: for him the visionary power of the imagination, its play and pleasure, constantly takes its flight from the real and it constantly stumbles against the unyielding, necessary laws of the business of living.

It is this discrepancy and kinship between art and life, whereby the two can never be thought of as fully apart nor as fully coincident with each other, which is the subject of the present study. These two terms, art and life, in a variety of ways (history and utopia, facts and values, foolishness and intelligence, pleasure and moral order) are the steady double focus around which the *Decameron* is woven. This discrepancy-kinship does not engender a literary mode that could be called tragic; on the contrary, it is a mode drawn under the sovereignty of play, which is both a stance and a style of effacement of the boundaries between the real and the make-believe, the serious and the unserious, the useful and the useless. It is a style that accounts for Boccaccio's humor, his willingness to articulate his vision within the conventions of laughter and comic deception—social dissimulations, duplicities, the illusory masks that are the recurrent pattern of life. It is a style whereby facts and fictions are not reassuringly separated for the readers' moral edification, for the sway of rational order is all too often made a dupe by the hyperboles of the numberless ironic fantasists who, undeluded, roam the great stage of the world. These fantasists remind us, in a text in which all illusions and formalizations are punctured, that the worst illusion of all is to believe we have no illusions.

More generally, this study maps Boccaccio's meditations on esthetics in the *Decameron*.[3] As a discipline of sensible appearances, esthetics is always involved in the transactions of the world—economy, medicine, law, politics and ethics (and this study affirms the importance of these traditions in the *Decameron*), but it never coincides with any of them. It is this odd position of the esthetic forms that makes Boccaccio suspicious of the grand designs of Dante's vatic voice; it makes him suggest that literature may possibly be no more than impotent daydreaming, but it also makes him claim that esthetics is the privileged source of knowledge for the play of illusion flowering in the imagination of his storytellers.

[3] A most important study on medieval esthetics and its links with ethics is Judson B. Allen, *The Ethical Poetic of the Later Middle Ages. A Decorum of Convenient Distinction* (Toronto: University of Toronto Press, 1982).

Because esthetics—and more precisely, literature—spuriously connives with and exceeds the other categories of the practical arts, it cannot be defined, to speak rigorously, within theoretical, abstract boundaries. There is, nonetheless, a tendency among scholars to drop philosophers' names (mainly that of Ockham) in order to frame Boccaccio within the climate of the radical intellectual speculations of his times. The gesture is understandable, but it would be justified only if it were accompanied by the critical awareness of the elusiveness and permanent displacement that the metaphor of play governing the *Decameron* engenders. This elusiveness, this game of hide and seek, one might add, is coextensive with the scandalous erotic charge of the *Decameron*. It may explain, finally, the reasons for the kind of book I think I have written. It is unfashionable, at a time when scholarship has turned to forging overarching theories of literature, to write a book on one writer, let alone on one book or parts thereof. Because Boccaccio in the *Decameron* trenchantly argues that the quality of literature is to be always resistant to formulaic pronouncements, he solicits not theoretical systems but the practice of reading, and thereby he seduces us into conversation.

I

PLAGUE AND PLAY

In the postscript to the *Decameron* Boccaccio dismisses the charge that some of its tales are too long. He states that brevity is appropriate for those students who sharpen their wits in the intellectual circles of Athens, Bologna or Paris, but is not desirable for his audience. The tales are written, he explains, for ladies, who, "oziose" (p. 4), have as much time on their hands as they fail to spend on the pleasures of love.[1]

The remark, even when viewed from all possible angles, is hardly unusual in the *Decameron*. We have been all too well prepared for the direct link established between the narrative and women provisionally out of love who are waiting to fall in love again. The subtitle to the *Decameron*, for instance, is "Galeotto," an explicit recall of the love book that Paolo and

[1] "Esse dentro a' dilicati petti, temendo e vergognando, tengono l'amorose fiamme nascose, le quali quanto più di forza abbian che le palesi color il sanno che l' hanno provate: e oltre a ciò, ristrette da' voleri, da' piaceri, da' comandamenti de' padri, delle madri, de' fratelli e de' mariti, il più del tempo nel piccolo circuito delle loro camere racchiuse dimorano e quasi oziose sedendosi, volendo e non volendo in una medesima ora, seco rivolgendo diversi pensieri, li quali non è possibile che sempre sieno allegri" (*Proem, Decameron*, ed. Branca, p. 4). The *Conclusione dell' autore*, to which we shall repeatedly return in the course of this study, picks up the motif of leisure: ". . . non m'è per ciò uscito di mente me avere questo mio affanno offerto all'oziose e non all'altre: e a chi per tempo passar legge, niuna cosa puote esser lunga, se ella quel fa per che egli l'adopera. Le cose brievi si convengon molto meglio agli studianti, li quali non per passare ma per utilmente adoperare il tempo faticano, che a voi donne, alle quali tanto del tempo avanza quanto negli amorosi piaceri non ispendete. E oltre a questo, per ciò che nè a Atene nè a Bologna o a Parigi alcuna di voi non va a studiare, più distesamente parlar vi si conviene che a quegli che hanno negli studii gl'ingegni assottigliati" (*Decameron*, pp. 962–963).

Francesca read in *Inferno* v.[2] At the same time, in the Introduction to the fourth day, to the critics, who advise him to remain with the Muses in Parnassus rather than lose himself by his "ciance" (p. 346) in the company of the ladies, Boccaccio replies that to him "le Muse sono donne," and that he never strays from the Muses when he is with the ladies.[3] Nor is the pairing of literature and wasted time all that unfamiliar. Boccaccio, who has an ironic insight into the values and profits of the marketplace, insists that the tales are to be told not in the "scuole de' filosofanti" (p. 960), but in the perimeter of the garden of delights, "ne' giardini, in luogo di sollazzo" (in gardens, in a place of pleasure, 6.960), where the ten young people retreat to escape the threat of the plague, the Black Death that was ravaging Florence in the spring of 1348.

None of this is unsettling, yet one can't but be intrigued by the overt suggestion in the self-defense of the epilogue of the unphilosophical nature of the *Decameron*.[4] In what must be their certain knowledge of the boundaries that delimit literature from philosophy, critics have not been noticeably ruffled by Boccaccio's juxtaposition. Probably deciding that, at least in appearance, the statement is simply right, they have kept from exploring both its value and its implications for the understanding of the *Decameron*. Their efforts to define its cultural context have been mainly directed to documenting the specifically rhetorical resources—the *artes dictaminis*—that mark the articulation of Boccaccio's prose.[5]

More frequently, however, critics have sought to identify the configuration of ideas sustaining the text. Following, by

[2] The reference is to *Inferno* v, 137. For a further discussion of the title and its implications, see below chapter 2 and n. 16.

[3] ". . . per che, queste cose tessendo, né dal monte Parnaso né dalle Muse non mi allontano quanto molti per avventura s'avisano" (*Decameron*, p. 351).

[4] "Appresso assai ben si può cognoscere queste cose non nella chiesa, delle cui cose e con animi e con vocaboli onestissimi si convien dire, . . . né ancora nelle scuole de' filosofanti . . . né tra cherici né tra filosofi in alcun luogo ma ne' giardini, in luogo di sollazzo, . . ." (*Conclusione, Decameron*, p. 960).

[5] Vittore Branca, *Boccaccio medievale* (Florence: Sansoni, 1956), esp. pp. 29–70; see also Alfredo Schiaffini, *Tradizione e poesia* (Roma: Ed. di Storia e Letteratura, 1969), pp. 193–203.

and large, the trails blazed by De Sanctis, they have assigned the *Decameron* to the bedrock of the so-called medieval naturalism, identifiable, in their views, as a body of thought which gives the instinctive life of sexuality a new moral sanction.[6] In the *Decameron*, as Erich Auerbach puts it, ". . . the thing which is diametrically opposed to medieval-Christian ethics, is the doctrine of love and nature which, though it is usually presented in a light tone, is nevertheless quite certain of itself. . . ."[7] This doctrine of nature, Auerbach, like De Sanctis, believes, had played an important role in the theological debate of the thirteenth century and had found literary expression in the second part of the *Roman de la Rose*. But no sooner is this background recalled than it is dismissed. Auerbach is forced to conclude that ". . . all this had no direct bearing on Boccaccio," whose prose fails to treat reality "problematically" and leaves by the wayside the complex intellectual and moral order that Dante's, on the other hand, had fully deployed.[8]

Clearly, even as the doctrinal substance of the *Decameron* is assessed, the nature of the claimed juxtaposition of literature and philosophy is largely ignored. It would be no doubt tempting to dismiss the projection of Boccaccio as a philosophically naive figure as the obvious move of philosophically conscious critics. One remembers, however, that Boccaccio's statement in the epilogue is addressed precisely to censors, who would be likely to find the intrusion of playfulness into the domain of philosophical knowledge too disruptive of the rhetorical canons of decorous language. My aim in this first chapter is twofold: most generally, I wish to examine Boccaccio's sense of this disruption, concealed in the claim that liter-

---

[6] Aldo D. Scaglione, *Nature and Love in the Late Middle Ages* (Berkeley and Los Angeles: University of California Press, 1963); see also Guido di Pino, *La Polemica del Boccaccio* (Florence: Vallecchi, 1953), esp. pp. 209–252. De Sanctis' views—and their limits—are stressed by Scaglione, *Nature and Love*, pp. 48–53. See F. De Sanctis, *Storia della letteratura italiana*, ed. B. Croce, 2 vols. (Bari: Laterza, 1958), I, chap. 9.

[7] Erich Auerbach, *Mimesis. The Representation of Reality in Western Literature*, trans. W. Trask (Garden City: Doubleday, 1957), p. 198.

[8] *Mimesis*, p. 198.

ature and philosophy are two separate forms in a rigorous hierarchy of knowledge; my more specific aim is to map out
with reasonable precision the cultural debate of the so-called
School of Chartres in which Boccaccio is directly engaged. I
shall do so by focusing on the two questions of plague and play
within which the narrative movement of the *Decameron* is contained.

The dramatic link between the plague and the world of play
is posited in the opening paragraph of the Introduction, as
Boccaccio, before turning to the stories, apologetically compels the attention of his audience, the "graziosissime donne"
(p. 9), to the memory of the horrors of the recent plague. The
reasons he gives for this detour are essentially esthetic; in a language that recalls the pilgrim's ascent to the Garden of Eden in
Purgatorio, he states that the climbing of a rugged mountain
makes more delightful lingering later on the plain; or in the
words of Proverbs 14:13 that "just as the end of mirth is heav-
iness, so sorrows are dispelled by subsequent joy."[9]

The claim that this detour is a formal strategy, a pretext to
justify the retreat of the "lieta brigata" (happy company, p. 29)
to a *locus amoenus* of feasting and merrymaking, is not a rationale that can altogether account for the complexity of the relationship between plague and play. The complication of this
pattern can be suggested, for the time being, by remarking
how Boccaccio rhetorically disguises the plague as a digression, a stage on the way to delight or "brieve noia" (p. 9)
(brief, he says, inasmuch as it is contained within few words).
Yet, thematically, the plague contains and surrounds the text
and largely determines its values. At the same time, the world
of play is the central burden of the *Decameron* and as it seeks to
exclude from its domain the memory of the plague, it comes
forth as a diversion, an experience that can only be itself sustained as a brief pastime. The design, which suggests, but not
quite, a chiasmus, will be explored by Boccaccio through a se-

---

[9] "Questo orrido cominciamento vi fia non altramenti che a' camminanti
una montagna aspra e erta, presso alla quale un bellissimo piano e dilettevole
sia reposto . . ." (*Introduzione, Decameron*, p. 9). See also Branca's note, p. 981.

ries of oblique figurative and thematic reversals throughout the text. For the moment, the Introduction gives an account of the plague as a hideous and intolerable interlude.

With striking clarity and a precision that physicians and historians of epidemics to this day find appealing, the general thrust of the Introduction is to describe the bubonic swellings, the vain hygienic measures taken by the officials to counter the spreading of the infection, and the disarray of social life in Florence.[10] The plague, we are told, wreaks its havoc in all directions, but Boccaccio's primary concern is to register what can be called the clinical semiotics, to use a word Hippocrates coined, of the disease.

He remarks that the symptoms vary as the plague moves from its starting place in the east to the west. In the east bleeding by the nose was "manifesto segno d'inevitabile morte" (a clear sign of inevitable death, p. 10); in the west, at first swellings would show at the armpits or at the groin in men and women alike; eventually, the signs change as the boils appear at random all over the body. Later on the distinctive trait of the infirmity (the word Boccaccio uses is "qualità," a technical designation in the current medical-philosophical vocabulary for that which is predicated of a substance) was the occurrence of black *or* livid stains, which, at times large and few, at times tiny and numerous, covered all the parts of the body and were infallible omens ("indizio," p. 11), of imminent death.[11]

From this tragic perspective of the rotting bodies and the

[10] For a historical-scientific reconstruction of what may have happened during the Black Plague, see Geoffrey Marks, *The Medieval Plague: The Black Death of the Middle Ages* (Garden City: Doubleday, 1971). See also J.F.C. Hecker, *The Epidemics of the Middle Ages*, trans. B. G. Babington (London: Woodfall, 1844), esp. pp. 1–83. The imaginative effects of the plague in the figurative arts have been examined by Millard Meiss, *Painting in Florence and Siena after the Black Death* (New York: Harper & Row, 1973). Cf. also, in a different key, Aldo S. Bernardo, "The Plague as Key to Meaning in Boccaccio's *Decameron*," in *The Black Death*, ed. D. Williman (Binghamton: Center for Medieval and Early Renaissance Studies, 1982), pp. 39–64.

[11] "E come i gavocciolo primieramente era stato e ancora era certissimo indizio di futura morte, così erano queste a ciascuno a cui venieno" (*Decameron*, p. 11).

shifty signs of the epidemic, the first few lines which introduce the plague mark Boccaccio's own intellectual predicament.

Dico adunque che già erano gli anni della fruttifera incarnazione del Figliuolo di Dio al numero pervenuti di milletrecentoquarantotto, quando nella egregia città di Fiorenza, oltre a ogn'altra italica bellissima, pervenne la mortifera pestilenza: la quale, per operazion de' corpi superiori o per le nostre inique opere da giusta ira di Dio a nostra correzione mandata sopra i mortali, alquanti anni davanti nelle parti orientali incominciata, quelle d'inumerabile quantità de' viventi avendo private, senza ristare d'un luogo in uno altro continuandosi, verso l'Occidente miserabilmente s'era ampliata.

I say then, that the sum of thirteen hundred and forty-eight years had passed since the fruitful Incarnation of the Son of God when the noble city of Florence, which is far nobler than any other Italian city, was visited by the deadly pestilence. This pestilence, which either through the influence of the heavenly bodies or because of our iniquitous ways descended upon the human race for our punishment, had started some years earlier in the east . . . (and) had unhappily spread westward.   (pp. 9–10)

If in rhetorical terms, the allusion to the Incarnation and the vernal equinox is a conventional device of exordium in a large number of medieval texts, here its thematic weight is to recall the experience of the body's redemption.[12] As Boccaccio chronicles the corruption of the plague, however, the redemptive resonance of the Incarnation ironically heightens the present bodily decay. The force of the epithet "fruttifera," moreover, is neutralized by the parallel epithet of like construction, "mortifera." At the same time, the quality of medieval chronicle—such as Matteo Villani's—that the text takes on scores the writer's own descent into what might be called an imaginative darkness, where data and surface appearances can be reported, but their process of signification remains caught in a

---

[12] See the remarks in chapter 2, n. 9.

stubborn unintelligibility.[13] For the possible significances of the plague, a punishment for man's sin or the influence of the stars, are in fact mutually exclusive alternatives. Whereas one posits a symbolic world sustained by a providential order, the other manifestly belies it by attributing the occurrence of the epidemic to the tyranny of chance.[14] More importantly, by the

[13] Matteo Villani (who continues his brother Giovanni's chronicle), *Cronica*, ed. F. Gherardi Dragomanni, 4 vols. (Florence: S. Coen, 1844–45). See on this Letterio di Francia, *Novellistica* (Milan: Vallardi, 1924), I, pp. 106–107.

[14] For Boccaccio's shifting attitude toward astrology, see Antonio E. Quaglio, "Andalò del Negro e Giovanni Boccaccio astronomi e astrologi," in *Scienza e mito nel Boccaccio* (Padua: Liviana, 1967), pp. 127–206. See also the excellent recent piece which focuses on medical themes in the *Decameron* by Marga Cottino-Jones, "Boccaccio e la scienza," in *Letteratura e scienza nella storia della cultura italiana* (IX Congresso dell'A.I.S.L.L.I.) (Palermo: Manfredi, 1978), pp. 356–370. Boccaccio's sense of astrology, and Andalò's doctrine, should be seen in the light of Petrarch's polemics against Arab thought. On this see, besides Quaglio, L. Thorndike, *A History of Magic and Experimental Science* (New York: Columbia University Press, 1934–58), IV, pp. 405–540. More generally, see T. O. Wedel, *The Medieval Attitude toward Astrology. Yale Studies in English*, 60 (1928, rep. 1968). For Petrarch's attack against astrologers, see his *Epistolas rerum senilium*, I, 4, 5, 7; II, 1; VIII, 1 in Giuseppe Fracassetti, ed., *Le senili*, 2 vols. (Florence: Le Monnier, 1869–70). Especially important is the letter (III, 1) to Giovanni Boccaccio from which I quote the following: ". . . these astrologers know well what they flourish before us, what they offer for sale, is nothing at all. . . . If they talk of the movements of heavenly bodies, of winds and rain, . . . they may be listened to with interest, . . . But where they prate of men's affairs, of men's future lot, which God alone knows, they are to be rejected as mere fabricators of lies." The translation is taken from *Letters from Petrarch*, trans. Morris Bishop (Bloomington and London: Indiana University Press, 1966), pp. 231–232. In the *Esposizioni sopra la Comedia di Dante* Boccaccio's position on astrology is close to Dante's own formulation: see, for instance, the brief digressions on canto II, esp. litt., 93–96; canto V, esp. litt., 162–163; and canto XV, esp. litt., 30–32: "Tocca in queste parole l'autore l'oppinione degli astrologhi li quali sogliono talvolta nella natività d'alcuni fare certe loro elevazioni e per quelle vedere qual sia la disposizione del cielo in quel punto che colui nasce. . . ." The quotations from the *Esposizioni* are taken from the edition by Giorgio Padoan in *Tutte le opere di Giovanni Boccaccio*, VI (Milan: Mondadori, 1965). For Dante's sense of the importance of astrology in God's scheme, see *Purgatorio* XVI, 67–81; *Paradiso* VII, 136–141. Dante's doctrine is partly a response to the astrological determinism debated at the School of Chartres. On this see Guillaume de Conches,

absence of a precise generative link between a cause and its effects, the law of causality is suspended.

There is an ironic counterpoint, it must be added, to these symbolic disjunctions in the body of Boccaccio's own prose structure. It is well known that the stylistic movement of this stretch of the text has generally been judged so contrived as to betray an imagination incapable of plunging, as Thucydides and Lucretius do, into the tragic mode that the horror of the plague would elicit.[15] In effect, the hypotactic arrangement of the sentences, the wealth of subordinates and the poised slow rhythm are symptoms of an intellectual effort to connect the dismembered appearances of the world into an intelligible pattern of order and hierarchy, which rhetoric manages to simulate, but which the plague literally effaces. The infection is perceived through a series of bewildering, unstable signs, which cannot even be construed definitively as signs of disease: the text is punctuated by repeated alternatives, either/or phrases

---

Glosae super Platonem, ed. E. Jeauneau, in *Textes philosophiques du Moyen Age*, XIII (Paris: Vrin, 1965), pp. 24–25. See also John Freccero, "*Paradiso* x: The Dance of the Stars," *Dante Studies*, 86 (1968), pp. 85–111. As far as the statement in the *Decameron* goes, my point is that Boccaccio dramatizes as mutually contradictory the position of the astrologers-physicians and the religious-moral view of the origin of the plague. I must also point out that the reference to astrology, as a way of referring to the "remote causes" of the pestilence, is a *topos* of medical tractates on the plague. Other *topoi* are diet, disinfection of the air, avoidance of baths and luxury. On this, see Dorothea W. Singer, *Some Plague Tractates (Fourteenth and Fifteenth Centuries)* (London: Bale, Sons & Danielsson, 1916), pp. 4ff.

[15] Giovanni Getto, "La peste del 'Decameron' e il problema della fonte Lucreziana," *Giornale storico della letteratura italiana*, 135 (1958), pp. 507–523. After Ugo Foscolo's suggestion of the Lucretian source in the *Discorso storico sul testo del Decameron*, N. Di Lorenzo, *La descrizione della peste in Tucidide, in Lucrezio Caro, nel Boccaccio e nel Manzoni* (Salerno, 1906) considers the texts in terms of parallelisms. The availability of Lucretius in the Middle Ages is questioned by E. Bignone, "Per la fortuna di Lucrezio e dell'epicureismo nel Medio Evo," *Rivista di filologia e di istruzione classica*, 41 (1913), pp. 230–262. See also I. Philippe, "Lucrèce dans la théologie chrétienne du IIIe au XIIIe siècle et spécialement dans les écoles carolingiennes," *Revue de l'histoire des religions*, 30 (1870), pp. 284–332.

and careful distinctions which sunder the appearances from any determinable, moral or even physical origin.[16]

This sense of the world out of joint, ostensibly, does not detain Boccaccio for too long, and his attention quickly turns to the practice of medicine, the discipline conventionally understood, in the words of John of Salisbury among others, as that by which "physicians foresee and declare the causes of sickness." Accordingly, the remedies, suggestions and dietary laws recommended by the prominent physicians of the time, such as Tommaso del Garbo, Guy de Chauliac and Dondoli da Oriolo, to ward off the threat of the infection, are alluded to in Boccaccio's account but only to dramatize their inefficacy. Very simply, the nature and causes of the disease remain unknowable, beyond diagnosis, to the physicians who did not know "da che si muovesse" (where it came from, p. 11). Their practice, actually, is grimly caricatured by the acknowledged presence of quacks among their ranks.

The drugs they prescribe are futile to prevent or cure the disease; the styles of life followed by the people reflect, in their patent contradictoriness, the physicians' lack of any positive knowledge. Exploiting the canonical definition of "medicina," etymologically from "modus" (moderation),[17] Boccaccio describes some people, who, to preserve their health, adhere to a sober diet, consuming a modest quantity of food in the belief that "il vivere moderatamente e il guardarsi da ogni superfluità" (living moderately and avoiding every excess, p. 12) will avert the infection. Others, on the contrary, live in reckless frivolity and a drink heavily, "senza modo e senza misura" (without moderation and measure, p. 13), in the dubious

---

[16] The text of the *Introduzione* is marked by disjunctive phrases. See, for instance, the following: ". . . e da questo appresso s'incominciò la qualità della predetta infermità a permutare in macchie nere o livide, . . . anzi, o che natura del malore nol patisse o che la ignoranza de' medicanti . . . non conoscesse da che si movesse . . ." (*Decameron*, pp. 10–11).

[17] "Nomen autem Medicinae a modo, id est temperamento, inpositum aestimatur, ut non satis, sed paulatim adhibeatur . . . Inmoderatio enim omnis non salutem, sed periculum affert" (Isidore of Seville, *Etym.*, IV, ii).

opinion that merrymaking is "medicina certissima a tanto male" (a most infallible antidote to such an evil, p. 12). Still others steer a middle course between the two just described and, in a distant echo of the views of Chauliac or Gentile da Foligno, who prescribe fumigation of the air, would move around holding in their hands fragrant herbs to protect themselves from the stench of dead bodies and medicine.[18] A fourth group callously makes the decision, which resembles that of the "lieta brigata"—though Boccaccio does not say so—to run away from the plague to the countryside. Like the other opinions, this turns out to be another trap of delusion and error, a further sign of medical ineptitude in the face of death.

So overwhelming is Boccaccio's sense of loss that the digression on the plague climaxes in the pathos of a series of *ubi sunt*, in the elegy for a world in which the pattern of generations and temporal continuity is broken up by the loom of death:

> *O quanti gran palagi, quante belle case, quanti nobili abituri per adietro di famiglie pieni, di signori e di donne, infino al menomo fante rimaser voti! O quante memorabili schiatte, quante ampissime eredità, quante famose ricchezze si videro senza successor debito rimanere! Quanti valorosi uomini, quante belle donne, quanti leggiadri giovani, li quali non che altri, ma Galieno, Ipocrate o Esculapio avrieno giudicati sanissimi, la mattina desinarono co' lor parenti, compagni e amici, che poi la sera vegnente appresso nell'altro mondo cenaron con li lor passati!*

---

[18] Guy de Chauliac is famous mainly for his ideas on the course of the plague. See *Chirurgia* (Lugduni: V. Portonari, n.d.), II, 5, p. 153. An excellent account of his role in the court of Pope Clement VI in 1348 at Avignon is available in A. M. Campell, *The Black Death and Men of Learning* (New York: Columbia University Press, 1931), pp. 2ff. But see "Flos Medicinae Scholae Salerni," pt. viii, cap. ix, *Collectio Salernitana ossia Documenti Inediti . . . raccolti da G.E.T. Henschel, Daremberg, De Renzi*, ed. De Renzi, 5 vols. (Naples: Sebezio, 1852–59), V, p. 77. Gentile da Foligno, *Consilium contra pestilentiam* (Padua: Laurentius Canozius, ca. 1475). Shorter *consilia* against the plague have been published by K. Sudhoff in *Archiv*, 5 (1913), pp. 83–86 and 332–337.

Ah, how great a number of splendid palaces, fine houses and noble dwellings, once filled with retainers, with lords and ladies, were bereft of all who lived there, down to the tiniest child! How numerous were the famous families, the vast estates, the notable fortunes, that were seen to be left without a rightful successor! How many gallant gentlemen, fair ladies, and sprightly youths who would have been judged hale and hearty by Galen, Hippocrates and Aesculapius (to say nothing of others), having breakfasted in the morning with their kinsfolk, acquaintances and friends, supped the same evening with their ancestors in the next world. (p. 19)

The dirge parallels, and in many ways reverses, a passage of Nature's Complaint in Jean de Meung's *Roman de la Rose*. The burden of Nature's speech is to focus on the endless tournament at which she jousts with Death. Nature evokes her role at the forge where she steadily fashions creatures to replenish the gaps opened by all-devouring Death. Death's sovereignty over the world of generation and corruption, we are told, can only be combated by sexual reproduction, while medicine is of no avail: "Not Hippocrates or Galen, no matter how good physicians they were. Rhases, Constantine and Avicenna have left their skins. . . . Thus Death, never satisfied, greedily swallows up individuals. By land and sea she follows them until in the end she buries them."[19]

---

[19] ". . . Nature, qui pensait des chose / Qui sont desouz le ciel encloses, / Dedenz sa forge entree estait, / Ou toute s'entente metait / En forgier singulieres pieces / Pour continuer les espieces; / Car les pieces tant les font vivre / car Nature tant li va près / Que Mort ne les peut aconsivre, / Ja tant ne savra courre après; / Car quant la Mort o sa maçue / De pieces singuliers tue / Cens qu'el treuve a sei redevables; . . ." (*Le Roman de la Rose*, ed. Langlois, vol. IV, ll. 15891–15905). The reference to the physicians is taken from a few lines down and the passage reads: "Mort, qui de neir le vis a teint, / Cueurt après tant qu'el les ataint; / Si qu'il i a trop fiere chace: / Cil s'en fuient e Mort les chace / Dis anz ou vint, . . . / E s'il peuent outre passer, / Cueurt ele après senz sei lasser, / Tant qu'el les tient en ses liens, / Maugré touz les fisiciens / E les fisiciens meïsmes, / Onc nul eschaper n'en veïsmes: / Pas Ypocras

For Jean, Nature's reference to the physicians, known as the philosophers of nature, is an overt strategy to expose as illusory the efforts of both art and other rational constructs to engender life or even shelter man from the mortal chase. Nature's claim, in turn, it should be added, is an ironic self-deception for she herself fails to found a rational order and is blind to the destructive impulses that lodge in her vast body. For Boccaccio, on the other hand, to turn to the physicians and their empirical prescriptions is to challenge radically the very basis of the Chartrian philosophy of Nature.

Students of the language and thought at the School of Chartres have generally recognized but not sufficiently explored the importance of Galenic medicine, along with the Platonic myth of creation, to the shaping of the doctrine of Nature in the twelfth century.[20] Yet it can be shown that the Galenic texts, brought to Chartres from Salerno by Constantinus Africanus, affected the early formulations of Adelard of Bath and Guillaume de Conches.[21] It is especially in the *Cos-*

---

ne Galien, / Tout fussent bon fisicien; / Rasis, Constantins, Avicenne / Li ront laissiee la coënne; / E ceus qui ne peuent tant courre, / Nes repeut riens de Mort rescourre" (ll. 15945–15964; *The Romance of the Rose*, trans. Dahlberg, p. 271).

[20] Heinrich Schipperges, "Einflusse arabischer Medizin auf die Mikrokosmos-literature des 12. Jahrhunderts," in P. Wilpert, ed., *Antike und Orient im Mittelalter. Miscellanea Medievalia*, 1 (Berlin, 1962), pp. 129–153. Cf. also Brian Stock, *Myth and Science in the Twelfth Century* (Princeton: Princeton University Press, 1972), esp. pp. 26–28, where the links between medicine and astrology are examined, and pp. 100ff. for the role medicine plays in the thought of Bernard Silvester. More generally, see D. Campbell, *Arabian Medicine and Its Influence on the Middle Ages* (London, K. Paul, Trench, 1926), 2 vols.; A. Castiglioni, *History of Medicine*, trans. E. G. Krumbhaor, 2nd ed. (New York, A. A. Knopf, 1947).

[21] Some interesting attempts to give a fuller picture of the School of Salerno and its role in the European sciences are Charles and Dorothy Singer, "The Origin of the Medical School of Salerno, the First University: An Attempted Reconstruction," in *Essays on the History of Medicine Presented to Karl Sudhoff* (Oxford: Oxford University Press, 1924), pp. 121–138; Paul O. Kristeller, "The School of Salerno," *Bulletin of Historical Medicine*, 17(1945), pp. 133–194; "Nuove fonti per la medicina Salernitana del secolo XII," *Rassegna storica Salernitana*, 18 (1957), pp. 61–75; "The School of Salerno: Its Development and

mographia of Bernard Silvester that Galenic theories find a
sharp literary adaptation.

Galen's assumption of a benevolent world of materiality, his
belief in the purposiveness and knowability of the natural
world, in the power of scientific reason, on the one hand, to
wrest and manipulate the secrets of nature, and on the other
hand, to reestablish health, understood as the harmonious relation of the four elements and humors—phlegm, melancholy, blood and choler—shape Bernard's allegory of creation
and man's education in it. For the primary concern of the
poem is to teach man, as the procession of the liberal arts exemplifies, the central values of Humanism: that man alone,
unlike the other beasts, can look up at the stars. And if this is
the index of his hubris, it also discloses the spark of the divine
in him.[22]

To be sure, Bernard's educational optimism is tempered by
the awareness of a lingering *malignitas* at the heart of matter,
which questions any facile celebration of the order Nature cre-

---

Its Contribution to the History of Learning," in *Studies in Renaissance Thought
and Letters* (Rome: Storia e letteratura, 1965), pp. 495–551; M. Steinschneider,
"Constantinus Africanus," *Virchowas Archiv*, 37 (1867), pp. 351–410; Richard
McKeon, "Medicine and Philosophy in the Eleventh and Twelfth Centuries:
The Problem of Elements," *The Thomist*, 24(1961), pp. 211–256; Theodore
Silverstein, "Guillaume de Conches and Nemesius of Emessa: On the Sources
of the 'New Science' of the Twelfth Century," in *Harry A. Wolfson Jubilee Volume*, 2 vols. (Jerusalem: American Academy for Jewish Research, 1965), II,
pp. 719–734. See Guillaume de Conches, *De philosophia mundi, PL* 172, cols.
39–102; Adelard of Bath, *De eodem et diverso*, ed. Hans Willner in *Beitrage zur Ge-
schichte der Philosophie des Mittelalters*, 4, no. 1 (1903). More generally see
Owsei Temkin, *Galenism. Rise and Decline of a Medical Philosophy* (Ithaca: Cornell University Press, 1973). Cf. Nancy Siraisi, *Taddeo Alderotti and His Pupils:
Two Generations of Italian Medical Learning* (Princeton: Princeton University
Press, 1981).

[22] On Bernard Silvester's *Cosmographia* and his context, see Tullio Gregory,
"L'idea di natura nella filosofia medievale prima dell'ingresso della fisica di
Aristotile: il secolo XII," in *La filosofia della natura nel Medioevo*: Atti del terzo
congresso internazionale di filosofia medievale, 1964 (Milan: Vita e Pensiero,
1966), pp. 27–65; Brian Stock, *Myth and Science in the Twelfth Century*; see also
The Cosmographia of Bernardus Silvestris, trans. Winthrop Wetherbee (New
York: Columbia University Press, 1973), esp. pp. 1–62.

ates from the shapelessness of Silva.[23] The world of Nature has
its eternal cycles of life and death, while man, the microcosm
and specimen of the harmony of creation, "ever liable to affliction . . . passes wholly out of existence with the failure of his
body. Unable to sustain himself, . . . he exhausts his life and a
day reduces him to nothing."[24] The possibility of a return to
primordial chaos is countered, nonetheless, by the vital role
played by the sexual organs. In a chapter (II, 14), which tex-
tually recalls Constantinus' *De communibus locis*, Bernard describes the perfection of the human body, "the masterwork of
powerful nature." After he illustrates the function of the five
senses and of the heart, brain and liver, we are told how "the
lower body ends in the wanton loins and the private parts lie
hidden away in this remote region. The exercise will be enjoy-
able and profitable. . . . They fight unconquered against death
with their life-giving weapons, renew our nature, and perpetuate our kind. . . . The phallus wars against Lachesis and carefully rejoins the vital threads severed by the hands of the
Fates."[25]

The assertion of the value of the genital organs recurrently
appears in the literary and intellectual debate on the regeneration of man among Bernard's followers. For instance, Alan of
Lille's moral allegory of man's fall from the order of Nature is
metaphorized as a venereal perversion. Venus, assisted by her
husband Hymen and Cupid regularly applying their productive hammers to the anvils, was wont to hold out the shield of
defense to the sword of Atropos and weave the continuity of
the human race.[26] But now, by her magic arts, Venus "de-
virat" man. The discourse of Raison in the *Roman de la Rose*,
where ostensibly the import of allegory is dismissed in favor

[23] *Cosmographia*, trans. Wetherbee, p. 50.

[24] *Cosmographia*, trans. Wetherbee, pp. 126–127.

[25] Constantinus Africanus, *De communibus medico cognitu necessariis locis*,
5.35, *Opera* (Basel: H. Petrum, 1539), p. 139. The translation is Wetherbee's,
p. 126. See also G. M. Nardi, *Problemi d'embriologia umana: antica e medioevale*
(Florence: Sansoni, 1938), esp. pp. 76ff.

[26] *Liber de planctu naturae*, PL 210, col. 459.

of experience, also valorizes the power of reproduction with which cullions and staff are endowed by God's wondrous foresight.[27]

Boccaccio's relation to this pattern of literary history, here briefly sketched, cannot be treated unequivocally in terms of simple parody, or polemics, and much less in the conventional language of indebtedness or originality. It is, rather, a case of thorough intellectual complicity to the point that disentangling its strands may turn out to be a redoubtable if not an altogether impossible task, more likely to betray the critic's bias than shed light on the strategies of the text.

It is possible to suggest, nonetheless, that at the beginning of the Introduction, Boccaccio departs from Bernard's stylized allegory of natural harmony or even from Alan's view of the metaphoric wounds inflicted by the "acuta febre" of Venus.[28] He strips off the veils of allegory and ostensibly turns to history, as he focuses on the literal, contingent plague in the city of Florence. This strategy, to be sure, is only provisional, for the *Decameron* will in turn probe, as we shall see later, the *aegritudo amoris* and will also evoke a golden world in the artifice of nature to which the *brigata* will retreat. At the same time, to Bernard's belief in the significant coherence of the moral allegory of Nature as *Mater generationis*, Boccaccio would seem to juxtapose a view of the corrupt constitution of nature, which engenders chaos and death and which, more generally, is more mysterious and less predictable than the Chartrians assumed. The attack against Bernard's allegory is made poignant, one should add, by the fact that the *Cosmographia* is extant because he, Boccaccio, in truly humanistic fashion, copied and handed it down to posterity.[29]

[27] ". . . Car volentiers, non pas enviz, / Mist Deus en coilles e en viz / Force de generacion, / Par merveilleuse entencion, / Pour l'espiece aveir tojourz vive / Par renouvelance naïve, . . ." (*Le Roman de la Rose*, ll. 6965ff.).

[28] *PL* 210, col. 460. The whole passage reads: "Behold, in wretchedness and lamentation, I have sung my song of complaint about mankind languishing from Venus' piercing fever." Alan of Lille, *The Plaint of Nature*, trans. James J. Sheridan (Toronto: Pontifical Institute for Mediaeval Studies, 1980), p. 165.

[29] Florence, Biblioteca Medicea Laurenziana, MS plut. xxxiii, 31, f. 59va.

Allegory, as the rhetorical vehicle of Bernard's vision, is primarily a mode by which the interpretability of the riddles and
enigmas of creation is stated; it also implies that enveloped in
Nature's garment there is a repository of moral norms that
man's reason can grasp; more pointedly, the presence of Galenic lore and other scientific myths drawn from astronomy,
geomancy and general Arab learning, remove the allegory
from the domain of fabulous narratives: they are tools by
which Bernard dramatizes his desire to charge the allegorical
scheme with a scientific and literal referent. In the *Decameron*,
by a sharp reversal, Nature's veils are shed, yet its literal designs remain unfathomable to the gaze of man, and appearances, in a narrative where every man is called upon to know
how to fashion and read appearances, are inscrutable.

Boccacio's foray into the boundaries of Bernard's figura-
tions is not kept, however, at this level of generality. If it were,
the *Decameron* would reenact the antiallegorical strain that critics believe Boccaccio or Jean, for that matter, elaborate in the
light of the complexity of experience and the value of the
body. Boccaccio, like Jean in this, deflates the myth of experience: he lays bare the movement whereby the plague wrecks
all the limbs of the body and, by alluding to the ulcers at the
groin and armpits, mocks the symmetrical arrangement celebrated by Bernard.[30] The word for groin, furthermore, is *anguinaia*, etymologically from *inguen*, which, "a loci vicinitate
dicitur de pudendis virilibus ac femineis."[31]

By the allusion to the diseased genital organs, Boccaccio dis-
mantles the theme of regeneration upheld by Bernard and
Alan and the tradition of Naturalism. In one sense, this perception puts him closely in touch with the classical texts on the

---

The manuscript was first brought to attention by Franco Munari, "Mediaevalia I–II," *Philologus*, 105 (1960), pp. 279–292.

[30] *Cosmographia*, II, 14.

[31] ". . . ma nascevano . . . a' maschi e alle femmine parimenti o
nell'anguinaia . . . certe enfiature . . ." (*Decameron*, p. 10). For the etymology
of *inguen* and its classical use, see *Totius Latinitatis Lexicon*, ed. E. Forcellini
(Prato: Aldiniani, 1865), III, p. 505. See also Isidore of Seville, *Etym.* IV, vi, 19.

plague by Thucydides, Hippocrates, Galen, Lucretius and even Gregory of Tours.[32] Uniformly, and by a move that effectively disregards the plague as a historical event (each literary elaboration repeats the earlier ones), they envision the epidemic as damaging the genitals. In *De rerum natura*, often and controversially considered to be a source of the plague's description in the *Decameron*, the infection is said to trigger the suppuration and successive self-amputation of the sexual organs.[33] There is in the detail a transparent, if sinister, reversal of the only possible foundation of life in this fictional world which comes into being under the aegis of triumphant Venus.[34] If the stability and health of this world of love are illusory, equally ironic is Lucretius' choice of the locale where the plague spreads unchecked: Athens, the city of philosophy, of the immortality of Philosophy, "A-thanatos,"—according to Boccaccio's own etymologizing in the glosses to the *Teseida*—plunges into madness and death.[35]

[32] "Huius tempore cum lues illa, quam inguinarium vocant, per diversas regiones desaeviret, . . ." (Gregory of Tours, *Historia Francorum, PL* 71, col. 272). Lucretius is very clear on this: "Profluvium porro qui taetri sanguinis aere / exierat, tamen in nervos huic morbus et artus / ibat et in partis genitalis corporis ipsa" (*De rerum natura*, VI, ll. 1205–1207).

[33] Vittore Branca, "Un modello medievale per l'introduzione," in *Boccaccio medievale*, pp. 209–213, shows how the description of the plague follows Paul the Deacon, *Historia Langobardorum*, II, 4. For the debate on Lucretius and Boccaccio, see note 15 above. I like to suggest that Lucretius' description of the plague—which I am using only as a textual parallel to the *Decameron*—was partly available from the scientific sections of Isidore's *Etymologies* and from Macrobius, *Saturnalia*, ed. J. Willis (Leipzig: Teubner, 1970). Book 6, chap. 2 is an external comparison of Vergil's description of the plague with Lucretius' *De rerum natura*, VI, ll. 1138ff. See ll. 1208ff. for the sexual self-amputation.

[34] The opening lines of *De rerum natura* are only too well known: "Aeneadum genetrix, hominum divomque voluptas, alma Venus, . . . quae terras frugiferentis concelebras, per te quoniam genus omne animantum concipitur . . ." (I, ll. 1–5).

[35] "Pallade, dea della sapienzia, et Nettunno, iddio del mare, fecero la città d'Attene, la quale fatta ciascuno voleva nomare a sua guisa. . . . Giove disse che Pallade la dovesse nominare. . . . Nominolla adunque Pallade Atene, la quale tanto vuole dire in latino quanto cosa immortale" (*Teseida*, ed. Salvatore Battaglia [Florence: Sansoni, 1938], VI, l. 71, p. 178).

In another sense, however, Boccaccio is also removed from Lucretius, for the *inguen* is only a term of proximity, a metonym for the sexual organs which remain unnamed just as there is not a proper name for the disease. His strategy is to elude a definition, and as such it reflects the fallibility of the effort to reckon with the central issue of the disease. The world of the plague is transformed into an ominous text, with its signs proliferating, shifting and only decipherable as presages of death.

While the epidemic continues to be an unknowable occurrence, there is another known disease in the *Decameron* which stands in a metonymic contiguity to the plague. This is, as hinted earlier, the *aegritudo amoris*, which Boccaccio evokes in the Proem to the narrative. Adopting a confessional stance, a seductive gesture by which he takes his readers, the charming ladies, into his confidence, Boccaccio refers to the distress which an immoderate love engendered in his mind.[36] While he had been floundering in this stormy passion, he found comfort to his anguish in the agreeable conversation offered by some friends. Now Boccaccio, in turn, offers solace to the women in love, who, brooding and lethargic, sit taciturn in apparent idleness weighed down by longing and melancholy.

As these conventional *signa amoris* are referred to, the text offers itself as a logotherapy, with Boccaccio ostensibly writing a version of Ovid's *Remedia amoris*, to what is known as the "disease of heroes."[37] The disease, melancholy or *atra bilis*, the

[36] "Per ciò che, dalla mia prima giovanezza infino a questo tempo oltre modo essendo acceso stato d'altissimo e nobile amore, . . . nondimeno mi fu egli di grandissima fatica a sofferire, certo non per crudeltà della donna amata, ma per soverchio fuoco nella mente concetto da poco regolato appetito. . . ." (*Proem, Decameron*, p. 3).

[37] The tradition of the lovers' malady has been stressed by John L. Lowes, "The Loveres Maladye of Hereos," *Modern Philology*, 11 (1913–14), pp. 491–546. See also B. Nardi, "L'amore e i medici medioevali," *Saggi e note di critica dantesca* (Milan-Naples: Ricciardi, 1966), pp. 238–267. More recently the issue has been reexamined by Massimo Ciavolella, *La 'malattia d'amore' dall'antichità al medioevo* (Rome: Bulzoni, 1976); see also his "La tradizione dell' 'aegritudo amoris' nel 'Decameron,' " *Giornale storico della letteratura italiana*, 147 (1970), pp. 496–517. See Edward C. Schweitzer, "Fate and Freedom in the *Knight's Tale*," *Studies in the Age of Chaucer*, 3 (1981), pp. 13–45. See also

quality that descends from Saturn, the father of Venus, is the condition of the mind clouded by fits of delusion and lust.[38] As a humor that obsesses the imagination, it had been the steady object of attention by both literary and medical authorities, and Boccaccio exploits the inconsistencies or agreements of the two strains. The physicians, such as Arnaldus of Villanova, Avicenna and Constantinus Africanus recognize, as Boccaccio does, that whereas man's melancholy is relieved by games and exercises of hunting, fowling and hiking, women's morbid fears and concealed passions are made worse by their being secluded without any diversion in the gloom of their chambers. As a therapy, they all recommend a change of environment, gymnastics, cheering conversation, amusements and music.[39] Further, the physician, according to Constantinus, must cure the disease with "reasonable and pleasant discourse, various kinds of music, and aromatic, clear and very light wine."[40] While Ovid plays the role of the *praeceptor amoris*

the excellent study by Mary F. Wack, *Memory and Love in Chaucer's* Troilus and Criseyde, Cornell Dissertation, 1982. For the links between medicine and philosophy, see also "La Glossa Latina di Dino del Garbo a 'Donna me prega' del Cavalcanti," ed. G. Favati, in *Annali della scuola normale superiore di Pisa. Lettere, storia e filosofia*, ser. 2, 21 (1952), pp. 70–103. Cf. A. C. Crombie, "Avicenna's Influence on the Medieval Scientific Tradition," in *Avicenna: Scientist and Philosopher*, ed. G. M. Wickens (London: Luzac and Co., 1952), pp. 84–107. Paul O. Kristeller, "Philosophy and Medicine in Medieval and Renaissance Italy," in *Organism, Medicine and Metaphysics: Essays in Honor of Hans Jonas on His 75th Birthday*, ed. S. Specker (Dordrecht: Riedel, 1978), pp. 29–40.

[38] R. Klibansky, E. Panofsky and F. Saxl, *Saturn and Melancholy. Studies in the History of Natural Philosophy, Religion and Art* (London: Nelson, 1964). Constantinus Africanus, *Libri duo de melancholia*, in *Opera* (Basel, 1536), I; also available in the edition by K. Garbers (Hamburg: H. Buske, 1977). Cf. also Robert Burton, *Anatomy of Melancholy*, ed. H. Jackson (New York: Random House, 1977).

[39] Constantinus Africanus, *Opera*, I, pp. 287–294. Arnaldus de Villanova, "De amore heroyco," in *Opera* (Lugduni: Fradin, 1504), 214r–215v.

[40] These are some of the suggestions provided by Constantinus: ". . . Adhibenda rationabilia et grata verba . . . tollendo quae in anima cum diversa musica et vino odorifero claro et subtilissimo . . ." *Opera*, I, p. 288. Cf. Panofsky, *Saturn and Melancholy*, pp. 82ff. Constantine adopts the doctrine of the

for the men betrayed by love and gives instructions whereby they can crush the baneful "seeds" of the disease, such as shunning of leisure, pursuit of husbandry and hunting, Boccaccio counters his lesson by writing for neglected women in love.

What is remarkable, however, is that the remedies for love melancholy physicians prescribe and Boccaccio echoes are exactly the same as the remedies that Tommaso del Garbo and Giovanni Dondoli recommend against the plague.[41] Tommaso, for instance, advises those at risk to flee the place where the pestilence is rampant and to take shelter in a spot where their thoughts can be delightful and pleasant and they can indulge in songs and entertainment.[42] Dondoli restates Tommaso's opinions but in a detailed language that closely recalls Boccaccio's formulations.

> *Non ne sia digiuno e ned patisca fame ne sete per nessun modo, ma temperatamente mangi, . . . Fuggansi abbracciamenti di femmine e tutti gli exercitii disordinati, . . . Anchora si fugghino tutti e puzzi di cose corrotte di corpi umani e d'animali o di gente inferma. . . . Anchora in quanto è possibile, studi l'uomo*

Salernitan School. See Brian Lawn, *The Salernitan Questions: An Introduction to the History of Medieval and Renaissance Problem Literature* (Oxford: Clarendon Press, 1963). See also S. De Renzi, *Collectio Salernitana* (Naples: F. Sebezio, 1852–59).

[41] A number of medical opinions on the plague (Del Garbo's, Dondoli's and Gentile da Foligno's) are available in Francesco Carabellese, *La Peste del 1348 e le condizioni della sanità pubblica in Toscana* (Rocca S. Casciano: Cappelli, 1897). For social background, see Raffaele Ciasca, *L'arte dei medici e speziali nella storia e nel commercio fiorentino dal secolo XII al secolo XV* (Florence: Olschki, 1927).

[42] The text by Tommaso del Garbo was recently shown to be part of Boccaccio's strategy by Letterio di Francia, *La novellistica*, p. 109. See also A. Scaglione, *Nature and Love*, p. 183. The passage which is usually quoted from *Consiglio contro a pistolenza*, ed. P. Ferrato. *Scelta di curiosità letterarie inedite o rare*, 74 (Bologna: Romagnoli, 1866), chap. 25, pp. 40–41, includes admonitions to have ". . . usanza . . . con persone liete e gioconde, e fugesi ogni maninconia, . . . e in giardini. . . ." It also prescribes avoiding solaces in baths and rivers, for which see the violation in *Conclusione, Decameron* VI, pp. 577–579. Glending Olson, *Literature as Recreation in the Later Middle Ages* (Ithaca: Cornell University Press, 1982), p. 175, returns to Tommaso's text. Cf. also Marga Cottino-Jones, p. 367.

di fuggire tutte quelle cose, che anno a contristare la mente. Im-
perochè per le passioni malinconiche il cuore sbigottisci, e li sogni
non turbano. . . . Ma per lo contrario studi a le e cose, che ab-
bono a conducere riso, donde lo cuore si dilecti, come è cantare e
sonare o udire cose giocose e vaghi narramenti. Mutare spesso
camicie bianche, usare belli vestimenti, giuochi di tavole o di
scacchi, nè altri giuochi non sono utili per lo fiato che rende l'uno
a l'altro. . . .

Do not fast nor in any way suffer hunger or thirst, but eat
moderately, . . . Avoid copulations with women and all
other disordered exercises. . . . Flee also the stench of
things corrupt, of human and animal bodies, or of sick
people. . . . Further, as far as possible, try to flee all those
things which sadden the mind, since melancholy passions
weigh on the heart and interfere with sleep. Seek on the
contrary those things that lead to laughter, by which the
heart delights, such as singing, playing instruments or listening to playful accounts and pleasant stories. Change
often the white shirts, dress smartly, play board games or
chess, but not those games which are not useful on account of the breath which goes from one player to the
other.[43]

It is plain how the two medical opinions are thoroughly
subsumed in the texture of the *Decameron*, which unfolds, as is
well known, with the ten young people resolving to go away
from the city to a pleasant natural spot. Here the tables are covered with "tovaglie bianchissime" (the whitest tablecloths, p.
29), dishes are daintily prepared, precious wines are at hand—
"le vivande dilicatamente fatte vennero e finissimi vini fur
presti" (dishes daintily prepared were brought in, very fine
wines are served, p. 29). During meals there is pleasant talk
and laughter; and while the young people live chastely, their
amusements are love songs, dances, storytelling, weaving
garlands, playing musical instruments and, at times, playing
with "tavolieri e scacchieri" (board games and chessboards, p.

[43] Carabellese, pp. 72–74.

30). Almost in mockery of Dondoli's explicit suggestion, the young people even fast on two Fridays in observance of Christ's passion.

Earlier in the text Boccaccio's attack against physicians was certainly unequivocal: their empirical remedies were inept, just as their control of the operations of nature was an imposture or, at best, a failure. Against their general claim that a metaphoric unity can exist between disease and cure, Boccaccio confronts an experience marked by an irremediable disjunction. Now, as he absorbs the medical precepts into the narrative of the *Decameron*, he empties their pronouncements—ironically identical for known and unknown ailments—of any scientific value and uncovers the fictional basis of their statements; he turns, in one word, the physicians into fabulators.

There is a tradition that conventionally views medicine as one of the "silent arts," as Vergil put it, or as John of Salisbury explains, "morbus non eloquentia sed remediis sanari."[44] Boccaccio, by contrast, evokes precisely the loquaciousness, acknowledgedly ineffectual, of the physicians. Medicine, it would seem, is important to him *because* it speaks: this means that he is enabled to exploit the resources of the physicians' illusory rhetoric and even to articulate the desire to give his literature a cathartic healing power. What is actually at stake is the connection between medicine and rhetoric, an insight which Plato had fully probed, but one which Petrarch, Boccaccio's interlocutor, had contested.

Plato held medicine and doctors in such a high esteem as to give them the pride of place among the practical arts. He admired their ethical code and viewed them as educators with a role akin to that of the philosophers, for the doctrine of virtue and health they teach is only a variant of the *arete* and of the order the philosopher pursues. It is especially in the *Phaedrus*

---

[44] *Aeneid* XII, 390ff. tells of Iapyx, disciple of Apollo and expert of the "silent arts"—healing and the power of herbs. For John of Salisbury, see his *Metalogicus*, I, 4, *PL* 199, col. 830. More generally, see Pedro Lain Entralgo, *The Therapy of the Word in Classical Antiquity*, trans. L. J. Rather and J. M. Shark (New Haven: Yale University Press, 1970).

that he argues in favor of envisioning medicine as the perfect model for rhetoric, for like medicine's, the task of rhetoric is to lead men to perceive what is most suitable for them.[45] Petrarch's position, however, is radically different. In the four books of his *Invectives against a Certain Physician* (which he sent to Boccaccio in 1357), written as a response to an angry physician's charge that he, Petrarch, knew no dialectic, had never read Galen's *Terapeutica*, and was only a poet, Petrarch questions the intellectual legitimacy of medicine and writes a defense of poetry.[46]

If Isidore or Petrus Hispanicus consider medicine a "secunda philosophia," for either art arrogates to itself the whole of man—by the one the body, by the other the soul is cured—Petrarch subscribes to the statement that medicine is a mechanical art, along with fabric making, agriculture and theatrics.[47] He acknowledges its utility, but rejects its claim to a divine origin or to the status of moral philosophy. In their attempt to supplant the power of rhetoric and poetry, physicians come forth as antihumanists, Averroists who observe the natural

[45] The description of Hippocrates—and the alliance between medicine and rhetoric—is in *Phaedrus* 270 c–d. More generally, see Jacqueline de Romilly, *Magic and Rhetoric in Ancient Greece* (Cambridge: Harvard University Press, 1975); for a more recent view, see Jacques Derrida, "La Pharmacie de Platon," in *La Dissémination* (Paris: Editions du Seuil, 1972), pp. 69–197; W. Jaeger, *Paideia: The Ideals of Greek Culture*, trans. G. Highet (New York: Oxford University Press, 1944), III, pp. 3–45. See also A. Castiglioni, *Il volto di Ippocrate* (Milan: Universitas, 1925).

[46] For Petrarch's correspondence with Boccaccio, see Ernest Hatch Wilkins, *Petrarch's Eight Years in Milan* (Cambridge: The Mediaeval Academy of America, 1958), pp. 141–146. See also D. C. Allen, "Petrarch and the Physicians," *Research Studies of the State College of Washington*, 3 (1935), pp. 37–47; E. Cerulli, "Petrarca e gli arabi," *Studi in onore di A. Schiaffini* (Rome: Rivista di cultura classica e medievale, 1965), I, pp. 331–336.

[47] Isidore of Seville, *Etym.*, IV, xiii, views medicine as incorporating all the liberal arts and concludes "Hinc est quod medicina secunda Philosophia dicitur." On this see the excellent bibliography in John M. Riddle, "Theory and Practice in Medieval Medicine," *Viator*, 5 (1974), pp. 157–184. But see *Invectiva contra medicum*, Testo latino e volgarizzamento di ser Domenico Silvestri, ed. Pier Giorgio Ricci (Rome: Storia e letteratura, 1950), esp. bks. III and IV, pp. 58–98.

world as an autonomous physical world and abide by its laws. And just as their knowledge is unreliable, their rhetoric is transparent: they wrap their errors and conjectures in vacuous lies and love empty emblems and ornaments. Their love for external symbols (Petrarch caricatures them for their pomposity in speech, dressing in purple and wearing fine rings) signals to him that they only care about the "putrid body" of man. By contrast the lies of poetry and rhetoric are veils sheltering the wisdom of the ancient and are valuable, he maintains, insofar as they are engaged in the analysis of the shadowy recesses of the soul.

Boccaccio shares, and in effect anticipates, Petrarch's view of the degeneration of medicine into a practice of appearances and dissemblance. Master Simon of Bologna (VIII, 9), as will be argued later in chapter 7, embodies in a way the very pretensions scorned by Petrarch; yet, his laughable stupidity, his naive belief in the existence of a symbolic bond between appearances and in effect nonexistent essences is for Boccaccio an imaginative value. In the brief story of another physician, Master Albert of Bologna (I, 10), on the other hand, the apparent foolishness of the physician can even turn out to be a source of wisdom. Master Albert is an old man, past his seventies, passionately in love with a beautiful widow. In terms of the courtly love of Andreas Capellanus, where the age limit of love is sixty, Albert's passion is a dementia and a social violation, for which he becomes the object of the widow's mockery.[48] The mockery, actually, reenacts the scene of the *gabbo*, the jest and derision in which the foolish lover is caught and which Dante dramatizes in the *Vita nuova*. At the same time, the story turns out to be a lesson on nature, as this *doctor amoris* explains to the widow that there cannot be an understanding of nature in terms of surface attributes alone.

Noteworthy, furthermore, is that the novella is framed by an introduction which has not been, to my knowledge, suffi-

---

[48] "Age is a bar, because after the sixtieth year a man and the fiftieth in a woman, although one may have intercourse his passion cannot develop into love; . . ." (*The Art of Courtly Love*, trans. Parry, I, v, p. 32).

ciently glossed. The storyteller Pampinea begins by positing a simile between, on the one hand, the ornaments of nature, stars in the sky and flowers in the fields, and, on the other, good manners and pleasant converse in women.[49] But women, she complains, adorn their bodies, as they go about heavily made-up and overdressed, and neglect the virtues of the mind and language. Blind to "Nature's intentions" they stand around dull witted like mute marble statues. The long digression proleptically bespeaks the fact that the physician, the master of love and nature, is a rhetorical figure that educates, compels, that is, the imagination to the properties of language, not as the pathway to knowledge, but as surface attributes and signs of beauty. More importantly, the story obliquely conjures up a view of speech which is valuable because it is at one with living: conversation gives life to the dumb statue and is a tool of erotic seduction.

This perception informs Boccaccio's own defense of literature in the *Genealogy of the Gentile Gods*, to which I must now briefly turn. Toward its final section, the mythological treatise is a response to the "blasphemers" who contend that poetry is inferior to philosophy, firstly, by denying that Plato banishes the poets from his republic; secondly, by refuting the charge that Boethius means to slander poetry when he expels the sluttish muses (*scenicas meretriculas*) from the bedside of the languishing prisoner.[50] Like Petrarch in the *Invectives*, Boccaccio

[49] "Valorose giovani, come ne' lucidi sereni sono le stelle ornamento del cielo e nella primavera i fiori ne' verdi prati, così de' laudevoli costumi e de' ragionamenti piacevoli sono i leggiadri motti, . . . Per ciò che quella vertù che già fu nell'anima delle passate hanno le moderne rivolta in ornamenti del corpo; . . ." (*Decameron* I, x, p. 83). The decay of rhetoric into cosmesis and made-up appearance is clearly seen as a departure from the norms of nature. This is a *topos* in patristic dismissals of the simulations of the theater.

[50] The passasge reads: "Amid clamor and discord they flourish the words of the most holy and learned Boethius, particularly those found near the beginning of his book on *Consolation*. It is the point where Philosophy speaks saying: 'Who hath let these drabs of the stage approach unto this man; for they apply no manner of remedy to his sufferings, but only nurse them with sweet poisons,' etc. . . . Little do they understand Boethius' words: they consider them only superficially; wherefore they bawl at the gentle and modest Muses,

interprets Boethius' statement to mean the bad muses who
nurse the sick with sweet poison (*dulce venenum*) and whom he
distinguishes from the good muses, trusted by the poets to
cure those sick of mind. It is the "poet-haters," he passionately
argues, who bawl at the "modest muses" as if they were
"women in the flesh" and accuse them of being "disreputable,
obscene, witches, harlots." Philosophy herself in *De consola-
tione philosophiae*, he concludes, cites "many a fragment of
verse and poetic fable to soothe and console Boethius."[51]

The *Decameron* obliquely refocuses on these issues and gives
them a crucial playful twist. If Boethius dismisses the strumpet
Muse of poetry (the *scenicas meretriculas*) because she disguises,
like actors on the stage, the abstract purity of philosophical
thought and because her *dulce venenum* corrupts the truth philosophy administers, lacks, that is, discursive rigor, and is
pleasurable only so long as it is heard, Boccaccio collapses this
concern. He writes a text, as he states in the Proem, which is
valuable because in its contingent unfolding it provides pleasure.[52] It is a text, furthermore, which is avowedly meretricious: its declared aim is for women brooding about love; it
comforts those who have lost love, but like the Galeotto, it is
also meant to procure new loves.[53] If for Boethius the only
remedy comes from philosophy, Boccaccio acknowledges
that his stories have no inherent remedial virtue and can be
either harmful or useful: "Chi non sa ch'è il vino ottima cosa
a' viventi, secondo Cinciglione e Scolaio e assai altri, e a colui

---

as if they were women in the flesh, simply because their names are feminine.
They call them disreputable, obscene, witches, harlots, and, forcing the
meaning of Boethius' diminutive, they would push them to the bottom of society, . . ." (*Genealogy of the Gods*, xiv, 20, in *Boccaccio on Poetry*, trans. Osgood, pp. 94–95).

[51] *Boccaccio on Poetry*, p. 96.

[52] "Nella qual noia tanto rifrigerio già mi porsero i piacevoli ragionamenti
d'alcuno amico e le sue laudevoli consolazioni . . . diletto delle sollezzevoli
cose in quelle mostrate . . . potranno pigliare" (*Proem, Decameron*, pp. 3–5).

[53] "Comincia il libro chiamato *Decameron* cognominato Prencipe Galeotto." *Title page*. On this see the discussion in chapter 2 below.

che ha la febbre é nocivo?" (Who will deny that wine, as Tosport and Bibber and a great many others affirm, is an excellent thing for those who are hale and hearty, but harmful to people suffering from a fever? p. 961.)

The rhetorical question echoes, I submit, "Temporis ars medicina est: data tempore prosunt / Et data non apto tempore vina nocent," from the *Remedia amoris*.[54] In this text, inspired by Apollo, the god of poetry and the art of healing (l. 76), and developed through the Platonic metaphoric bond of medicine and rhetoric, Ovid gives precepts (avoid theater and love-literature, never drink wine in moderation, either abstain or overdo it, do not eat onions) which, taken together, are a transparent burlesque of the rhetoric of pedagogical treatises and in themselves are useless to control the unbounded play of love (ll. 23–24). This Ovidian recall, with its playful insistence that remedies do not cure the diseases of love, both carries the brunt of Boccaccio's own insight that remedies are word games freed of any therapeutic power and enacts a strategy by which he undoes Boethius' claims. For just as he had stated in the *Genealogy of the Gentile Gods*, Boethius may have banished poetry and its lure, but poetry never quite left: Lady Philosophy herself was always a figure of poetry in disguise, and the *Decameron* ends up both bringing women on stage, as it were, and miming the formal structure of *satura*, an alternation of gloss and poems around which the *Consolation of Philosophy* is structured.

By this elaborate series of conceptual and figurative counterpoints, Boccaccio, against Boethius, marks the ongoing complicity between literature and philosophy, and literally makes a joke of the *Consolation of Philosophy*. Its ludicrous aims are exposed as he exploits the semantic weight of *consolatio*, et-

---

[54] Lines 131–132. The whole passage reads in English: "The art of being timely is almost a medicine: wine timely given helps, untimely harms. Nay, you would inflame the malady, and by forbidding imitate it, should you attack it at an unfitting time" (Ovid, *The Remedies of Love*, trans. J. H. Mozley [Cambridge: Harvard University Press, 1969], p. 187).

ymologically a *solatium*, the play and leisure which are everywhere in the *Decameron* and are even its central narrative category.

In the remaining pages of this chapter I shall explore Boccaccio's imagination of play, the idle wasting time the ten
young people choose as a way of countering and escaping the
horror of the plague. The dramatic juxtaposition between
plague and play is certainly not unusual nor is it confined to
therapeutics of medicine. Livy and St. Augustine, for instance,
account for the origin of the *ludi scenici* as a response to the epidemic which devastates the city of Rome.[55] More precisely,
the theatrical representations were an attempt to purge the
bane of the disease, after all other remedies and propitiations
of the gods failed. Though without its specific theatrical overtones, the world of play in the *Decameron* is yoked, as hinted
earlier, to a quite scrupulous observance of religious ritual, and
is also turned into a space of simulation in which Elissa, Dioneo, Filostrato and their companions are masks, names of
disguises for concealing their identities.

There is another, in a sense more earnest, simulation that the
storytellers enact in the closed order of play. This is the game
of utopia, which is to be understood as the imaginative project
to reverse and parody the corruption of the city they have left
behind. Thus, if the shape of the body politic in Florence is
crumbling; if the authority of the law, conventionally under-

---

[55] ". . . pestilentia fuit . . . et cum vis morbi nec humanis consiliis nec ope
divina levaretur victis superstitione animis ludi quoque scaenici, . . . caelestis
irae placamina instituti dicuntur." Titi Livi, *Ab urbe condita*, ed. H. J. Muller
(Zurich / Berlin: Weidmannsche Verlag, 1965), VII, 2, p. 105. The notion is
picked up by St. Augustine, who writes: "Know then, . . . that the scenic
games, exhibitions of shameless folly and licence, were established at Rome,
not by men's vicious cravings, but by the appointment of your gods . . . the
gods enjoined that games be exhibited in their honour to stay a physical pestilence; their pontiff prohibited the theatre from being constructed, to prevent
a moral pestilence" (*The City of God*, trans. M. Dods [New York: The Modern Library, 1950], I, 32, pp. 36–37). See also the brilliant piece by a modern,
A. Artaud, "Theatre and the Plague," *The Theatre and Its Double* in *Collected
Works*, trans. V. Corti (London: Calder and Boyars, 1974), IV, pp. 7–21.

stood as the medicine of the body politic, is transgressed; if the foundation of moral life is shattered; if the most elementary works of mercy, such as the burial of the dead and the caring for the sick, are neglected; if community can only be defined by the communication of the infection; if the exercise of reason, eclipsed in man, seems the attribute only of animals who roam freely through the fields and, unguided, return in the evenings to their quarters—now, the *brigata* is in a pastoral natural landscape, a place where its members have not to wrestle with nature nor do they have to obey the laws of necessity. Work is excluded from this bower of bliss in favor of that "festa, quell'allegrezza, quello piacere" (entertainment, that delight and that pleasure, p. 22) that they can take. These pleasures do not entail a surrender to licentious impulses; or, to put it differently, their game is not Jocus, the perverse love or *ludus instabilis*, born of the adultery of Venus and Antigamus in Alan's *De planctu naturae*.[56] It is a game in which, against Jean who explicitly ridicules celibacy and chastity, the practice of physical love is banished and the dictates of reason are said to be followed.[57]

As Pampinea starts persuading the other young women she meets in the Church of Santa Maria Novella to leave the city, she appeals to reason and to their natural right to preserve their lives. Later she urges her companions to abide in the garden "senza trapassare in alcun atto il segno della ragione" (without

---

[56] *PL* 210, col. 455. In the meter, Love as Sport accounts for the oxymora and the general reversal of all terms: ("Pax odio, fraudique fides, spes iuncta timori, Est amor . . . Dulce malum, mala dulcedo . . . mors vivens, moriens vita . . ."). For the identity of Jocus, see also this other passage: "Two sons were given, then, to Dione's daughter, different by discrepancy of origin, dissimilar by law of birth, unlike in their moral reputation, different by diversity of skill. . . . He begat from Venus a son, Desire. On the other hand the buffoonish Antigenius, sprung from an ignoble line, in rakish fashion fathered, in adultery with Venus, a bastard son, Sport" (*The Plaint of Nature*, trans. J. J. Sheridan, pp. 164–165).

[57] See, for instance, *Le Roman de la Rose*, ll. 19505ff. Cf. also Venus' speech: " 'May I perish in a miserable death,' she said, 'that may take me straightway, if I ever let chastity dwell in any woman alive, . . .'" (*Roman*, ll. 15830 ff.; trans. Dahlberg, p. 268).

trespassing in any action the mark of reason, p. 23). Though
reason in the *Decameron* is a confused designation under which
one can easily smuggle the most disparate opinions, one gathers from the context that "ragione" is to be understood as restraint, rather than as an abstract rationality which would conform either to the order of nature, which in reality is sheer
chaos, or to the order of the garden to which they move, for
the garden is an artifice of nature. But the phrase has a more
complex resonance: it echoes, I would like to suggest, the lines
of *Paradiso* XXVI, 115–117: "Or, figliuol mio, non il gustar del
legno / fu per sé la cagion di tanto essilio, / ma sólamente il tra-
passar del segno" (Now, my child, not the tasting of the tree,
but the trespassing of the mark was the cause of such an exile).
The passage, which in its original context describes Adam's
fall from the Garden of Eden, discloses Boccaccio's irony: as
the youngsters move into the idyllic space, halfway between
reality and a fantasy world, they seem to reverse Adam's experience of the fall; at the same time, there is an intimation of
precariousness, a hint that the safe bounds of the garden are
just as illusory for them as they were for Adam.

The oblique textual recall also gauges the distance between
what one could call the Games of God and the leisure of the
storytellers. In the eternal playing of God, Adam in the Garden is its centerpiece and the promise of a paradise to be re-
gained is God's sign to man that he may return home and play.
Clearly, as the storytellers make it to the garden, they are not
governed by what could be called a theology of play, a view of
jocunditas as a moral virtue, as Aquinas understands it.[58] Their
playing is, in a way, an imitation of the philosopher, who in
his *schole*, literally in his leisure, seeks wisdom as its own esthetic end; it is an instance of a deliberate shirking of work and
duties, a truancy, which, while it relieves from the anxieties of
the plague, asserts the players' freedom and mastery, by the
imagination, of the space they occupy in the midst of the
world's dereliction.

[58] St. Thomas Aquinas' understanding of relaxation is treated in chapter 9.
See below nn. 44–48 for further references.

It has been said in recent times that man is wholly man when he is at play.[59] There are, in effect, few other things (love, death) that, for Boccaccio, completely engage the imagination, will and body of man with the intensity of play. In the play of the *Decameron*, however, the body is absent, either misshapen and disfigured by the plague or held at bay during the two weeks of the escape to the garden. In the stories, the free play of the imagination constantly stumbles against the passions of other imaginations as the "beffa" (joke) which the beautiful widow Elena plays on the young scholar Rinieri (VIII, 7) shows.[60] After years of studying in Paris "la ragione delle cose e la cagione d'esse" (the reason of things and their cause, p. 711) Rinieri returns to Florence. In need of diversion he goes to a banquet where he sees and quickly falls in love with Elena. He puts aside his philosophical meditations, while Elena seems to encourage him, but in effect decides to play a trick on him. She promises to receive him in her room, and one night in the dead of winter, while Rinieri is kept outside freezing to death, she cavorts with her lover till the early hours of the morning. The text turns into a transparent parody of the medieval erotic *alba*, and as Rinieri perceives that he has been duped in the vigil, he changes his love into hatred and makes elaborate plans for securing his revenge. It is by chance, however, that he will gratify his longing for "giusta retribuzione" (just retribution, p. 710), the law of Dante's Hell. It has happened in the meantime that the foolish widow has lost her lover and asks the scholar whether with his knowledge of magic arts he can help her to get him back. Overjoyed, the scholar agrees to help by necromantic conjuration. He directs the woman to go by night to a stream, dip naked into it while holding an image

[59] Frederick Schiller, "Letters on the Aesthetical Education of Man," trans. in *The Works of Frederick Schiller* (New York: Lovell Co., 1886), IV, esp. Letters XIVff., pp. 75–125.

[60] For other aspects of the novella, cf. M. Leone, "Tra autobiografismo reale e ideale in 'Decameron VIII, 7,' " *Italica*, 50 (1973), pp. 242–265; Guido Almansi, "Alcune osservazioni sulla novella dello scolaro e della vedova," *Studi sul Boccaccio*, 8 (1974), pp. 137–145.

of her lover in her hands and then climb to the top of a nearby tower. While she carries out the instructions, the scholar, who has been hiding behind a bush, removes the ladder from the tower. He keeps the woman on the platform under the heat of the blazing sun for a whole day and, finally gratified, lets her go.

Though the scholar vies with the strumpet, each comes through as the mirror reflection of the other. The symmetrical design of the two *beffe* discloses their essential interdependence. The second half of the story is arranged as a pointed reversal of the metaphors that organize the first half: night, thus, is changed into day, winter into summer, snow into heat, etc. These turnings find a counterpart at a thematic level as desire turns into aggression, philosophy into madness, learning into weapon of power, promises of either scholar or strumpet into deceptions. The reversals dramatize the insight that love and knowledge never quite coincide; as each of the principals is no doubt different from the other, both of them are caught in the same moves: they are blind to each other's deceptions, and at the end, more generally, they are both in need of medical treatment.

The phrase at the outset of the novella, "l'arte è dall'arte schernita" (art is mocked by art, p. 710), which translates "ars deluditur arte," an aphorism from the *Distica Catonis*, draws attention to the balanced, retributive order that the *beffa* enacts.[61] It also conceals, however, the violence, the menace of the passions which lie under and quickly can surface from the world of play. The play, in turn, far from being governed by a set of fixed conventions, is set in motion by the strumpet, a figure who at first disrupts the game of courtly love; who later is an emblem of free play, never allowing herself to be won, offering and denying herself, perverse and gullible, always herself by feigning, and whom the scholar fails to possess but succeeds in punishing. It is by concealing the dangers under-

[61] *Distica Catonis*, I, 26.

neath the jokes, or by feigning that a balance can be reestablished, that the *beffe* become pleasurable pastimes.

Pastime, in effect, is the essence of the *Decameron*, which the category of play discloses. This "passing time" is to be understood in the sense of diversion, of "wasting time," (possibly even with the deluded knowledge that time is wasting us as we think we waste it) of enjoyment of the sensuous and frivolous qualities that the text lavishly evokes. The diversion brings with it, in the same breath, the playful knowledge of what could be called the truth of time as the flight of time.

In the prelude, introduction and throughout the *Decameron*, Boccaccio warns us that essential is not to learn, for knowledge comes too early or too late to be of any real use. Essential is to love. He also tells us that love is a disease and a child of time (as the mythic account of Venus' origin from Chronos' emasculation shows), and is bound, that is, to a temporal scheme of memory and imagination. The first two sections of the text display abundantly the presence of this pattern. Love is said in the Proem to be subjected to the "processo di tempo;" (movement of time, p. 3); the memory of a past love gives an abiding pleasure; the plague, a temporary anomaly, has, first, to be recollected and, later, forgotten. In the epilogue, finally, the unstable world of time, opposed to the permanence of God, is its explicit thematic concern. All together these are metaphors that focus on the radical contingency of every experience in the *Decameron*, by which the absolute truth of philosophy and its body of thought are not necessary; they are not even so important when compared to the involuntary insights of the disguised strumpet Muse into the ruptures of time and the shifty surface values of worldliness.

In this world of time and numbered days which the *Decameron* literally is, each moment is contiguous to the other, each is disjunct and partitioned from the other; each experience is both a digression from and a frame to another, the plague for the play, and the play for the plague, without ever intersecting as in a chiasmus, though they well might. Caught in this predicament, the young people of the *lieta brigata*, who had met by chance in the church, play and tell stories in simulated obliviousness of the surrounding chaos. And as they play chess or checkers and dice to pass the time, there is the flicker of a dark premonition that they themselves may be pawns in the Game of Death, or its shadow, the agon of Time.

THE MARGINALITY OF
LITERATURE

There has been no sustained examination of Boccaccio's reflections on the meaning of literature in the *Decameron*. Probably because Boccaccio himself in his Introduction places his fiction in a garden, critics have often spoken of the *Decameron* as nothing more than escapist literature.[1] The plague that necessitates the escape is seen to provide the literal alibi that makes any serious concern with the world irrelevant.

If this were all, the *Decameron* would still be in itself a substantial cultural achievement. An intimation of what can be at stake in the choice of a garden as the frame for the stories can be obtained by a quick comparison with one corresponding aspect in the narrative structure of Chaucer's *Canterbury Tales*. The point of departure for the pilgrims on their way to the shrine in Canterbury is the Tabard Inn.[2] This locale is primarily the stage for the pilgrims' convivial indulgences: as the po-

---

[1] An overt espousal of this view is to be found in Charles S. Singleton, "On Meaning in the *Decameron*" *Italica*, 21 (1944), pp. 117–124. See also Francesco De Sanctis, *History of Italian Literature*, trans. John Redfern, 2 vols. (New York: Harcourt Brace, 1931), I, p. 359, where he states that art is the only thing in life Boccaccio takes seriously. This critical line is extended in Erich Auerbach, *Mimesis: The Representation of Reality in Western Literature*, trans. Willard R. Trask (New York: Anchor Books, 1957), pp. 177–203.

[2] "Bifil that in that seson on a day, / In Southwerk at the Tabard as I lay / Redy to wenden on my pilgrymage / To Caunterbury with ful devout corage, / At nyght was come into that hostelrye / Wel nyne and twenty in a compaignye, . . ." *The Canterbury Tales*, General Prologue, 11. 19–24, quoted from *The Works of Geoffrey Chaucer*, ed. F. N. Robinson, 2nd ed. (Boston: Houghton Mifflin Co., 1957).

etic texts of a Cecco Angiolieri or Dante himself have it, the
tavern is the place where devilish *ioca* are enacted.[3] But the inn
is also the emblem of the precariousness of man's earthly
dwelling place and, in general, of the pilgrimage of human
life.[4]

The double value of this initial metaphor is a powerful hint
of Chaucer's ironies fully articulated throughout his *Tales*.
Boccaccio's strategy in making the garden the locale for the
storytelling is different but no less imaginative a move. To
quit the arena of history and voluntarily lapse into intransitive
esthetic fruition is perhaps a fundamental revision of St. Augustine's Christian doctrine that the esthetic experience be in-
strumental to man's spiritual ends; that literature like the prophetic writings be the nexus between man and God.[5] But

[3] "Tre cose solamente mi so' in grado, / le quali posso non ben ben for-
nire: / ciò è la donna, la taverna e 'l dado; / queste mi fanno 'l cuor lieto sen-
tire." I am quoting from *Sonetti burleschi e realistici dei primi due secoli*, ed. Aldo
Francesco Massera, 2 vols. (Bari: Laterza, 1920), I, p. 112. Cecco Angiolieri's
taste for taverns and gambling appears in IX, 4 of the *Decameron*. On the novella, see M. Baratto, *Realtà e stile nel Decameron* (Vicenza: Pozza, 1970), pp.
234–237. The importance of this "realistic" literary tradition has been studied
by Salvatore Battaglia, "L'estro del Boccaccio," in *Giovanni Boccaccio e la riforma della narrativa* (Naples: Liguori, 1969), pp. 195–213; Mario Marti, *Cultura e stile nei poeti giocosi del tempo di Dante* (Pisa: Nistri-Lischi, 1953). See also
the general treatment by Antonino Pagliaro, *Poesia giullaresca e poesia popolare*
(Bari: Laterza, 1958). For Dante's place in the tradition, see Marti in the volume just cited. One could also point out the protasis of *Inferno* XXII, which,
after the comedy of the devils, describes the devils' noise in terms of drums
heard at tournaments and jousts. The simile issues into the lines: "Ahi fiera
compagnia! ma ne la chiesa / coi santi, e in taverna coi ghiottoni" (*Inferno*
XXII, 14–15).

[4] "At contra justi . . . sic . . . refoventur subsidio, sicut viator in stabulo
utitur lecto: pausat et recedere festinat; . . . Nonnumquam vero et adversa
perpeti appetunt, in transitoriis prosperare refugiunt, ne delectatione itineris a
patriae perventione tardentur . . ." (Gregory the Great, *Moralia in Job*, PL 75,
cols. 857б–858б).

[5] St. Augustine, *On Christian Doctrine*, trans. D. W. Robertson, Jr. (Indi-
anapolis: The Library of Liberal Arts, 1958), bk. I, chap. 3. The view, very
pervasive in medieval theories of esthetics, is of considerable influence on the
last two books of Boccaccio's *Genealogia deorum gentilium*. See on this, Francesco Tateo, "Poesia e favola nella Poetica del Boccaccio," in *"Rhetorica" e
"Poetica" fra Medioevo e Rinascimento* (Bari: Adriatica, 1960), pp. 62–202.

Boccaccio, paradoxically known as *Joannes tranquillitatum*, is radically unable to rest content with the formulation of an absolute and stable antithesis between the esthetic order and historical existence just as he is equally unable to accept the Christian view of a creative unity between literature and life. Far from being an evasion into frivolity, the retreat to the garden is a dramatic strategy that enables Boccaccio to reflect on history and to find, in this condition of marginality, of provisional separation from the historical structures, a place for secular literature.

Literature, one could agree, is always written on the margin, where there is an emptiness, and in the desert, outside the city of life: the patristic writings are *marginalia* to the Logos, commentaries around the biblical text. The *Divine Comedy* is the journey of literature across the desert to the City of God. Writing glosses is also the most conventional activity of the humanists. When Boccaccio, for instance, finished writing his *Decameron*, he compiled a mythological dictionary and footnotes to Dante.[6] But the *Decameron* itself is not an exegesis of the Logos, the way Dante's *Comedy* in many ways is. Yet its mode of being is one of marginality in relationship to existing literary traditions, cultural myths and social structures, to that which, in one word, we call history.

The dramatic relation between literary marginality and history does not have a clear-cut configuration in the *Decameron*, both because the world of history is seen as absolute negativity, corroded by the plague, and because Boccaccio intentionally writes secular literature. In the absence of the Logos, what meaning can literature possibly have? What is its function in this world of death? What does it accomplish in the neutral area Victor Turner calls "betwixt and between?"[7]

---

[6] I am referring, of course, to the completion of *Genealogia deorum gentilium libri*, ed. Vincenzo Romano, 2 vols. (Bari: Laterza, 1951) and to his lectures on the *Divine Comedy*, for which see *Giovanni Boccaccio: Esposizioni sopra la Comedia di Dante*, ed. Giorgio Padoan, in *Tutte le opere di Giovanni Boccaccio*, VI (Milan: Mondadori, 1965).

[7] Victor Turner, *The Forest of Symbols* (Ithaca: Cornell University Press, 1970), pp. 93ff. See also Victor Turner, *The Ritual Process* (Chicago: Aloline

Within this context, we must reject Auerbach's remarks that the *Decameron* never transcends the purely phenomenal aspects of historical experience and that it "becomes weak and superficial as soon as the problematic or the tragic is touched upon."[8] Boccaccio's primary concern is rather to reflect on the continuities and discontinuities between literature and history. He clearly understood that literature always has a historical dimension, yet its historicity is deliberately impoverished, shrunk to the unserious and the banal. When literature fails in its impulse to capture and interpret the mass of empirical fragments in a significant historical structure, it brings itself into being as a degraded object of erotic mediation. The *Decameron* is, in many ways, a reflection of the essential discontinuity between literature and historical reality and on the deliberate self-reduction of literature to the ontological status of a "thing."

Boccaccio pursues these problems throughout the *Decameron*. In this chapter, I propose to isolate and examine, on the one hand, some crucial passages in the Introduction, the Introduction to the fourth day and the Conclusion; on the other hand, I propose to relate to these passages some *novelle* where literary self-reflexiveness and historical awareness are openly dramatized.

Undoubtedly, the pastoral mode constitutes the primary strategy of Boccaccio's fiction. He attempts to weave and subsume into the continuity of the pastoral structure the various levels of the book. The retreat of the *brigata* to the *locus amoenus* to tell stories, away from the terror of the plague-stricken city, finds its counterpart in the author's own distance from an inordinate love of the past. The *fluctus concupiscentiae* that threatened his life was also averted by the "piacevoli ragionamenti d'alcuno amico" (the pleasant conversations of some friends, p. 3). Accordingly, the *Decameron* is consistently traversed by a double pastoral: the pastoral of the garden corresponds to

---

Publishing Co., 1969). The two terms, marginality and liminality, which Turner keeps separate, tend to be confused, in sometimes too facile a manner, in some recent works on Dante and Boccaccio.

[8] *Mimesis*, p. 202.

historical chaos and the pastoral of the author to erotic chaos. Since literary entertainment is common to both of them, we shall speak of a pastoral of literature. The pastoral of literature goes beyond the author's esthetic recollection of the radical disorders of the flesh; it absorbs the readers who must be distracted from the despair of love into its own rhetoric of evasion. In all these cases, the absolute presupposition of the literary garden is death; literature is seen as the positive vehicle by which to transcend the experiment of death, by forgetting it.

The retreat into the garden is, thus, obviously an effort to cope with loss and a conversion to life. Aptly enough, the *Decameron* begins with a dramatic emblem of life, with a reference to the anniversary of the Incarnation, the symbolic date of the beginning of the world:

> *Dico adunque che già erano gli anni della fruttifera incarnazione del Figliuolo di Dio al numero prevenuti di milletrecento quarantotto, quando nell'egregia città di Fiorenza, oltre a ogn' altra italica bellissima, pervenne la mortifera pestilenza; la quale per operazion de' corpi superiori o per le nostre inique opere da giusta ira di Dio a nostra correzione mandata sopra i mortali, alquanti anni davanti nelle parti orientali incominciata . . . verso l'Occidente miserabilmente s'era ampliata.*

> I say, then, that the sum of thirteen hundred and forty-eight years had passed since the fruitful Incarnation of the Son of God when the noble city of Florence, which is far nobler than any other Italian city, was visited by the deadly pestilence. This pestilence, which either through the influence of the heavenly bodies or because of our iniquitous ways descended upon the human race for our punishment, had started some years earlier in the East . . . (and) had unhappily spread Westward. (pp. 9–10)

I have examined the passage in the previous chapter. Let me now add that while Boccaccio attempts to situate the plague in historical space and time, he uses what in medieval rhetoric is a conventional topos of exordium. The vernal equinox, occur-

ring on the Feast of the Annunciation, 25 March, is the emblem of the beginning of the world, the fall of man and his redemption. The date stands at the exact center of the historic
process and is a typological recapitulation of the great events
of salvation history. Conventionally, medieval works of fiction begin with this typological *ab initio*. More prominently,
the *Divine Comedy* and the *Canterbury Tales*, with significant
differences, employ this rhetorical device as a deliberate sign
that the book is a synopsis of the pilgrimage of human history
and a way of creatively participating in the *renovatio mundi*.[9]

The use of this *topos* in the *Decameron* also transcends mere
rhetorical interest. Its conceptual function is clear in the description of the plague. The plague, rooted in the historical
particularity of 1348, is expanded by Boccaccio into a metaphor for the totality of history. By describing it as a continuous east-west movement, Boccaccio is applying to the plague
the Christian interpretation of the historic process. The doctrine of history as a spatial-temporal *translatio* from east to
west, patterned on the movement of the sun, with the Incarnation at its center, is inverted in order to dramatize the totality of history *sub specie mortis*.[10] No redemption, therefore, is
intended by the reference to 25 March. The intensification of
the fecundity engendered by the Incarnation through the epi-

---

[9] For Dante, see *Inferno* I, 37–43. Benvenuto da Imola, *Comentum super Dan-tis Aldigherij Comoediam*, ed. Giacomo Filippo Lacaita, 2 vols. (Florence: Bar-beri, 1887) comments on these lines as follows: "Dicunt enim astrologi et theologi quod Deus ab initio saeculi posuit solem in ariete, in quo signo facit nobis ver." The opening lines of the General Prologue of the *Canterbury Tales*, ed., F. N. Robinson, also use the astronomical reference for the pilgrimage motif. More generally, see Macrobius, *Commentarium in somnium Scipionis*, ed. J. Willis (Leipzig: B. F. Tuebner, 1970), I, chap. 21.

[10] The metaphor of the *translatio* for the movement of history is explicitly mentioned by Boccaccio in the *Decameron*, II, 8, in the novella of the Conte d'Anguersa, treated extensively below in chapter 3. For a documented history of this doctrine, see P. Van den Baar, *Die Kirchliche Lehre der Translatio Imperii Romani* (Rome: Analecta Gregoriana, LXXVIII, 1956); W. Goez, *Translatio Im-perii* (Tubingen: J.C.B. Mohr, 1958); E. R. Curtius, *European Literature and the Latin Middle Ages*, trans. W. R. Trask (New York: Harper Torchbooks, 1963), p. 29.

thet "fruttifera" only underscores the ironic disparity between the typological abstraction and the reality of death. Typology, which is the prophetic interpretation of the structure of history, is annihilated in the world of death.

It is this general vision of history as absolute death that compels Boccaccio to search for a pastoral heterocosm and to claim for the *Decameron* what might be called a metahistorical autonomy. The very word *Decameron* has in itself a symbolic resonance that can hardly escape students of the Middle Ages. The title is patterned, as has been commonly acknowledged, on the medieval *Hexamera*, schematized accounts of the succession of events in the history of the world which were modeled on the six days of creation. Boccaccio secularizes the title by significantly altering the six days into ten days. In medieval numerical symbolism, moreover, ten is the number of temporal perfection, of self-enclosed totality.[11] With its claim to be sufficient and coherent enclosure the *Decameron* is projected as an antiworld, an atemporal esthetic garden juxtaposed to the history of mutability and death.

The secularization of this seemingly privileged literary cosmos is stressed by two other correlated motifs. The first is the transition from the corrupt city of the world to the garden of literature which takes place through the Church. The Church is an enclosed garden, commonly described as the *hortus conclusus*, a Christian variant of the pastoral mode because it is interpreted as the typological figuration of the Garden of Eden.[12] It is in the Church, in itself a liminal place because it is the space where disjunctive experiences converge (time-eternity), that the *brigata* convenes and decides to escape to a pagan refuge, a *locus amoenus*. This narrative move is not an abstract polemic, nor is it a formal strategy without a particular cultural reference. It ought to be stressed, I would suggest, that Iacopo Passavanti in his *Specchio di vera penitenza*, a series of sermons de-

[11] Curtius, *European Literature*, pp. 501ff. See also V. H. Hopper, *Medieval Number Symbolism* (New York: Columbia University Press, 1938).

[12] This motif is common to most homiletic expositions of *Apocalypse* 21: 2–11; see St. Augustine, *PL* 35, col. 2450. See also Bede, *PL* 93, cols. 194–195.

livered at the height of the plague in the church of Santa Maria Novella, was passionately urging his audience to give up worldly delights and lead an ascetic life if they cared to save their souls. The plague to him was a sign of God's wrath and the proper response to it was a spiritual conversion.[13] As Boccaccio's *brigata* meets in the very church where Passavanti preached and leaves it behind, Boccaccio marks how the garden of literature begins as a parody of institutional liminality.

Although this first detail reinforces our general interpretation that the *Decameron* is a provisional conversion to a secular order, I would not emphasize its importance if it were not part of a consistent pattern of changes of locale. At the end of the sixth day, the *brigata* moves into the "Valle delle Donne" (valley of the ladies, p. 577), an idyllic landscape where on the seventh day, ironically, the discussion is of the deceits within the structure of marriage; the ordered idyllic background is a mockery of marriage, because marriage, ever since St. Paul and the patristic allegorizations of the *Song of Songs*, is the sacramental figure of an immanent experience of edenic unity.

This second detail which emphasizes the process of secularization of the literary garden is more important because it brings into question the aim of this literary venture. While still in the church, the *brigata* decides to structure itself as a hierar-

---

[13] Iacopo Passavanti, *Specchio di vera penitenza*, 2 vols. (Milan: Società Tipografica de' Classici Italiani, 1808). The link between Passavanti and Boccaccio, which was accepted, as the preface to this edition shows, even in the sixteenth century, was suggested in our time by L. Di Francia, *La novellistica* (Milan: Vallardi, 1924). Di Francia quotes the following passage from Passavanti's *Specchio*: "Va, o uomo d'altura, quando vaneggi nella mente tua, e considera la viltà della sepoltura. Va garzone, giovane altiero e sanza freno quando t'allegri co' compagni, e vai in brigata sanza temperanza, seguitando i voleri, e poni mente i sepolcri pieni di bruttura, e di puzzolente lordura. Va, donna svaliata e leggiadra, quando ti diletti d'essere guatata, e giovati d'essere pregiata e tenuta bella, sguarda nelle fosse de' cimiteri le carni verminose e fracide. Va, donzella vezzosa, che studi in bel parere, azzimandoti e adornandoti, per avere nome e pregio di bellezza, o d'essere dagli amanti amata, e specchiati n'e monimenti, pieni d'abominevole fracidume." This passage occurs in volume two of the present edition of the *Specchio*, Trattato dell'umiltà, chap. 4, pp. 117–118.

chical *communitas*, turning the experience in the *locus amoenus* into an ironic reversal of the city:

> *Disse allora Elissa: "Veramente gli uomini sono delle Femine capo e senza l'ordine loro rade volte riesce alcuna nostra opera a laudevole fine . . . !"*

> Then Elissa said: "Man is truly the head of the woman and without a man it rarely happens that an enterprise of ours comes to a worthy conclusion. . . ."   (p. 24)

The biblical allusion in this passage, like its irony, is transparent. St. Paul in the *Letter to the Ephesians* wrote of the mystical body of the Church as follows:

> Wives, be subject to your husbands, as to the Lord; for the husband is the head of the wife, even as Christ is the head of the Church.[14]

The Pauline doctrine of the mystical body, expressed through the marriage analogy, is uniformly used as the rationale of the body politic in the political theology of the Middle Ages.[15] The irony, of course, consists in the fact that Boccaccio secularizes St. Paul's vision of order precisely in the Church, and thus goes into a double mockery of the City and the Church, which theoretically incarnate that order. The whole of the *Decameron* is, in a sense, a quest for order and unity achieved, somewhat ambiguously, through marriage. In the story of Griselda, marriage itself is the metaphor for the reinstatement of opposites to a prelapsarian and sacramental unity.

The Pauline allusion to the edenic myth of order and hierarchy makes manifest the utopian impulse of the escape and connects the escape dialectically with history: the literary experience is an antiworld, disengaged from history only in order to reflect from this marginal state both on itself and on the chaos of the world, and ultimately to return to the world with a vitally renewed apprehension of its structures. In this con-

---

[14] *Ephesians* 5: 22–23.
[15] E. Kantorowicz, *The King's Two Bodies* (Princeton: Princeton University Press, 1966), pp. 194ff.

text, the irony we have stressed is not the simple irony of reversed meaning, but a systematic and all-encompassing mockery of the structures of society. The very chastity of the *brigata*
in the *locus amoenus* is a brilliant parodic counterpoint to the
frank sexuality of some of the tales, possibly a self-mockery of
the storytellers, in the same way that the vision of order formulated in the church is, as we have seen, a parody of the lawlessness and anarchy of the city.

The view of literature as a middle ground between two ab-
sences, between utopia and social structures, as a provisional
retreat from the city in an atemporal space, is intensified by the
brigata's ritual of return, at the end of the storytelling, to the
church where its members had originally met. The *brigata* dissolves at the end because no finality is possible for the pastoral
interlude.

There is, however, a radical disproportion between, on the
one hand, this view of literature mediating between order and
chaos and aspiring to be an alternate world and, on the other,
the systematic degradation of the text to the role of a "Galeotto." The very subtitle of the *Decameron* reads "prencipe
Galeotto" (Prince Gallehault). Boccaccio's own gloss on "Galeotto fu il libro e chi lo scrisse" of *Inferno* v establishes a clear
perspective on the inner form of the *Decameron*.[16] Dante's Gallehault is the book in its function as intermediary of love between Paolo and Francesca, the dramatic equivalent of Pan-
darus in Chaucer's *Troilus and Criseyde*. Aware of literature

---

[16] Dante's line, as is known, occurs in *Inferno* v, 137. Boccaccio in his *Esposizioni sopra la Comedia*, writes: "Scrivesi ne' predetti romanzi che un prencipe Galeotto, il quale dicono che fu di spezie di gigante, sì era grande e grosso,
sentì primo che alcuno altro l'occulto amor di Lancialotto e della reina Gine-
vra; . . . ad aprire questo amore con alcuno effetto fu il mezzano: . . ." (ed.
Padoan, p. 324). See the recent musings on the discrepancy between Dante's
ethical perspective and Boccaccio's commentary in Wesley Trimpi, *Muses of
One Mind. The Literary Analysis of Experience and Its Continuity* (Princeton:
Princeton University Press, 1983), pp. 349–361. See also for bibliography,
Robert Hollander, *Boccaccio's Two Venuses* (New York: Columbia University
Press, 1977), pp. 102–107 and 225–228.

as an erotic snare—a commonplace of medieval romances[17]—
Boccaccio seems intent on assigning to this text the role of
erotic mediator, and thus unmasking the threats and seduc-
tions of his own artifact.

The audience itself that Boccaccio chooses, the women who
sit "quasi oziose" (of leisure, p. 4), exposes the trap of the literary act. In a way Boccaccio is alluding to and playing with a
convention that came to full flower with the poets of the Sweet
New Style, chiefly among them, Dante. In the *Vita nuova*, the
poem that is said to signal a radical shift in poetic style evokes
exactly the audience of women. The song "Donne ch'avete in-
telletto d'amore" strives, among other things, to bring together in the figure of the women, who are apostrophied, love
and intellect, two terms that Cavalcanti, for instance, in a
poem also addressed to a woman ("Donna me prega"), sees as
inexorably sundered from each other.[18] Within this context,
Boccaccio's gesture of addressing the *Decameron* to the women
of leisure is a coy claim and, concomitantly, an admission of
estheticism and futility. Even St. Augustine's esthetic doctrine
of the *uti et frui*, to which I have alluded in my preliminary remarks, is depreciated: women who will read the tales "diletto
delle sollazzevoli cose in quelle mostrate e utile consiglio potranno pigliare . . ." (will be able to derive pleasure from the
entertaining matters as well as useful advice . . . , p. 5). The
world of pornography is revealed as the essential structure
which supersedes the impossible effort to write serious literature.

Boccaccio, therefore, clearly establishes in his introduction
a state of tension between two types of literary mediation, the
erotic mediation and the prophetic mediation. What is the link

[17] Denis de Rougement, *Love in the Western World*, trans. Montgomery Belgion (Greenwich, Connecticut: Fawcett Publications, 1966).

[18] A clear, if well-known, formulation of both Dante's and Cavalcanti's
imaginative understanding of the figure of the woman, as it is to be found in
their poetry, is provided by G. Favati, *Inchiesta sul dolce stil nuovo* (Florence: Le
Monnier, 1975), esp. pp. 225–226.

between them? Is Boccaccio inviting us to read the text simultaneously on two levels? Or does the reduction of the text to the role of procurer serve to question literature itself and its vital role in the reordering of the world? These questions are explored in some of the novelle to which we now turn.

The very first novella of the *Decameron* throws into focus several aspects of the relationship between typology and literature to which I have alluded. Critics have chosen to read it in ways that cripple and sterilize it. They have emphasized the credulity of the friar confessor, the shrewd bourgeois cynicism of the merchants, or more subtly, the *arte di vivere* of the protagonist.[19] The novella, to be sure, is so rich that it can sustain a great many commentaries. Here, we shall try to read it as a deliberate metaliterary act, or more precisely, as a tale about the deception of language. Boccaccio, in other words, at the strategic and crucial moment of venturing into a universe of tales, stops to unveil the possible mystifications of literary creation and its links with history.

The preamble to the tale uncovers its thematic basis. There is a statement on the flux and corruption of the temporal order; and there is a formulation of the efficacy of prayer to mediate between the confusion of the world and the stability and unity of God. These two problems are pivotal to the inner structure of the tale because its thematic core, by contrast, is the attempt of the language of man to order and formalize the chaos of experience.

The tale is articulated in two ironic halves: in the first half, we are given an impersonal and objective account of the life of Ser Cepparello: through the rhetorical figure of *adynaton*, the reader is emphatically asked to discern in this figure an inver-

---

[19] The phrase is by Giovanni Getto, *Vita di forme e forme di vita nel Decameron* (Turin: G. B. Petrini, 1958), p. 77. Getto's chapter on the first novella is still valuable. See also Luigi Russo, *Letture critiche del Decameron* (Bari: Laterza, 1977), pp. 51–68; for a sharp understanding of the novella, in moral terms, see Millicent J. Marcus, *An Allegory of Form. Literary Self-Consciousness in the Decameron*, Stanford French and Italian Studies 18 (Saratoga, Calif.: Anma Libri, 1979), pp. 11–26.

sion of the human order. His total alienation is dramatized through the transparent emblems of his being a foreigner, a usurer, a sodomite and a sinner. The second half is a rewriting of the first, a palinode, so to speak, in the sense of a symmetrical ironic reversal of the first half. On the point of death, Ser Cepparello makes his confession, during which he goes into a consciously falsified retrospective account of his life.

The pretext for the confessional falsification is to simulate a Christian life in order to avert exposing his hosts, two Florentine usurers, to public contempt. In a sense, the confession becomes a distorted self-creation, the last act of an existence of uninterrupted forgery and decepion which, therefore, gives a paradoxical coherence to Ser Cepparello's whole life of blasphemy. The confession is an act of usury because it is an unreal production; Ser Cepparello reproduces a mere appearance, an unreal image of himself, and usury, in its primary symbolic value, is always the parody of *poiesis* because it is an emblem of imaginary unreal productivity.[20] Ser Cepparello's verbal self-fabrication becomes an unquestionable reality to the friar who listens to his confession. The friar, in turn, after the death of Ser Cepparello, builds a sermon on the false confession and proclaims him a saint. The self-loving man who was alien to the world and who lived in profanation of the world, is sanctified and becomes, through his verbal disguise, the center of cohesion and stability of the community of men.

There is, no doubt, a great irony in this reversal. Cepparello's subversion of Christian values leads to his being absorbed in the canon. It is as if cultural order and its subversion always implicate and reinforce each other. More to our concern, Boccaccio is not interested in the problem of the triumph of perversion or in bourgeois cynicism except in a peripheral way.

[20] This sense of usury as the mockery of production and art can be found in Dante's *Inferno*. In the exposition of the moral system of Hell, one remembers, usury is said to offend the divine Goodness in that it violates the productive processes of nature (*Inferno* XI, 94-105). For an Aristotelean-Thomistic analysis of the issue, see Jacques Maritain, *Art and Scholasticism and the Frontiers of Poetry*, trans. Joseph W. Evans (New York: Scribner's Sons, 1962), pp. 10-37.

He is raising, at the heart of the tale, the problem of the truth of language, its proliferation and contagiousness, its uses and role within history. He underscores the ambiguity of the confession by using a double perspective on what Ser Cepparello says: from the friar who is listening to the confession the description rapidly shifts to the adjacent room where the two Florentine brothers are overhearing the verbal exchange and laughing at the lies of their friend. More directly, during the sacramental confession, the problem of truth is more explicitly raised:

> *"Padre mio, di questa parte mi vergogno di dirvene il vero, temendo di non peccare in vanagloria." Al quale il santo frate disse: "Dì sicuramente, che il vero dicendo nè in confessione nè in altro atto si peccò già mai. . . ."*

> "Father, I am loath to tell you the truth on this matter, fearing that I sin in vainglory." To which the holy friar replied: "Speak out freely, for one can't sin by telling the truth either in confession or otherwise."   (p. 38)

This allusion to the truth is picked up at the end of the confession, where the verbal performance is linked to the problem of faith in language:

> *Veggendo il frate non essere altro restato a dire a Ser Ciappelletto, gli fece l'absoluzione e diedegli la sua benedizione, avendolo per santissimo uomo, sì come colui che pienamente credeva esser vero ciò che ser Ciappelletto avea detto: e chi sarebbe colui che nol credesse, veggendo uno uomo in caso di morte dir così?*

> When the friar saw that Ser Ciappelletto had nothing more to say, he gave him the absolution and blessed him thinking that he was a most holy man. He was convinced that all Ser Ciappelletto had said was true; but then, who would not have been convinced, on hearing a dying man talk in this fashion?   (pp. 43–44)

The friar believes in the confession, and the people believe in the holiness of Ser Ciappelletto, because there is a shared faith in the Word that gives sense to words and sustains them. But to understand more fully the relationship between secular and prophetic literature, we have to analyze the literary traditions which constitute the fundamental structure of the tale. The tale is simultaneously a parody of the hagiographic mode, of the confessional mode and of the religious sermon. It is because of the parody of these rhetorical genres that we can consider the tale a metaliterary act. Boccaccio connects the two genres of hagiography and confession and exploits them in order to raise the problem of the relationship between a literary making of the self and history. The confessional element, probably because it appears as a sacrament, has been neglected as a literary form. Like most literary confessions, the tale gives, albeit in a grotesque inversion, an autobiographical review of the significant events in the life of Ser Ciappelletto from the vantage point of death; it shows the conversion of the hero and his reconciliation with history; finally it attests to the hero's explicit purpose of "saving" his friends. The confession is a lie, and Boccaccio's distinctive aim is to degrade and parody the confessional form. The conversion, which is the crucial turning point in the novel of confession, is reduced in the tale to a mere change of name. Ser Cepparello is changed to Ser Ciappelletto, which means "ciappello, cioè ghirlanda" (hat, that is garland, p. 34). The new name, in other words, does not dramatize an inner change; rather, it becomes an ironic allusion to the halo of the protagonist's future sainthood through Boccaccio's own etymologizing. The hagiograhic mode is the basis for the parody of the process of reconciliation of the self with history.

As has been shown,[21] hagiography provides the blueprint for the dramatic process of the tale insofar as the story of Ser Ciappelletto is essentially structured on a saint's life. But hagiography also provides the historical dimension for various reasons. It makes possible the transition from the private confession to the world of history because it makes Ser Ciap-

---

[21] Enrico de' Negri, "The Legendary Style of the *Decameron*," *The Romantic Review*, 42 (1952), pp. 166–189.

pelletto the center of the community. More fundamentally, it constitutes in itself a typological structure. The *Legenda aurea*, on which the tale is patterned, is essentially the history of the chain of saints from Abel to the Last Judgment. It is a typological mode because it defines the process of extrapolating from the multifariousness of historical reality the significant inner events of history. In its general structure, therefore, it provides the true history of the city of God on earth; its particular function in the tale is to provide the nexus between the self and the prophetic history of the world.

The sermon is the last rhetorical target of the tale. Language is again the chief performer. Because of the sermon, the focus is on language in its direct prophetic function: after the esthetic self-dramatization, patterned on typological and sacramental modes, language is used as a prophetic proclamation. The derivation of the sermon from the confession shows how one rhetorical form is generated from another: in the tale, in effect, we move from confession to the sermon and finally to the popular legend in a continuous process of fictional excrescence. This rhetorical proliferation, and its effects on listeners, forcefully dramatizes the inherent ambiguity of language. Like the plague, literary language is contagious; it has an autonomous and treacherous existence, organically multiplying itself and drawing into its inauthenticity the whole audience. There is the implication, furthermore, that a link between the self, history and God, through literary typology, may exist only if there is a faith in the *Logos*. But the whole tale subverts the literary forms in which a typological structure of reality is envisioned. It demystifies and empties of its faith-content the myth of the unity of literature and life.

In the preamble to the tale, as we pointed out, the emphasis falls on the general chaos of the world, followed by a statement on the efficacy of prayer to bridge the gap between God and man. At the basis of typological literature there is an impulse to counter this chaos. The function of secular literature, by contrast, seems to be one of consumption of literary artifacts, a way of placing these rhetorical modes within the general confusion and duplicity of life. Secular writing involves itself, furthermore, in this pervasive corrosion and, significantly, contracts itself into the unseriousness of a "joke." What remains intact and vital in the general dissolution of forms in the tale of Ser Ciappelletto is the trick played by him on the friar in order to save his Florentine hosts.

There is an obvious incongruity between the brilliance of the literary forms concocted and parodied and the pretext from which the fictional mechanism originates and which alone is preserved. Boccaccio subtly discloses how the domain of parodic literature is narrowed down to the "trick." The analogy with the problems set forth in the Introduction is striking. Set in the context of death, literature is in the impossible situation of providing truth and permanence. It can only actively confront the mythic literary forms and dissolve itself into cheap and trivial uses.

It might be objected that this tale is, after all, not so serious, that its tone is unmistakably comical and, therefore, that it might even be difficult and artificial to superimpose similar responsibilities on a fundamentally funny story. To answer these imaginary objections, let us turn briefly to a consideration of these problems in the sixth day of the *Decameron* and particularly to another novella, which is equally funny, that of Frate Cipolla (vi, 10).

The sixth day, in general, is very important in terms of our discussion because its declared focus is the uses of language; the tales gravitate around the concept of literary taste and literature as part of human leisure. In the tale of Cisti (vi, 2), language is endowed with efficacy to redeem Cisti in the social hierarchy in the sense that the language he uses with Geri levels the social differences between them. But Boccaccio prefaces this redemptive view of language with an apt description of Fortune not as the random, blind chance of the pagans, but as an Intelligence of God. The world is given a metaphysical coherence, in other words, and within this context, language has its efficacy. The story of Frate Cipolla, on the contrary, amplifies the problems of the inherent theatricality and duplicity of language treated in the tale of Ser Ciappelletto. In a sense, it supplements the first tale because the verbal illusionism, this time, comes from a friar.

This tale is at the basis of Thomas Mann's *Mario and the Magician* and a brief analysis of Mann's long short-story is in order here because it provides a heuristic tool for an interpretation of Boccaccio's tale. The factual correspondences between the two tales range from the identity of the consummate *magus* (Cipolla), to the histrionics of both (one from the pulpit, the other from a stage), to the more profound questions of the function of literature within the social order.

Mann's tale is primarily a blatant political allegory: the magician is the demagogue and his deception is the deception of political language. The tale itself, furthermore, functions as a sustained dramatic counterpoint to the hypnosis engendered by Cipolla's rhetoric: the impersonality of the narrative provides the rational and critical distance necessary to demystify the irrationality and incantations of the magician. At the same time, it reveals the fascination of the writer with what is for him a possibility of being. Mann dramatizes in depth the confrontation between these two radically antithetical modes of viewing literature.

The whole experience takes place during the narrator's holiday in Italy: the critique of leisure that is implied concerns, however, Cipolla as well because he stands for pastoral evasion into a world of illusoriness. The pastoral motif gives momentum, in addition, to the tragic finale of the tale. Mario, a young waiter who, like the narrator, had been a detached observer of Cipolla's manipulative rhetoric, hypnotized and threatened with being absorbed into the homoerotic world of the clown, kills him. Ultimately, Mann is talking about the painful inadequacy of literature. It is Mario who kills the tyrant, while the writer is doomed to inaction. His language, to be sure, is the primary medium for the disclosure of lies and, in a sense, its inadequacy vouchsafes its privileged role and its truth.

The tale of Frate Cipolla in the *Decameron* is even more radical than Mann's story. Boccaccio involves the whole world of rhetoric in his tale and discloses the absurdity of metaphoric language in his parody. The friar, in fact, "sì ottimo parlatore e pronto era, che chi conosciuto non l'avesse, *non solamente un gran rettorico l'avrebbe estimato, ma avrebbe detto esser Tullio medesimo o forse Quintiliano*" (was such a fast and great talker, that anybody who was not acquainted with him would have taken him not only for a great rhetorician, but for Cicero himself or perhaps Quintilian, p. 566).

The irony of the passage is extraordinary, for Cipolla is identified as a friar of Saint Anthony. Anthony is the saint of the gift of tongues.[22] Cipolla, in an overt degradation of St. Anthony's prophetic language, is a rhetorician. Accordingly, the world of rhetoric is carefully thematized in the tale: the sermon turns into a brilliant exposure of the possibilities for deception in fictive language. When Frate Cipolla manipulates his listeners by the sermon, the focus falls upon the parody of the metaphoric language in which religious mysteries are represented:

> *Egli primieramente mi mostrò il dito dello Spirito Santo così intero e saldo come fu mai, e il ciuffetto del serafino che apparve a san Francesco, e una dell'unghie de' gherubini, e una delle coste del Verbum-carofatti-alle-finestre. . . .*

> First of all he showed me the finger of the Holy Ghost, as straight and firm as it ever was; then the forelock of the seraph who appeared to St. Francis; and one of the cherubim's nails, and one of the ribs of the Word-made-flesh in the pan. . . . (p. 572)

If metaphor attempts to unite the separate elements of the world and discover the fundamental identity of things, in this context it is an absurdity, because its literalness annihilates the symbolic language of religious experience. As in the case of the tale of Ser Ciappelletto, social cohesion is not affirmed by

---

[22] For bibliography, see "Antoine de Padoue," in *Dictionnaire de théologie catholique* (Paris: Letouzey, 1909), I, 1445.

the verbal acrobatics of a mystifier, because the community, by virtue of its shared faith in God, antecedes the experience of language. On account of this fundamental futility, the sermon readily dissolves into cant.

Boccaccio, furthermore, exposes the mechanism of deception in language by the ingenious interaction of a subplot in which the friar's servant, Guccio Imbratta, attempts to seduce the maid of the inn where they live. The dramatic function of this subplot is clear: by the confrontation, Boccaccio creates a doubling of plots, each mirroring and dissolving the other; by crude eroticism, it exposes the master's own seduction of the people in the church. We might even point out how this master-slave relationship, which is part of a more complex dialectic in the *Decameron*, is anticipated in the very introduction to the sixth day in which the *brigata* of young people and their servants mirror each other in the act of storytelling. The self-reflection implies a suspension of social hierarchy at the moment in which they are involved in the marginal world of books.

The tale of Frate Cipolla, like that of Ser Ciappelletto, comes into being from an extraliterary impulse. At the heart of the tale there is the trick that two friends play on the friar by substituting charcoal for a feather. Throughout the sermon they remain dissociated from the people, outside the seduction of language but fascinated by the friar's cunning. The trick of the two friends and their admiration for the sermon dramatize the whole process of literary creation, from the cheap reality of its intent to the mystification of representation. At the same time, their detached perspective on the fiction and the theatricality of Frate Cipolla's mark the degradation of language as prophecy to language as sheer performance.

In the light of this novella, it is time to return to the imaginary objections which we formulated after the discussion of Ser Ciappelletto. This story is also a flagrant joke, as funny as the story of Ser Ciappelletto: we cannot minimize it. How do we account, then, for the comical tone of two tales? In a sense, Boccaccio has internalized in the two tales the possible response of the reader, first through the two Florentine brothers, secondly through the two tricksters. But the fun is also the storytellers'. It is the index of the ambiguous fascination of the storytellers, because they are midway between detachment and involvement with the artifices of reality they create. The verbal performances are temptations because they are possible ways of being for the *Decameron* itself, in the same sense that Francesca, for instance, is a temptation to Dante because she is Dante's possible self.[23] Furthermore, Boccaccio intentionally degrades the status of the tales to the frivolous and idle because by being jokes they can question all reality around them without themselves claiming a privileged mode of being. What is involved in all of this is the whole nature of the playful and comical in the *Decameron*. Boccaccio devotes the entire seventh day to the motif of the joke or *beffa*. These jokes are ludic moments, literally illusions, experiences in which not only is reality doubted, but in which illusion and reality inextricably overlap, an absolute space where the real and the imagined, the inner and the outer, are systematically confused.[24]

But Boccaccio will not deal with the problem of the function of literature within history uniformly in a comical vein. Immediately preceding the story of Frate Cipolla and in dramatic contrast to it, is the tale of the poet Cavalcanti (VI, 9). This short novella begins with a statement of nostalgic evocation of the social harmony reigning in the Florence of old: a drastic contrast to the fragmentation of plague-ridden Florence. The rhetorical formula of *laudatio temporis acti* proves to be somewhat shallow when we are told that the poet Cavalcanti lives in a condition of radical estrangement from the

[23] For the interpretive importance of the Dantesque episode, see the discussion, with extensive bibliography, in my *Dante Poet of the Desert. History and Allegory in the Divine Comedy* (Princeton: Princeton University Press, 1979), pp. 160–170. This "metaliterary" line of analysis can be found in Guido Almansi, *The Writer as Liar: Narrative Technique in the Decameron* (London and Boston: Routledge and Kegan Paul, 1975).

[24] The implications of the *beffa* are amply treated in chapter 6 below. For now, let me mention the thematic account of the dialectics of illusion and reality provided by Giovanni Getto, "Le novelle dello scambio di illusione e realtà," in *Vita di forme e forme di vita*, pp. 164–187.

Florentine community. An Epicurean, he is given to metaphysical speculation, rejecting the belief in the immortality of
the soul and in God's existence.[25] The contrast between the
community, unquestionably immersed in leisure, and the isolation of the poet is dramatized by the fact that the poet with-
draws for his reflections to a graveyard, at the periphery of life,
in a symbolic space of ontological ambiguity, the boundary
line of death and life. This dramatic contrast alludes to and al-
ters some general views held about the Epicureans. Whereas in
traditional Christian apologetics, in the wake of Cicero's polemics against the Epicureans, they are indiscriminately
viewed as "hogs'" given to sensual pleasures, Boccaccio (and
in this he seems to follow Dante, who separates the gluttons
such as Ciacco from the dignified heretics in *Inferno* x) pointedly distinguishes the two opposed strands of Epicureanism
and no real contact is posited between them. On the one hand,
there is Epicureanism as vulgar sensuality; on the other, there
is an Epicureanism exemplified by Guido's intellectual prob-
ings.[26]

[25] For an understanding of Boccaccio's fascination with Guido's thought,
see A. E. Quaglio, "Prima fortuna della glossa garbiana a 'Donna me prega'
del Cavalcanti," *Giornale storico della letteratura italiana*, 141 (1964), pp. 339–
369. See also the recent reading of Boccaccio's novella and Cavalcanti's intellectual concerns by Robert M. Durling, "Boccaccio on Interpretation: Guido's Escape (*Decameron* VI, 9)," in *Dante, Petrarch, Boccaccio. Studies in the Italian Trecento in Honor of Charles S. Singleton*, eds. Aldo S. Bernardo and
Anthony L. Pellegrini (Binghamton, N.Y.: Medieval and Renaissance Texts
and Studies, 1983), pp. 273–304. Mario Baratto, *Realtà e stile nel Decameron*
(Vicenza: Pozza, 1970), pp. 336–340 gives a more conventional view of the
story somewhat in line with Luigi Russo, *Letture critiche del Decameron*, pp.
217–223, and Giovanni Getto, *Vita di forme*, pp. 156–159.

[26] What I have in mind here is the fact that Dante distinguishes between the
"hogs" of gluttony—and Ciacco in *Inferno* VI is manifest emblem of vulgar
sensual gratification—and the adherents to an intellectual variety of Epicureanism, such as those who do not believe in the immortality of the soul (*Inferno* X, 13–15). For the conventional moralistic dismissal of Epicureanism as
sensual self-indulgence, which is crystallized in the formula *Epicuri de grege
porcorum*, see Emerson Brown, Jr., "Epicurus and Voluptas in Late Antiquity:
The Curious Testimony of Martianus Capella," *Traditio*, 38 (1982), pp. 75–
106. It could be pointed out that the presence of Guccio Balena or Guccio
Porco in the *Decameron* VI, 10—which is an ironic allusion to St. Anthony's

When Betto and his *brigata* approach the poet to mock him by asking him why he wants to prove that God does not exist, the poet simply replies: "Signori, voi mi potete dire a casa vostra ciò che vi piace" (Gentlemen, you can say to me whatever you like in your house, p. 564). Betto finally interprets the cryptic line to mean that he and his *brigata* are "peggio che uomini morti" (worse off than the dead, p. 564). This is clearly a serious tale: Boccaccio examines in it the way in which secular poetry acts on history. The poet dissipates the illusions of the *brigata* and brings its members to an explicit awareness of their common finitude. At the same time, a reflexive self-disclosure is laid bare. The marginality of the poet is an essential feature: his role is to be in contact with a universe of death.

The critical cliché that the *Decameron* is escapist literature, an evasion into a pastoral world, is in this tale ostentatiously reversed. It is the historical world that lives in the irreality of a land of Cockayne and hides the truth of its existence. We find in this tale, furthermore, a dramatic inversion of the general frame of the *Decameron* where the golden world is the literary garden, while the historical world is the one of death. The inversion actually points to the one essential similarity between the two visions: the inevitable discontinuity between literature and history. Literature can have only a negative and critical relationship with history and it can only perform its service of demystification by being in an alienated region.

This purported discontinuity between literature and life is the opposite of what Boccaccio explicitly states in his Introduction to the fourth day, where the universe of his fiction is consciously examined. There is, in this Introduction, a declared faith in the continuity between literature and the reality of the world. Within the context of a defense of the *Decameron* from the charge of eroticism, Boccaccio formulates his views of the essential unity of sense and idea (through the *exemplum* of Filippo Balducci) and simultaneously of the unity of life and literature through the equation of muses and women:

---

traditional figuration with a pig at his feet (cf. *Paradiso* XXIX, 124–126 for the motif)—can also be taken as the contrasting pole to Guido Cavalcanti's detachment from worldly pleasures related in VI, 9.

*Le Muse son donne, e benché le donne quel che le Muse vagliono
non vagliono, pure esse hanno nel primo aspetto simiglianza di
quelle, . . . per che, queste cose tessendo, né dal monte Parnaso
né dalle Muse non mi allontano quanto molti per avventura
s'avisano. . . .*

The Muses are women, and although the women do not
rank as highly as Muses, still they resemble them at first
sight . . . and so, in weaving these stories, I do not stray
as far from Mount Parnassus or from the Muses as many
people might be led to believe. . . .   (p. 351)

Boccaccio, furthermore, claims that through his writing he
does what love poets such as Dante, Cino and Cavalcanti have
done. The tale about Cavalcanti that we have analyzed contra-
dicts the view of an unproblematical unity between the poet
and history. If on the other hand Boccaccio alludes in his statement to the stilnovistic intuition of the unity of man and God
through the vehicle of love and literature, various tales of this
fourth day are pointed parodies of the *Dolce stil nuovo*. This
claim of the continuity of being and rationality is made within
the *Decameron* as a defense against the charge that it is erotic,
debased literature. We must thus account for the process of
degradation of literature into pornography.

This contradiction exemplifies Boccaccio's view of literature in the *Decameron*. Literature aspires to shape a coherent
sense of reality, to express a unitary world view, but the poetic
process undermines this assumption. This is not the discrepancy between conscious statements and unconscious meanings
in the tales, a dialectical and yet generic antinomy ultimately
to be dissolved into a wider structure of discourse. This very
contradiction is the fundamental historical feature of Boccaccio's ideology and is consciously dramatized in the tale of Gentile de' Carisendi (x, 4).

The tale reproduces the world of romance, the transition
from death to life, but has also other discreet literary allusions.
Some motifs from the code of courtly love (love for a married
woman, unrequited love, despair of love, etc.) inform the

structure of the tale and are exploited to introduce its central myth: the descent of the lover into the underworld. Under the compulsion of love, Gentile enters the tomb where the woman he loved is buried, kisses her, and brings her back to life. The story appears, unmistakably, as the reenactment of the Orpheus theme because of the myth of death and resurrection which constitutes its dramatic center. Gentile mediates between life and death, and, unlike Orpheus, succeeds in recovering Catalina. But this new Orpheus alienates himself from creation and, in the presence of the community, gives back to her husband the woman he evoked back to life.

The theatricality of the public restitution points to the ritual of order which subtends the whole experience in the sense that the spectacle organized by Gentile is an esthetic ritual mediating between discontinuities: Catalina returns to her family, Gentile returns to the world after the estrangement caused by his erotic despair. But, paradoxically, Gentile's reintegration into the community is possible *because* he renounces what he has brought back to life. If, on the one hand, this shows how the demands of the social fabric are irreconcilable with Gentile's private world, on the other hand, a new gap is established. There is a transparent irony in the fact that Catalina's child is named Gentile, an emblem of the purely symbolic and oblique continuity of the lover in the newly reconstituted family. As soon as the new Orpheus conquers the shadows of death, he must step out of the ordered social structure. Boccaccio, again, is intent on erecting a hiatus between the poet and the social order, immediately after the esthetic experience has provisionally mediated between them.

Although the general dramatic configuration of the tale is that of an idealized quest-romance, it is impossible to ignore Boccaccio's revisions of the underlying Orpheus myth. Catalina was not actually dead, only in a state of apparent death; Gentile's descent into her tomb verges on the necrophiliac. In a sense, this temptation of the flesh is the dragon Gentile must kill so that he is purified and finally spiritually resurrected along with Catalina; at the same time, the world of romance is vitiated by these dramatic impurities. The romance does not give a representation of plenitude: the dialectic of presence and absence is unceasing; an absence is filled and simultaneously, a void is created. The domains of literature and history are always discontinuous.

All the tales we have analyzed have this much in common: the inevitable marginality of the literary act which, therefore, should confine itself to efface the fictions—literary and spiritual—of society. We cannot resist the temptation to extrapolate a line that condenses this view of art: "l'arte è dall'arte schernita" (art is mocked by art, p. 710), as Boccaccio writes. This marginality of literature shows that the literary act is neither entirely tautological and self-enclosed nor in an unproblematical continuity with reality. The ambiguity inherent to the tales is the center of the *Conclusione dell'Autore* in which Boccaccio attempts to define the mode of existence of the book as a mediator of love.

His major concern in this conclusion is to relegate the *Decameron* to the garden, bracketed and disconnected from the world of reality, to change the area of transition into a garden of self-absorption. Like Cervantes who addresses his *Quixote* to a "desocupado lector," Boccaccio addresses his *Decameron* to the "donne oziose." They both make the ironic claim that literature is of no serious use and that the text occupies the interstices of active life. Yet, Boccaccio reveals, at the same time, that literature is an erotic snare and women are possessed by it. The eroticism of literature is necessarily connected with its failure to function in its vital historicity upon the world: pornographic literature, in other words, is that literature which is an intransitive esthetic experience, which has been reified, preserved and *used to be enjoyed*. In the presence of this blurring of any moral hierarchy, the reader and book form a closed narcissistic circuit, a private little garden of complacency shutting out the world. Because of this, the reader has only a virtual and illusory centrality.

More explicitly, in the conclusion Boccaccio abdicates responsibility for the effect of the book on the audience, tries to disclaim authorship for the tales and finally releases them in a moral vacuum as neutral and autonomous objects to be interpreted by the reader. The marginality is total, which is to say another void; the reader is abstracted from history waiting to reemerge into history; the writer even denies any centrality for himself.

The first two tales we have examined revolve around the opposition between prophecy and literature. Literature was the negation of prophecy, its mockery. In a sense, literature seems to be possible precisely when prophecy fails or to indicate the failure of prophecy. In the process of subversion of mythic forms, literature involves itself in the general failure; its self-annihilation is the index of its privilege and its specificity. Yet, when Boccaccio compares in the conclusion sacred and secular forms of scriptures, the opposition can no longer be sustained because there is a universal leveling by death. Along with the assertion of his own instability, Boccaccio's final words are a statement on the ontological instability of the world: "Confesso nondimeno, le cose di questo mondo non avere stabilità alcuna, ma sempre essere in mutamento, e così potrebbe della mia lingua essere intervenuto . . ." (I acknowledge, nonetheless, that the things of this world do not have any stability, but are always shifting and this may have happened to my tongue . . . , p. 964).

The *Decameron* began with the plague and ends with this jocular-serious vision of flux. Literature, because of this, is explicitly self-consolatory, an elegy for the precariousness of the literary experience itself: "nobilissime giovani," Boccaccio writes, "a consolazione delle quali io a così lunga fatica messo mi sono . . ." (most noble young women for whose consolations I have undertaken this taxing work, p. 959).[27]

---

[27] On the tradition of consolation—and its conceptual and figurative correlatives, such as *iocus, otiositas, medicina*, etc.—see Peter Van Moos, *Consolatio. Studien zur mittellateinischen Troistliteratur über den Tod und zum Problem der Christlichen Trauer* (Munich: Fink, 1971–72). Cf. also Sister Mary Edmond Fern, *The Latin Consolatio as a Literary Type*. (St. Louis, Mo., St. Louis University, 1941).

Written with the assumption that the social foundations are shaking and that there is no firm ground in the moral cosmos, the *Decameron* fails to be a lasting sacrosanctum and is equally insufficient to order life. Unable to do either in the face of metaphysical annihilation, it contracts under Boccaccio's reductive impulse to the necessary role of the devalued and the useless: a perennial marginality. In this tension, the *Decameron* stands halfway between the universe of plenitude and sense of the *Divine Comedy* and the programmatic non-sense of *Orlando Furioso*.

By way of epilogue, let me add a historical note to the foregoing considerations. After the *Decameron*, Boccaccio wrote no more imaginative literature, except for the satirical *Corbaccio*. He dedicated himself to what used to be venerable humanistic pursuits (a commentary on Dante, a mysogynistic treatise, book collecting, etc.). What is more important for the present discussion is that he finally finished his treatise on the *Genealogy of the Gentile Gods*. In this text, Boccaccio writes an organic history of the world in terms of moralized literary myths and ends with a passionate defense of allegorical writings. In the defense, while strongly upholding that poetry which expresses unequivocally a moral truth, he does not hide a flagrant contempt for "useless" literature. The "uselessness" of literature will turn out to be, as the next chapter will argue, literature's profound value, with its power to challenge, even as it is fascinated with, the utilitarian, "real" values that have currency in the social world.

We can perhaps grasp the reasons for Boccaccio's change from the imaginative, "useless" writing to this act of faith in literary myths as tools to formalize and interpret the history of the world. In a sense, Boccaccio had no choice; after experiencing the dangers and precariousness of the esthetic imagination, he could turn for certainties only to philology, the discipline of objective facts, the mythic world of literature. Only when the *Decameron* is over does the pastoral of the author begin: now, "è da dare alla penna e alla man faticata riposo" (it is time to give rest to the pen and the weary hand, p. 959).

THE RIDDLE OF VALUES

A definite point of agreement among scholars in recent years is that in the *Decameron*, although shying away from overtly political concerns, Boccaccio has a sure grasp of the realities of the social world. Because so many of the novelle move within the horizon of business ventures, Boccaccio has come to be known as a writer whose originality lies in his power to gauge the interests and passions at the heart of the city of man.[1] In the construction of the so-called "social morality" of the *Decameron*, the obvious point of reference is Dante. Whereas Dante views commerce and spirituality as terms of a tragic dilemma and denounces "la gente nova e i subiti guadagni," Boccaccio's posture marks a radical novelty in intellectual perspective.[2]

[1] The sociological concerns of the *Decameron* are emphasized, correctly even if too complacently, by G. Petronio, "I volti del *Decameron*," in *Boccaccio: Secoli di Vita. Atti del Congresso Internazionale: Boccaccio 1975*, eds. Marga Cottino-Jones and Edward F. Tuttle (Ravenna: Longo, 1977), pp. 107–124. Within this context it is appropriate to mention some bibliographical items that describe the social background of the times: H. Pirenne, "L'instruction des marchands au Moyen Age," *Annales d'histoire économique et sociale*, I (1929), pp. 13–28; A. Sapori, *Studi di storia economica (sec. XIII–XIV–XV)* (Florence: Sansoni, 1953); C. Bec, *Les Marchands écrivains: affaires et humanisme à Florence* (Paris-Hague: Mouton, 1967). An impressive study of the links between the *Decameron* and society is given by Vittore Branca, "L'epopea mercantile," in *Boccaccio medievale* (Florence: Sansoni, 1956). See also Giorgio Padoan, "Mondo aristocratico e mondo comunale nell'ideologia e nell'arte di Giovanni Boccaccio," *Studi sul Boccaccio*, II (1964), pp. 81–216, and now reprinted in his *Il Boccaccio Le Muse Il Parnaso e l'Arno* (Florence: Olschki, 1978), pp. 1–91; Mario Baratto, *Realtà e stile nel "Decameron"* (Vicenza: Pozza, 1970).

[2] Dante's lines are from *Inferno* XVI, 73ff. But it is in *Purgatorio* XIV and XV that the distinction between material and spiritual goods is dramatized. Dante's ideals of Franciscan poverty can be gauged by the recent study by Ga-

Writing, as he does, at that critical juncture of history when the old chivalric code is being supplanted by a bourgeois mythology of profit, he responds, we are told, to history's shifts by celebrating the energy and compulsions of the merchants, the "new paladins," of whom he is the inspired rhapsodist.[3]

It is certainly undeniable that the marketplace, the area of the city where goods are exchanged, prices are fixed, money is alternately made and lost and, more generally, a utilitarian morality holds sway, is a privileged space of Boccaccio's imagination. In fact there is so little in the *Decameron* that is not absorbed within the nomenclature of economics or is not, at least, affected by it, that the "ragion di mercatura" is taken to be nothing less than the ground of all values, the implied paradigm by which loyalties, social bonds, love and even literature itself are appraised.

Though it does not necessarily follow, one suspects that it is precisely because of the openly declared importance of the economic realities in the text that the various interpretations of the *Decameron*, however rigorous they may be, predictably end up in the impasse of a broadly conceived sociology of literature. What this means is that whether the scholars marshal a rich inventory of facts to establish a correspondence between the mercantile themes of the narrative and the concrete features of history, or study the rhetorical strategies and forms that Boccaccio adapts in his representation of the contradictory prov-

---

briele Di Giammarino, *Il concetto dei beni in Dante* (Naples: Fratelli Conte, 1979). See also Judith Schenck Koffler, "Capital in Hell: Dante's Lesson on Usury," *Rutgers Law Review*, 32 (1979), pp. 608–660; John Noonan, *The Scholastic Analysis of Usury* (Cambridge, Mass.: Harvard University Press, 1957). For a more general view, see Marino Damiata, *Guglielmo d'Ockham: povertà e potere, I: Il problema della povertà evangelica e francescana nei sec. XIIIe XIV. Origine del pensiero politico di G. D'Ockham* (Florence: Studi Francescani, 1978).

[3] The phrase is Branca's, from his *Boccaccio medievale*, who refers to the merchants as "ulissidi degli scambi economici" (p. 75). In rhetorical terms the shift from a transcendent, "medieval" view to an immanent, modern one is studied by Salvatore Battaglia, "Dall'esempio alla novella," in *Giovanni Boccaccio e la riforma della narrativa* (Naples: Liguori, 1969), pp. 21–81. A sustained analysis of this shift is Baratto, *Realtà e stile*, which is in the same spirit of Mario Marti, "Interpretazione del 'Decameron,' " *Convivium*, 25 (1957), pp. 276–289.

inces of his moral world, in effect they share the assumption that, directly or indirectly, literature is a mimesis of society. They all agree, that is, in making the text an oblique but still reliable chronicle of the times, a quasi-documentary reflection of the complexities of reality.[4]

The desire to pin literature to history is understandable. What is disturbing in these various critical procedures, however, is the ease with which they completely bypass what is truly radical in the *Decameron*, and what I would like to explore in this chapter, namely the insight that the imagination is the faculty governing the bonds and transactions in the economy of the world. This social role of the imagination is not given, to be sure, a solid and explicit formulation in the text. It appears, nonetheless, obliquely as the force by which various

---

[4] This type of analysis is overtly inspired by G. Lukacs, *Realism in Our Time: Literature and the Class Struggle*, trans. J. N. Mander (New York: Harper, 1971), and L. Goldmann, *Essays on Method in the Sociology of Literature*, trans. W. D. Boelhower (St. Louis, Mo.: Telos Press, 1980). What these theories miss is the problematical nature of the literary mediation. They proceed, by and large, as if a direct link can be established between the order of reality and its mimetic double. The way I understand the imagination remains to be seen in the analyses of the various novelle in this chapter as well as in the other chapters. I hesitate to bring in medieval speculative texts on the imagination and its operations because the body of opinions is everything but homogenous. Anyone familiar with Dante's *Vita nuova* and its extraordinary insistence on the tension between imagination and knowledge, or dreams and their interpretations, will understand the present restraint. I will mention, however, some recent items on the problem: M. W. Bundy, *The Theory of Imagination in Classical and Medieval Thought*, University of Illinois Studies in Language and Literature 12. 2–3, (Urbana: University of Illinois Press, 1927); see also, for the problem of the imagination as it figures in Old French love poems, Douglas Kelly, *Medieval Imagination: Rhetoric and the Poetry of Courtly Love* (Madison and London: University of Wisconsin Press, 1978). There are two articles that deserve special mention. One is by Winthrop Wetherbee, "The Theme of Imagination in Medieval Poetry and the Allegorical Figure 'Genius,'" *Medievalia et Humanistica*, N.S. 7 (1976), pp. 45–64. If Wetherbee gives some of the twelfth-century musings on the imagination, Alastair J. Minnis, "Langland's *Ymaginatif* and late medieval theories of imagination," *Comparative Criticism. A Year Book*, 3 (1981), pp. 71–103, addresses himself to the scholastic debate. Excellent bibliography is also available in J. S. Wittig, "*Piers Plowman*, B, Passus IX–XII: Elements in the Design of the Inward Journey," *Traditio*, 28 (1972), pp. 211–280.

frames of social order either crumble or are sustained. My first concern here is to describe the two major emblems of social order in the *Decameron*, the aristocratic court and the marketplace, both of which are founded on the assumption of a law whereby contracts, pledges, promises and commodities are invested with a literal value which alone keeps the social fabric from tearing at the seams. These structures of order that Boccaccio envisions, I shall argue, are steadily marked by antinomies of value (wealth, love, and honor almost always, for instance, interfere with each other).

But I will also show that what truly disrupts the system of social equivalences is the excess of the imagination. To illustrate: the marketplace, the privileged realm of values because there properties are traded, is also the locus where the crisis of exchange occurs on account of the fantasies of power, imaginary self-constructs, private interests, passions and unbridled desires which converge in and lie under all deals merchants strike. It is within this perspective of the imagination as it acts in the world that Boccaccio can advance the claim that literature is alone equipped to confront and probe the workings of social life, not because it is the mirror of life, but because the boundaries between the two are forever blurred.

To be sure, Boccaccio never stakes openly such a claim for his own text. *The Genealogy of the Gentile Gods* states, on the contrary, that poets cannot dwell in "places like the greedy and mercenary market, in courts, theatres, offices or public squares, amid crowds of jostling citizens and women of the town."[5] These are spots that so many of the stories of the *Decameron* consistently evoke, yet the general narrative impulse stems from the storytellers' retreat from history in the face of the plague and the bankruptcy of the social order. If anything, the stories are meant for despondent women out of love and in

---

[5] This motif, which Boccaccio shares with Petrarch (cf. *De vita solitaria*, 2.7.2) and which echoes a long established classical tradition (for which cf. Gustav Riedner, *Typische Aeusserungen der Romanische Dichter*, Inaugural Dissertation, Nuremberg, 1903), is voiced in *The Genealogy of the Gentile Gods*. I am quoting from *Boccaccio on Poetry*, trans. Osgood, XIV, 11, p. 55.

need of relief from melancholy afflictions. In them the women
will find, Boccaccio says, echoing the Augustinian and classical doctrine of delight and utility engendered by the work of
art, "diletto" and "utile consiglio."[6]

The meaning of "utile consiglio," which Boccaccio, who
had received it in turn from some of his friends, dispenses to
the ladies, is suspended between two possibilities: its usefulness can consist either in teaching how to avoid the pangs of
love, or it can be seen as a promise that the text can show how
to retrieve an old love or acquire a new one. In any case, the
Decameron at the outset promises entertainment, is a commodity to be used for diversion by idle ladies. As such, it seems
both to mock and imitate the world of men's business with its
production of real wealth and lure of real adventures. The
novelle come forth as an explicit counterpart to men's diver-
sions. Whereas women, stifled by silent passions, can turn to
reading literature, men lift the burden of their passions by
"uccellare, cacciare, pescare, cavalcare, giucare o mercatare"
(fowling, hunting, fishing, riding and gambling or attending
to their business affairs, p. 5), because these are pursuits with
the power of engaging men's minds and diverting them from
gloomy meditations. What is striking in this catalogue of remedies to amorous frenzy is that "mercatare" is also viewed as a
pastime, as much as literature is for women. They are both, in
short, tied by Boccaccio to an imaginary economy of desires.

This world of private concerns is the steady focus of the sto-

---

[6] The quotation is from the Proem, p. 5, and it echoes the Horation principle of mingling "utile dulci." This principle is later formulated as *ioca seriis mis-
cere*, a commonplace which has been delineated by E. R. Curtius, *European
Literature and the Latin Middle Ages*, trans. W. R. Trask (New York: Harper
Torchbooks, 1963), pp. 417–435. The usefulness of *ioca* has been stressed by
G. Olson, "The Medieval Theory of Literature for Refreshment and Its Use
in the Fabliau Tradition," *Studies in Philology*, 71 (1974), pp. 291–313. For the
value of *utilitas* and *delectatio* in the medieval commentaries, see *Accessus ad auc-
tores; Bernard d'Utrecht; Conrad d'Hirsau*, ed. R.B.C. Huygens (Leiden: E. J.
Brill, 1970); Fausto Ghisalberti, "Medieval Biographies of Ovid," *Journal of
the Warburg and Courtauld Institutes*, 9 (1946), pp. 10–59. From Boccaccio's perspective, the utility need not be understood only as moral edification.

ries. The importance of this private sphere is heightened by
Boccaccio's deliberate departures from the larger public structures of history to the passions that lie behind them, as if
through them only could the public events be made intelligible. Thus, it would certainly be possible to extrapolate from
sundry places in the text traces of the conventional central
myths of history. The novella of the Count of Anguersa (ii, 8)
begins, for instance, with a recall to that time when the Roman
Empire had moved from the French to the Germans ("essendo
lo 'mperio di Roma da' franceschi ne' tedeschi transportato,"
p. 185). The overt allusion is to the *translatio imperii*, traditionally a shaping principle of medieval historiography.[7] This
principle, along with other elements such as the failure of friars
to bring about the *renovatio* of the world, or the breakdown of
law and authority in the *Divine Comedy*, are for Dante part of
a coherent ideology of history.

What for Dante is a sustained vision of moral decay becomes
for Boccaccio the repertory of narrative motifs and resources
and circumstances of plot. In the unfolding of the novella of
the Count of Anguersa, for instance, there is a drastic shift
away from the political strife dividing French and Germans to
the private boundaries of the royal household, where the count
has been left to look after the affairs of the kingdom while the
king is abroad waging war. As the narrative focus turns to the
court, Boccaccio dramatizes not so much the failure of an abstract pattern of history as the power of private passions to en-
danger the stability of the political frame of order.

The count embodies the idealized virtues of the perfect
worldly courtier: elegantly dressed, he is a man of handsome
looks and manners, who performs his duties of managing the
state for his lord with prudence and skill. But the order of the
court is quickly shattered by the mad love the wife of the
king's son develops for the count. If the king's war abroad ostensibly removes violence from the court to a distant battlefield, the woman's passion brings it right back. Actually the

---

[7] For bibliography, see above chapter 2, n. 10.

court, the symbolic locus of rationality, turns, as it almost always does in the *Decameron*, into a corrupt place of unreined desire which eclipses reason's sway.[8] Thus, ironically, the lady's attempted seduction of Gualtieri proceeds as if it were a rational demonstration. To justify her surrendering to love's promptings, she first claims the privilege of rank and lists, then, some conventional *topoi* of courtly love, such as the valor and wisdom of the lover, her husband's absence, the frailty of her sex, the secrecy of her passion. The rationalizations punctuating her discourse, which largely resembles a formulaic speech in *De arte honeste amandi*, are belied by the repeated echoes in the scene to *Inferno* v, the canto where the lust of the flesh preys on the rigor of reason and overturns it. There is a way in which Dante's vision always touches the edges of Boccaccio's narrative: in this context *Inferno* v is the perspective which discloses as illusory the claim of order at the court.

The lady's sexual advances make of the story a drama of conflicting demands on Gualtieri. There is no neutral standpoint available to him: his double bind is that to fulfill her desire would mean violating the loyalty he owes the king. The value scheme the count chooses is the chivalric code of honor on account of which he takes the way of exile along with his two children, disguised and stripped of all trappings of power, wealth and identity. As he is thrown into a harsh world where he will survive by begging or working as a groom and servant in someone else's house, his worth is the secret he can never share, and yet it shines through the endurance of his ordeals.

It is a mistake—the novella's overt morality seems to be—to construe the value of the self as dependent on the favors of unreliable Fortune. In this sense, the count's virtue in knowing

---

[8] What I have in mind here are Dante's lines in *Inferno* v, ". . . i peccator carnali, / che la ragion sommettono al talento" (38–39). Theirs are courtly sins and the list of sinners includes the queens, Semiramis, Dido, Cleopatras. The abstract rationale for the court as the seat of reason, of which Dante and Boccaccio are giving negative counters, is to be found in John of Salisbury, *Policraticus*, ed. C.C.I. Webb (Oxford: Clarendon, 1909), v, 2, pp. 282–283. This is the chapter in which John expounds the theory of the body politic, whereby the parts of the body correspond to particular offices.

how to withstand Fortune's buffets, however conventional an *exemplum* it may be, suggests the presence of a stabler order of values countering the contingent privileges granted by Fortune. These are values that belong to the moral order of the chivalric world: as the count is an outcast, a noble lady generously offers to take care of Giannetta; eventually the queen of France, having fallen seriously ill, confesses at her deathbed the great wrong she had perpetrated on the count and requests that he be rehabilitated; Giannetta is the cause of Giachetto Lamiens' lovesickness but ends up marrying him; Perotto, who is a "prod'uomo e valente" (strong and valiant man, p. 197), becomes the king's marshal.

These moral values, which appear variously as loyalty, patience, generosity and honor and which mark the articulation of the story, certainly triumph at the end. Yet Boccaccio also wants to show that these values are always open to the insidious encroachments of desire: Giannetta's protectress, for all her benevolence toward the girl, does attempt to induce her to become her son's mistress. What is truly dangerous about desire is that it comes forth as sheer madness, as in the case of the queen, or, as in the case of Giachetto, as an uncontrollable disease which borders on death. This desire hovers forever over any provisional form of order and threatens to derange it.

That the happy ending is not final is made evident by the fact that in the story it does not even grow from the spontaneous development of the plot. The happy ending is unexpected and a direct allusion to the designs of the Divine Providence to impart a surprising turn to Gianetta's destiny bears it out: "Ma Idio, giusto riguardatore degli altrui meriti, lei nobile femina conoscendo e senza colpa penitenza portare dell'altrui peccato, altrimenti dispose . . . e acciò che a mano di vile uomo la gentil giovane non venisse, si dee credere che quello che avvenne egli per sua benignità permettesse" (But God, who rewards all according to their deserts, knowing her to be a noble woman doing penance for another's sin, arranged matters differently . . . one must believe that, to prevent the woman from falling into the hands of a commoner, He allowed, out of his kindness, what actually happened, p. 192). More generally, the heading of the second day announces that the discussion turns upon those who, after suffering a series of misfortunes, are brought to a state of unexpected happiness. The theme describes what by grammarians is known as anacoluthon, the rhetorical figure expressing the reversal of sequence in the narrative pattern or, more precisely, the disconnectedness in the construction of a sentence. Consistently, the interruption of the order of causality is figured in the unpredictability and randomness of Fortune's movements which introduce the story of Alessandro (II, 3).

The preamble to the story tells of Fortune's inscrutable permutations. Fortune, Pampinea states, controls all the affairs we unthinkingly call our own, moving them now in one direction, now in another, without following any discernible plan. The description is a clear echo of Dante's representation of Fortune as the agency of distributive justice and of the order lying behind the mutabilities of the sublunary world.[9] But Boccaccio also recalls the dramatic context which surrounds the digression on Fortune in *Inferno* VII. This is the canto of the avaricious and prodigals, the sinners who have violated the circulation of goods either by overvaluing or scorning the gifts of Fortune. The contrary excesses of the sinners are for Dante tantamount to a disruption of the natural economy of the world for theirs was a deluded attempt to appropriate what must forever be exchanged. Ironically, in this ridge of Hell they are doomed to move around in clashing semicircles, ex-

[9] "Valorose donne, quanto più si parla de' fatti della fortuna, tanto più, a chi vuole le sue cose ben riguardare, ne resta a poter dire: e di ciò niuno dee aver maraviglia, se discretamente pensa che tutte le cose, le quali noi scioccamente nostre chiamiamo, sieno nelle sue mani, e per conseguente da lei, secondo il suo occulto giudicio, senza alcuna posa d'uno in altro e d'altre in uno successivamente, senza alcuno conosciuto ordine da noi, esser da lei permutate" (*Decameron*, p. 108). Branca in his notes (p. 1057) rightly points out that Fortune is here a providential agency. For more bibliography, cf. Howard R. Patch, *The Goddess Fortuna in Medieval Literature* (Cambridge, Mass.: Harvard University Press, 1927); see also V. Cioffari, *The Conception of Fortune and Fate in the Works of Dante* (Cambridge, Mass.: Dante Society, 1940).

changing insults, each group of sinners the parodic double of the other, like the opposing unnatural waves of Scylla and Charybdis.

Exploiting Dante's metaphoric yoking of Fortune and economy, Boccaccio also places the passage on Fortune's workings within an account of the economic entanglements of the Agolanti family. Alessandro is the scion of a noble and wealthy family, whose substance has been dissipated by the prodigality of other heirs. He restores the family wealth by lending money to English aristocrats, till, unpredictably, he loses all his possessions when "nacque in Inghilterra una guerra tra il re e un suo figliuolo, per la quale tutta l'isola si divise" (In England broke out a war between the king and his son which split the whole island into factions, p. 110). The reference is to the historical event of the English war of succession, which for Dante becomes the emblem of the sinister reality of history and through which, in *Inferno* XXVIII, he both shows the crumbling of the political order and enunciates the law of the *contrapasso*, the principle of moral retribution linking sin and its punishment. The tragic resonance of the disintegration of family and political bonds in the war between father and son is bracketed by Boccaccio. The historical crisis is in the novella a fortuitous point of intersection between the two main strands of the plot: Alessandro, who in absolute penury is on the way home, meets the daughter of the king of England, who disguised as an abbot is traveling to Rome ostensibly to be confirmed by the pope "nella dignità," the worth and rank of the office.

The abbot is at first attracted by Alessandro's beauty and after they converse together she is inflamed by passion for him, till one night while they chance to sleep in the same room, she asks Alessandro to lie down by her. Alessandro reluctantly complies suspecting that the abbot might "forse" be "da disonesto amor preso," (perhaps be seized by dishonest love, p. 114) but is relieved when he is told that the abbot is in reality a woman in disguise. Still concealing her true identity, she tells him that she has chosen him to be her husband, convinced, as she will tell the pope later, that his "costumi e . . .

valore sono degni di qualunque gran donna, quantunque forse la nobiltà del suo sangue non sia così chiara come è la reale" (character and valor are worthy of any lady, though perhaps the nobility of his blood is not as pure as that of a person of royal lineage, p. 116). The pope celebrates the marriage, and after Alessandro reinstates his uncles to their former position of wealth, he returns with his wife to England where he brings peace between the king and his son and eventually, "con senno e valore" (with wisdom and valor, p. 118), he conquers Scotland and becomes its king. The phrase translates *sapientia et fortitudo*, a classical and medieval commonplace describing the attributes of the hero.[10]

But the word *valore*, as well as the reference to the royal rank Alessandro attains, brings to the fore the underlying issue of values in the novella. The story Pampinea tells is one in which material possessions are too precarious to be trusted; family and natural bonds are too insecure, as children rebel against fathers, as everyone seems to do in his own way; the social structure, as the political rebellion looming in the background shows, far from being an inviolable order of rank is vulnerable to usurpation and strife. The pope is the unquestioned authority who grants recognition and legitimacy to the status of men, but the real source of value is the accident of sexual attraction. To be sure, as Boccaccio pokes fun at the readers' prurient expectations by equivocating over the type of sexuality involved in the first encounters between the "abbott" and Alessandro, there is the intimation that sexuality cannot be conceived within conventional norms of naturalness. Nonetheless, sexuality is acknowledged as the powerful impulse which subverts the hierarchical arrangements of social life, because by virtue of it the usurer Alessandro is enabled to be-

[10] The *topos* has been traced for the Renaissance by Curtius, *European Literature*, pp. 178ff. Its medieval recurrence has been investigated by R. E. Kaske, "*Sapientia et Fortitudo* as the Controlling Theme in *Beowulf*," *Studies in Philology*, 55 (1958), pp. 423–457. For a general description of the hero in Boccaccio, see V. Branca, "The Myth of the Hero in Boccaccio," in *Concepts of the Hero in the Middle Ages and the Renaissance*, eds. M. T. Burns and C. J. Regan (Albany: State University of New York Press, 1975), pp. 287–291.

come king. In this world subjected to Fortune's mockery all values are contingent on her playful schemes. Sexual attraction, which is both fortuitous and "natural," is, from a social point of view, an indeterminate value because it can variously be both creative and disruptive of the balance of the world (as Gualtieri's and Alessandro's experiences make clear). The effort must lie in finding the manner by which it can be accommodated to the conditions of social life.

So strong is Boccaccio's sense of the extent to which various forms of desire interfere with the social structures that many novelle explicitly focus on the antinomy of values such as those of wealth and love. The story of Federigo (v, 9), the lover who wastes all for love and is finally rewarded by winning Monna Giovanna, is probably too well known an instance of the contrast between the scorn the hero feels for material possessions and the importance he assigns to his object of desire to be rehashed here. In no less sharp terms, the novella of Nastagio degli Onesti (v, 8) exemplifies Boccaccio's insight both into the clash between social and erotic values and into the process by which desire is accommodated to the demands and pressures of reality.

In rough outline this is the story of Nastagio who loves a woman of higher social station and, desperate because his love is not reciprocated, squanders his fortune and thinks of killing himself. The narrative unfolds in the city of Ravenna, but the specific locale of the climactic action is the woodland of Chiassi, the metaphoric landscape through which Dante had figured the Garden of Eden. There are some unmistakable textual recalls of Dante's representation, but what matters to our concerns is Boccaccio's complication of what for Dante is the imaginative experience of the world of romance. Boccaccio preserves Dante's sense of the garden as a place of visionary encounters, but at the same time shatters the idyllic appearance of the pastoral form. In the garden of love at the top of *Purgatorio* the pilgrim meets Beatrice, while the poet celebrates, among other things, the bounty and pure giving of harmonious nature. By contrast, Boccaccio's garden is a veritable space of horror, where Nastagio, walking despondently, sees the savage inversion of the medieval commonplace of the chase of love: a beautiful young woman running naked while pursued by two mastiffs and a knight on a horse piercing her with a rapier every time he catches up with her. When Nastagio tries to rescue the woman from the punishment inflicted on her, the knight fends him off telling him that this was a woman who did not return his love; that, because of her indifference, he killed himself; that he is now suffering among the damned in Hell just as is the woman for refusing to love; that the punishment he is witnessing is a ritual reenacted every Friday.

The violence ritualized in this visionary experience derives mainly from two texts. The hellish spot echoes, first of all, the desolation of the wood in *Inferno* XIII, the canto where suicides and those who have squandered their property are damned.[11] At the same time, from the point of view of the woman's sin this is also the other world of lovers described by Andreas Capellanus. In an overt inversion of Christian values, Andreas' code envisions a place of delight beyond the grave for the women who have surrendered to love's precepts; one of eternal punishment for those who on earth have preferred a life of chastity.[12]

[11] Since the story takes place in the locale of Ravenna, the forest which Dante uses as the image of the Garden of Eden, *Purgatorio* XXVIII, 2ff., is the text lying behind Boccaccio's figuration. Yet *Inferno* XIII, with the wood of the suicides, and the dog chase, is a text ironically superimposed on the image of Earthly Paradise.

[12] Andreas Capellanus, *De amore libri tres*, ed. E. Trojel (Munich: *Eidos Verlag*, 1964). Here is the text from *The Art of Courtly Love*, trans. Parry: "While we were talking thus we had gone a good distance and had come to a most delightful spot, where the meadows were very beautiful and more finely laid out than mortal had ever seen. The place was closed on all sides by every kind of fruitful and fragrant trees, each bearing marvelous fruits according to its kind. It was also divided concentrically into three distinct parts. . . . This section, the inner one, was called "Delightfulness.". . . The second part was called "Humidity.". . . The third and last part was called "Aridity" and with good reason for water was completely lacking, the whole place was arid, and the heat of the sun's rays was intense, almost like fire, and the surface of the earth was like the bottom of a heated oven. All about the place were innumerable bundles of thorns. . . . Then, at the same place entered the third and last throng of women—those who would not have pity on the soldiers of Love—and they came as far as the edge of Humidity; but when they found no en-

These two textual strands are drawn together by Boccaccio to emphasize the violence of desire as well as the contradictoriness of the ethical norms which attempt to structure it. In terms of the plot, the vision prompts Nastagio, who perceives the experience of Guido degli Anastagi to be a thinly disguised parable of his own possible destiny, to stage in that very place a banquet on a subsequent Friday to which he invites the whole Traversari family. While they are all sitting for the meal, the scene of the love chase is repeated and, because of the fear it inspires, the girl changes her hatred of Nastagio into love and consents to marry him. In other stories marriage is dramatized, consistently with commonplace exegetical tradition, as the typology of the unity of the Garden of Eden.[13] In this novella marriage, the emblem of order, results from a desire to subdue the imaginary violence that the pageant in the garden represents. At the same time, just as in the other stories we have looked at earlier, here, too, Boccaccio senses how order is a containment of possibilities, at once terrifying and wondrous, which desire generates. With the resolution of the tale, what is driven home is Boccaccio's steady insistence on the difference between the experience of romance and its domestication: the world of romance is unlivable, and actually the expectations of comfort in the garden are shattered through the juxtaposition of pastoral edenic conventions and violence. The world of reality and order restored by marriage appears as an inevitable reduction, a retrenchment from the mystery and terror that the vision in the garden conveys.

This separation between romance and reality is not exclu-

---

trance, they commenced to spread through Aridity, since that was the place prepared for them from of old" (bk. I, chap. 6, pp. 78–80). For the debates around the question of "courtly love," see R. E. Kaske, "Chaucer and Medieval Allegory," a review of D. W. Robertson, Jr., *Preface to Chaucer*, in *English Literary History*, 30 (1963), pp. 175–192. See also Francis L. Utley, "Must we abandon the Concept of Courtly Love?" *Medievalia et Humanistica*, 2 (1972), pp. 299–324.

[13] A good bibliography on this point can be found in Henry Ansgar Kelly, *Love and Marriage in the Age of Chaucer* (Ithaca: Cornell University Press, 1975), pp. 245ff.

sively accountable in terms of the formal design of this novella. In effect, the contrast between the seemingly safe bounds of daily life and the experience of sudden disruption of that safety, whereby the characters are displaced into a land of adventures before arbitrary Fortune settles again the score, sustains all the stories we have examined so far. The formal pattern finds a consistent thematic extension in the links Boccaccio forges between economy and the passion of love. Thus the Count of Anguersa, forced to leave the court, lives in utter poverty his days of exile; Alessandro loses all, but through love he regains and multiplies his fortunes; Federigo, to honor the "valore" of Giovanna serves her the falcon, his last possession, and Giovanna, in turn, remembering Federigo's own "valore" calls him to share her love and wealth; Nastagio's love leads him to squander his riches. The general point, no doubt, is that the values of love, for all its madness, are more important than those of economy, and love can even turn out to be a good economic investment. The point is of some moment because it marks Boccaccio's deliberate departure from the major ideological preoccupations in *De arte honeste amandi*, a text which directly appears in these stories.

There is considerable evidence suggesting that the bulk of *De arte* is probing the interplay between desire and economy. By and large critics have neglected this thematic link, which, nonetheless, Andreas states with his usual forcefulness. His first move is to keep the two spheres distinct and view love as other than possession. Thus, money, as the means by which to obtain love, is firmly rejected. At length are we told that love can impoverish man, while advice is liberally given to the wise lover. The wise lover, actually, is he ". . . who does not throw wealth as a prodigal spender; usually he does, but he plans his expenditures from the beginning in accordance with the size of his patrimony."[14] Andreas will even inject, under the guise of a hard-gained personal wisdom which might make his case even more persuasive, that he knows "from personal experi-

[14] The quote is from *The Art of Courtly Love*, trans. Parry, I, 2, p. 30. See also the extended reflections on "Love got with Money," I, 9, pp. 144–148.

ence that, when poverty comes in, the things that nourished love began to leave, because poverty has nothing with which to feed love."[15] He certainly acknowledges that a true lover would rather be deprived of all his money and of everything that the human mind can imagine as indispensable to life rather than be without love, yet, the steady concern is to place love outside the scheme of economic values: the unequivocal definition is that love is "a gracious thing arising out of nobility of the heart and liberality of the mind, and should be given to everybody without cost and with no idea of payment, although lovers may for mutual solace honor each other with certain gifts."[16]

The polarization between economy and love, however simplified it might appear, has justifications that go to the heart of Andreas' vision. On the one hand, this is an overt strategy to preserve love passion intact from worldly impurities, forever shrouded in the dark language of adultery's secrets. Hence the injunction to shun the love of prostitutes, figures who set a price for love, are available to everyone and, in making love a marketable commodity, cause the glamor of passion and the illusions of romance to vanish. On the other hand, the opposition between love and economy betrays Andreas' plan to contain the articulations of a desire which, if set loose, threatens the stability of the social order. For desire always announces, as the man of the middle class, say, falls in love with a member of the nobility, the arbitrariness of all distinctions and ranks in a world in which, as in a Platonic Great Chain of Being, rank is value or, more precisely, the value of the individual depends on the position he occupies in the social structure. By formalizing the rules of love, then, Andreas allows eros to exist, but on condition that its radical subversiveness be neutralized: he acknowledges it as a transgression and sweeps it away from the public gaze. From this standpoint the doctrine of the "double truth" to which the text has often been assigned, is extended to cover the double values of private desires and public morality.[17]

---

[15] I, 2, Parry, p. 30.   [16] I, 6, Parry, p. 131.

[17] A. J. Denomy, "The *De Amore* of Andreas Capellanus and the Condem-

The *Decameron*, by contrast, features an eloquent recasting of Andreas' assertion of an experience divided between the social and the erotic functions. Boccaccio ponders exactly what can be called the politics of desire, not in the naive belief that it can ever simply be accommodated within the bounds of material economy, rather because he knows that both the world of the merchants' pursuits of wealth and the world of sexual desire are part of a shared imaginary movement. I shall explore this link by turning to three stories of the second day.

The novella of Bernabò of Genoa (II, 9), for all the unpredictable turns of the plot, begins with the evocation of ordinary circumstances. To relax from the day's pressures while in Paris on business, some Italian merchants get together and, after dining, end up talking about the women they have left behind at home. In the tone of people used to facing facts and that one imagines at once crude and complacent, the merchants flaunt their sexual profligacy, sure as they are that their wives back at home would never resist other men's advances.

The mixture of cynicism and self-indulgence notwithstanding, the vignette conveys an unmistakable impression of pleasant conviviality. The facade, however, cracks when Bernabò objects to the views his friends hold about the guile and unreliability of women. His own wife's beauty, he maintains, is without equal in the whole of Italy, and her skills in writing and bookkeeping rank above those of the average merchant. When he finally claims, more to the point, that she is a most chaste and honest woman, Ambrogiuolo, one of the merchants, blasts him. On the strength of the aphorism, *casta quam nemo rogavit*, Ambrogiuolo challenges Bernabò's remarks with the assertion that man is the most noble and perfect of God's mortal creatures, while woman is naturally his physical inferior, fickle and vulnerable to the manipulations of an intellectually more resourceful and more willful man.

The speech rephrases a commonplace of classical Human-

---

nation of 1277," *Mediaeval Studies*, 8 (1946), pp. 107–149. See also D. W. Robertson, Jr., *A Preface to Chaucer* (Princeton: Princeton University Press, 1962), pp. 391–448.

ism, the Neoplatonic doctrine of the worth and dignity of man given currency by, among others, Bernard Silvester.[18] Man, the doctrine states, is the measure of things and the excellence of creation. Wrapped in a haze of divinity, he is a molder of himself, capable of fashioning himself in whatever shape he chooses. Such is his sovereignty that he is made to symbolize, in conventional Augustinian terms, the higher faculty of reason, while the woman is the figure for the lower appetites.

Bernabò's reply to Ambrogiuolo's theories is sharp: "Io sono mercatante e non fisofolo . . . e come mercatante risponderò. . . ." (I am a merchant, not a philosopher . . . and I shall answer as a merchant, p. 207.) The answer is probably nothing more than Bernabò's polemical weapon to stress the value of his own private world and dismiss as empty talk Ambrogiuolo's presumptions about creation and its hierarchy of values. Nonetheless, both Ambrogiuolo's argument and Bernabò's dismissal allow us to perceive a sudden broadening of perspective on the world of business. The merchants come forth not as mere entrepreneurs who exchange wares: theirs is a world where they obliquely claim, in however crude a style, that more general values are affirmed and tested.

It is not, one can infer from this exchange, that philosophy, in this city of philosophy, has simply descended from the academy to the *agora*: what Bernabò's remark implies is that the disinterested, abstract speculations philosophers conduct into the universal order of things are paltry when measured against the merchants' real risking their wealth for their values and beliefs.

The claim that commerce occupies a legitimate place in the scheme of knowledge is not to be found uniquely in the *Decameron*. In Hugh of St. Victor's organization of the theoretical,

[18] "The human condition is utterly unique. . . . Human nature has been wrought with all possible care into a whole . . . for it would have been improper for the future abode of intellect and reason to suffer imbalance or disruption through any uncertainty in its design. . . . Man was formed with masterly and prudent skill, the masterwork of powerful Nature" (*The Cosmographia of Bernardus Silvestris*, trans. Winthrop Wetherbee [New York: Columbia University Press, 1973]. pp. 120–123).

practical, mechanical and logical arts, for instance, commerce is viewed as an art, ". . . a peculiar sort of rhetoric—strictly of its own kind—for eloquence is in the highest degree necessary to it. Thus the man who excels others in fluency of speech is called a *Mercurius*, or Mercury, as being a *mercatorum kirrius* (=kyrios)—a very lord among merchants. Commerce penetrates the secret places of the world. . . ."[19] We shall soon see which secret place Ambrogiuolo will penetrate. For now, let us point out that their argument moves away from words to real concerns. Against the lengthy "questionar con parole" (arguing emptily, p. 208) as Bernabò says to Ambrogiuolo, who claims he knows the truth of his statements, miming the philosophers' language, "per naturali e vere ragioni" (by cogent and logical arguments, p. 208) they wager five thousand florins, with the understanding that Ambrogiuolo will try the virtues of Bernabò's wife, Zinevra, to furnish proof of his assertion.

Through the wager Zinevra is turned into a pawn in the two men's power game; through it philosophy is also trivialized, for the merchants, more than being figures supplanting the philosophers' hollow arguments, are in effect like pimps, who, betting over the woman's chastity, turn their ideals of honor into a pretext for gain.

From the perspective of the mercantile ethos, however, the pledge is the symbolic bond, a token of the trust merchants must put in each other's word either to seal a contract or to secure a future transaction. In either case the pledge shows that in the economy of the marketplace words are commodities, have even a definite value because there is an assumption of the necessary correspondence between the promise one makes verbally and the fulfilling of it by future deed. There is, in a sense, a metaphoric structure that organizes the laws of the marketplace, and in this rhetorical-symbolic universe Bernabò comes forth as a naive literalist. He will accept as a settled truth

[19] *The Didascalicon of Hugh of St. Victor*, trans. Jerome Taylor (New York: Columbia University Press, 1968), II, 23, pp. 76–77. See also pp. 205–206 for references to Remigius of Auxerre and Fulgentius.

everything Ambrogiuolo will report to him, blind to the possibility that, underneath the seemingly most persuasive evidence, Ambrogiuolo may be lying. And, in effect, Ambrogiuolo's humanistic ideals turn out to be a thorough falsification of the world of fact. This is not to say that Boccaccio maligns the ideal; rather, he shows how the point of view his character upholds about the moral superiority of man leads him not to a morally virtuous action, but to a distortion of the very idea of virtue.

Boccaccio's sharp sense of the sprawling variety of life cannot but make us suspect that Ambrogiuolo's deceptions verge on being a self-deception. He plunges us into a series of frauds beginning with his enlisting the help of an old maid. He then secretly enters at night Zinevra's bedchamber, and gazes, while she is asleep, at her nakedness to use what he sees as signs of his intimacy with her, so that he can win the wager. As he manufactures the evidence, Ambrogiuolo, indeed, comes forth as a consummate plot maker, the molder and master of the reality he constructs and, in this sense, he bears out the truth of the cliché he had announced. Throughout he is unaware, however, that his is a morally degraded version of the humanistic model he proclaims. If for Ambrogiuolo to master is to deceive, Zinevra's experiences provide a trenchant reversal of his practices.

Spared from the death Bernabò had destined her by a servant's sword, she takes on the guise of a man, Sicurano by name, and enters the service of the Sultan of Alexandria. She understands, by impersonating what she is not, as Ambrogiuolo does, that impersonation will be the source of her power. But unlike Ambrogiuolo's, her deception is a way of survival in the grubby and lonely world of men's affairs; and as by her work and abilities she manages to become a trustworthy agent of the Sultan, she shows, against Ambrogiuolo, that the value of self is not dependent on sexual identity. There is not a fixed, biological determination for the value of the self because, as she adapts to changing circumstances and takes on different roles, wifely, menial and, finally, that of confidant, we witness how multiple *personae* inhabit the presumed integrity of the self.

What brings the novella to a denouement is the chance encounter between Sicurano and Ambrogiuolo at a fair in the East. Among the items Ambrogiuolo has displayed for sale, Sicurano notices "una borsa e una cintura" (a purse and a belt, p. 214) which he identifies as having belonged to him. There is a special dramatic aptness in Boccaccio's reference to the "cintura." In medieval mythography the "cintura" or *ceston*, as in the commentary to *Inferno* v Boccaccio calls it, is the emblem of sexual continence, and its removal is the clear sign of unbound desire.[20] When Sicurano feigns interest in buying the items, Ambrogiuolo explains that he got them from madonna Zinevra after sleeping with her and that he also won the pledge of five thousand florins from her husband Bernabò.

What are the reasons for the lies he weaves to one he perceives as a stranger and which are his undoing? In a way he is a conventional *alazon* and his boast is his downfall. But there is a special insight in Ambrogiuolo's figment, for he recognizes that the value of objects is never absolute, but it depends on the desires and fantasies they arouse. As he invests the girdle and purse with the erotic charge of his personal life (the

[20] "Alla qual cosa con più evidenzia dimostrare è da sapere che, tra gli altri più ornamenti che i poeti aggiungono a Venere, è una singular cintura, chiamata 'ceston,' della quale scrive cosi Omero nella sua *Iliada*: 'Et a pectoribus solvit ceston cingulum varium, ubi sibi voluntaria omnia ordinata erant, ubi certe amicitia atque cupido atque facundia, blanditie que furate intellectum, studiose licet scientiam.' etc. E vogliono i poeti, con ciò sia cosa che a Venere paia dovere apartenere ogni congiunzione generativa, che, quando alcuni ligittime e oneste noze celebrano, Venere vada questa congiunzione cinta di questa sua cintura detta 'ceston,' a dimostrazione che quegli li quali per santa legge si congiungono sieno constretti e obligati l'uno all'altro da certe cose convenientisi al matrimonio, e massimamente alla perpetuità d'esso; e per ciò che Venera similmente va a' non ligittimi congiugnimenti, dicono che, quando ella va a quelli così fatti, ella va scinta sanza portare questa sua cintura chiamata 'ceston': e quinci ogni congiunzion non ligittima chiamarono 'incesto,' cioè fatta sanza questo 'ceston' " (*Esposizioni sorpra la Comedia di Dante*, ed. G. Padoan in *Tutte le opere di Giovanni Boccaccio* vi [Milan: Mondadori, 1965], pp. 341–342).

whole thing said, one suspects, most confidentially), he points to the imaginary structure governing our desires. The irony in Ambrogiuolo's gesture is that he takes at face value, like Bernabò earlier, Sicurano's query and does not know that, independently of his own fantasizing, the two articles are valuable to Sicurano precisely because they belong to the story of his secret life. Ambrogiuolo, in all this, may be acting out of raw profit motive. The lies he tells also suggest, however, the powerful hold of the imagination, over and beyond economic gain, on this man, who manipulates at will the world of appearances, for whom reality can be easily concocted, and who freely substitutes lies for facts. There are no agreements or equivalences that he cannot or does not violate: as a figure of pure transgression (and in this he resembles a host of other perverse "esthetes" in the *Decameron*, such as Ser Ciappelletto) he is the threat to the marketplace's system of ideally fixed correspondences in that he reveals what the social contract cannot bear to see: the simulation at the heart of all traffics.

It is not surprising, then, that Ambrogiuolo should be punished so fiercely. His possessions, valued at over ten thousand doubloons, are passed on to Zinevra, who also receives from the Sultan gold and money coming to a further ten thousand doubloons in value. Ambrogiuolo is tied to a pole, smeared with honey, is slain and his flesh devoured by mosquitoes, wasps and horseflies.

From a moral point of view, Ambrogiuolo certainly would belong to cantos xxix and xxx of Dante's *Inferno*, which features counterfeiters, falsifiers of words and impersonators. What gives the connection weight is that the punishment Dante reserves to these sinners is to suffer itching and disfiguration of limbs. The brooding core of Dante's vision is the threat impersonators constitute to the principle of identity. If in *Inferno* xxix the sinners are referred to as "persone" (l. 72), literally the hollow masks of actors on the stage, the passing allusion to Narcissus' mirror of *Inferno* xxx, 128, the water where the mythical boy saw reflected his own face, draws attention to the illusoriness of self revealed by their artifices. They are truly, as Dante implies, *simiae naturae*, engaged, like apes, in a literal unproductive exchange of make-believe for reality. Quite in keeping with the principle of *contrapasso*, which establishes a symmetrical balance between sin and punishment, the sinners are represented as they literally suffer the loss of their original figure.

In the steady displacement of all things that Ambrogiuolo's imagination operates, Boccaccio represents the disruption of the order at work in the economy of the marketplace. Ambrogiuolo also embodies, like the sinners in Dante's cantos, the crisis of metaphor, for to him there are no proper values, no firm resemblances, no reliable exchanges, no stubborn identities. Everything can be literally converted into everything else. To punish him with a death that literally disfigures him seems unavoidable from the point of view of the continued existence of the social order. And with his death, all things finally return to their "proper" place: Sicurano resumes her real identity; she returns to Bernabò and both of them retrieve their money and place in the restored economy of the world. The social order does not tolerate the dizzying circulation of the imagination; rather, as Ambrogiuolo's savage punishment illustrates, it will violently expel all figures of transgression.

That the social world constantly represses the turns of the imagination in favor of a precarious literal surface is a motif that explicitly recurs in the tale of Landolfo Rufolo (II, 4). The narrative opens with the description of the landscape along the seashore between Reggio and Gaeta and closes in on Ravello, one of the towns in that area. The topographical precision in the evocation of the mythic bay of Baiae, a symbolic place of benign and controlled nature, where Landolfo and many other wealthy merchants live, alludes to the defined and identifiable boundaries of a contained and safe world. The sense of repose and order that the landscape evokes also prepares, by contrast, the frenzied reality of mercantile life which the novella proceeds quickly to relate. Impelled by a desire to double his already considerable wealth, Landolfo goes to Cyprus with his whole merchandise.[21]

In a way, his intrepid quest over the familiar and yet dangerous sea-lanes of the Mediterranean casts him as the hero of real, bourgeois adventures in pursuit of wealth and self-mastery. As such, he gives in to his drives, but sets out only after making the preliminary rational calculations merchants make in similar circumstances. Within the brief space of the same paragraph, however, Landolfo discovers that, as a merchant, he cannot control the circumstances of the world: this is the day of Fortune's ambushes and the goddess mocks his designs of wealth. What happens is that other merchants had carried the same goods as Landolfo to Cyprus, and he is forced to sell his merchandise at a loss before it goes bad. We are given, in passing, a glimpse of an elementary law of the economic circuit, namely that excess of available goods reduces their value. At the same time, Boccaccio unveils the operation of time in the value system: since goods are perishable, their value cannot but depend on the timeliness of the transaction, on the merchants' ability to "seize the time." From this point of view the merchant comes forth as a figure who is caught in an authentic temporal predicament, and whose aim is to fight off or, at least, be a step ahead of impending death, as well as to circumvent the subterfuges of Fortune, which, as the figure of time's circles, holds sway over perishable goods.

Faced with financial ruin, Landolfo plots to take the high road of piracy, willing to die rather than return home poor. The glitter of the adventure is not tarnished by an overt moral reflection either on the oblique equation between wealth and life (or bankruptcy and death), or on the sovereignty of self-interest, which makes this into a predatory world. Landolfo accumulates wealth, only to become himself prey to the violence of other pirates who will strip him of all his possessions. While he is a captive at sea a dramatic reversal occurs. The locale could not have been more appropriate for the shift, for the

---

[21] It is of interest to stress that Cyprus is the island associated with Venus. Cf., to mention the most obvious case, "la bella Ciprigna," *Paradiso* VIII, 2.

sea, from Boethius to Alan of Lille and Dante, is the very emblem of Fortune's fluctuations: the boat founders in a storm and Landolfo is shipwrecked.[22] In the description of his experience there is a great deal of irony in the echo from Aeneas' shipwreck in the first book of the *Aeneid*: "essendo . . . il mare tutto pieno di mercatantie che notavano e di casse e di tavole, come in così fatti casi suole avvenire . . ." (As is usually the case where this happens, the sea was all littered with floating merchandise and chests and planks, p. 122). The precise sense of the resonance is difficult to establish.[23] Is Boccaccio, as he sets up a parallel between the two storms, implying that Landolfo is the modern version of the epic hero; or, and by the same stroke, is he showing how wide is the gap between the schemes of political power of the Trojan hero and the gratuitous private passions of the merchant; or, finally, is the point that Aeneas is really no better than a modern pirate? Confronted with all these interpretive possibilities, a reader might well suspect that the allusion does not have a *proper*, direct rationale, as if Boccaccio wants to leave these semantic possibilities open. One thing is clear, though, from the passage: the storm is the occasion for the comedy of Fortune's dissembling. While Landolfo swims ashore by clinging to a plank, he sees a chest floating on the sea's surface being tossed against him. Fearful of being injured, he tries to push it away from him. When a sudden squall causes Landolfo to lose his grip and go under, on resurfacing he finds that the plank is some distance away from him and to keep afloat he sprawls across the chest which is close at hand. In this fashion, he reaches the coast of the island of Corfu, where he is sighted by a peasant woman,

---

[22] If the wheel is the conventional emblem of Fortune, the tempest and sea waves are also part of her iconography. See, for instance, *The Consolation of Philosophy*, trans. H. F. Steward (Cambridge, Mass.: Harvard University Press, 1968), II, 2, p. 181; see also Alanus de Insulis, *Anticlaudianus*, ed. R. Bossuat (Paris: J. Vrin, 1955), VII, 397–457; Dante, of course, introduces the long digression on Fortune in *Inferno* VII with a reference to the contrary waves of Charybdis and Scylla (22–24).

[23] *Aeneid* I, 118–119: "rari nantes in gurgite vasto Arma virum tabulaeque et Troia gaza per undas."

who carries him in her arms "come un piccol fanciullo" (like a small child, p. 123) to her hut, revives him and nourishes him with wine and food.

The scene of the rescue, with its simple and direct charity in taking care of the derelict's needs of food and shelter, clearly escapes the logic of the market, and affords a respite from the treachery of the high seas. "La buona femina" (the good woman, p. 124), as she is repeatedly referred to in the final paragraph of the story, hands over the chest to Landolfo, who opens it to discover that it contains a number of precious stones which he recognizes as being "di gran valor" (extremely valuable, p. 124). To make sure that he can take "quelle cose" (those things, p. 124) safely home, he asks the woman for some rags in which to wrap them and tells her to keep the chest, if she so likes. The woman is glad to comply with his request: dissembled as a poor man, he makes it to Trani, where he meets some cloth merchants to whom he relates his adventures, saying nothing about the chest, and who out of compassion fit him with new clothes. Once he is back in Ravello, he realizes that he is now twice as wealthy as he was before leaving: after sending some money to the peasant woman "per merito del servigio ricevuto" (as a reward to the services received, p. 125) and to the cloth merchants, he decides to give up commerce.

The decision is a gesture of repression of the violence behind the surface world of social order. Once power and rise in the social hierarchy are achieved by the stones, trade is abandoned. The precious stones function in the text primarily as an extension of Boccaccio's insight into the temporality to which the merchant's condition is bound: unlike perishable goods, the stones, in their permanence, crystallize time and are, as it were, the simulacrum of eternity. The fascination with them is such that Landolfo knows that he must conceal them and avoid speaking about them. If they are kept hidden, however, they have no value, for they are objects that have no use in a world of needs. Paradoxically, it is their great value that demands that they be kept invisible, because they have the power to represent everything they are not. Like fetishes, which are empty of any inner value, they are metaphors of universal exchange, invested with a magic value by the general desire to possess them. Social order, in one sense, is the investing of metaphors with a literal value. More than that, social order has a metonymic relation to what can subvert it: it represses, supplants and forgets the insights gained in what could be called the space of romance.

Unsurprisingly, the ending of this novella, with Landolfo repaying the woman and the cloth merchants, jars with the violence at the core of the adventure. There is a certain irony in his deciding what the right price is for their saving his life; more precisely, the payment is a recognition of bonds which his experience as a pirate had ruthlessly violated. The rift between the two moments of the story may well point to the opposition Landolfo wants to establish between the dangerous world of the quest and the social structure; at the same time, it also hints at how illegitimate are the foundations of the political order. But what is essential is that the ending, with the circulation of precious stones, exemplifies Landolfo's desire to assimilate everything into his world of exchange, to draw his benefactors into his own system of metaphors and values of which he is the master.

If Landolfo's gesture shows that to assign values is to master and create one's reality, there is in the *Decameron* the awareness of another reality that always escapes the circuit of exchange and mastery. This is what can be best described as the value of the esthetic experience. Boccaccio probes the issue in the story of Alatiel (II, 7), the woman who, by the sorcery of her beauty, dazzles all those who gaze at her. For Thomas Aquinas beauty is "id quod visum placet."[24] For Boccaccio beauty disorients, opens up a radical crisis in the value system.

In its general movement—Alatiel's journey from her fa-

---

[24] *Summa Theologiae*, I, 5, ad. 1. For the debate on the beautiful in St. Thomas, see U. Eco, *Il problema estetico in Tommaso d'Aquino* (Milan: Bompiani, 1970). See also Jacques Maritain, *Creative Intuition in Art and Poetry* (Cleveland and New York: Meridian Books, 1961), pp. 122–151.

ther's house in Babylon to Spain and back home—the novella evokes the epic adventures into an alien world. Alatiel is the heroine caught in a strange periplus, though as the "trastullo della Fortuna" (Fortune's plaything, p. 178) she is the heroine turned inside out: hapless and passive after the shipwreck she becomes the pure object of general fascination in a foreign land. From the point of view of her reduction to the condition of object, the story does not provide any significant shifts, for at the outset of the narrative Alatiel is already cast as a pawn in the transaction between her father and her future husband, given away with a dowry to seal an alliance between the two.[25]

But in her new condition of lonely survivor her reification is ostensibly complete. When, after the storm, Pericone's man reports to him what had been found in the ship, Pericone arranges for the woman to be brought ashore along with the other valuable items that could be salvaged. Deprived of social context (she is a Muslim in a Christian world), she knows no language and is outside the structure of communication. More generally there is in the story a tragic repetition of lovers who attempt to possess her and steal her away, along with her other precious possessions, from the others.

For what secret reason are all enthralled by the powerful spell her appearance casts? Her secret, in the first place, is that she has no secret: as a naked and silent object, she represents herself (not status or family, for instance), and there are no false resemblances or lies in her. Her silence and passivity probably even arouse the illusion of power in those who behold her. Finally, she is different from everybody else in this alien world: as the outsider who brings fantasies of far-away romances into the daily world, she is the frontier of difference, the enigma of appearance. Her spell cannot be explained solely by providing a series of likely reasons, for Alatiel is also a figure through which an ironic reversal of any definite rationale

---

[25] Cesare Segré, "Comicità strutturale nella novella di Alatiel," *Letteratura e critica. Studi in onore di Natalino Sapegno*, vol. II (Rome: Bulzoni, 1972), pp. 193–206. See also Millicent Marcus, "Seduction by Silence: A Gloss on the Tales of Masetto (*Decameron*, III, 1) and Alatiel (*Decameron*, II, 7)," *Philological Quarterly*, 58 (1979), pp. 1–15.

takes place. Thus, though she is different from all, she ironically establishes a difference among those who desire to possess her. At the same time, she can never really be possessed: all the efforts to own her are ironically twisted: it is her beauty that possesses and haunts the men; a derelict object, she gives value to them; she must be kept hidden, but like gold, everyone is compelled to show her; even her silence seems to mock the sense of mastery of those who possess language. It could be said that her silence is the obverse mirror of her beauty: it conceals impenetrable depths, speaks the unfathomable riddle of her value; reveals the dizzying reality of desire and imagination. In short, Alatiel's beauty is that strangeness which, though part of the world of desire and provisional enjoyment, can never be assimilated into the structure of exchange. Through her Boccaccio figures the appearance of the enigma which disrupts all loyalties (friends here betray friends, servants their masters, brothers kill brothers), which can never be contained in any formula and only engenders death.

When after many vicissitudes Alatiel comes home and regains her language, she simulates to her father. There is in her account a profusion of deceptions: she tells him that she spent her time in "uno monastero di donne secondo la lor legge religiose; e quivi, che che essi dicessero, io fui da tutte benignissimamente ricevuta e onorata sempre, e con gran divozione con loro insieme ho poi servito a San Cresci in Valcava, a cui le femine di quel paese vogliono molto bene . . ." (in a convent of nuns who practice [these men's] religion; here, whatever it was they said to the nuns, I was kindly received by everybody and was always treated with respect. While I was there, I joined them in the worship of St. Stiffen, for whom the women of that country possess a deep affection, p. 181). The transparent lies, which barely cloak the reality of her experience and teasingly recollect her past pleasures, certainly lower the tragic intensity of the preceding adventures. The point, however, is that the Sultan believes this story of modesty of Alatiel tells and arranges to have her sent safely to the re del Garbo as his wife, according to the original plan, as if her ordeals could be effaced.

The lie is at the origin of order. In a larger sense, social bonds are made to depend on deception or on what can be called metaphors which are accepted as true. All the stories we have analyzed show that the foundation of order is exactly a literalization and a forgetting of predatory action, violence or savagery. This literalization is an act by which we displace and repress the imaginative excesses which do not fit the balance sheet of everyday life. The lies make life for Boccaccio a fundamentally esthetic phenomenon, a beautiful appearance which in its superficiality and shimmering falsehood masks the terrible depths of imagination and desire. This superficiality is, paradoxically, the profound wisdom of Boccaccio's text.

The *Decameron*, conceived as a gift of Boccaccio's liberality to relieve the erotic crises of housebound women, is an object to be used and enjoyed, but its power transcends these reductive confines. All the stories examined in this chapter steadily probe the effort to contain the imagination, and steadily discover that the imagination always exceeds all efforts at containment, and that ruses, feints and simulation are at the heart of all forms of social living. It is because of this double vision that Boccaccio's text may be said to be political, but also to lie beyond politics. Dante writes explicitly political texts, and he does so with the perception that the sovereignty of evil forces him, as well as us, into a recognition of necessary but forever suspect allegiances to the secular world. Boccaccio overtly refuses, as we know from his explicit critique of Dante's political engagement, the possibility of a direct link between politics and literature. In these stories, however, he nags us into gauging the ambiguities of the imagination, which is simultaneously in complicity and at odds with history. This predicament forever haunts the foundation of the social world in the *Decameron*.

ALLEGORY
AND THE PORNOGRAPHIC
IMAGINATION

Several tales of the *Decameron* feature an allegorical structure which, though essential to Boccaccio's narrative, has been somewhat neglected by critical commentaries. This is possibly due to the belief that the importance of the *Decameron* lies precisely both in Boccaccio's act of rescuing his stories from the ponderous allegorical mechanisms which figure in other medieval texts and in his attempt to recover the texture of reality in its rich and random literalness.[1] Within this perspective, allegorical structures, much like other codes that formalize experience, such as courtly love and stilnovism, are stressed only in so far as they are subverted by Boccaccio's mimetic art and are held up as objects of ridicule.

But Boccaccio's literary subversiveness is much more radical than is commonly recognized, and my aim here is to map the ruses of his strategy. The primary focus is the allegory of the Earthly Paradise as it is dramatized in the Introduction to the third day and the tales of Masetto (III, 1) and Griselda (X, 10). In the tale of Griselda, Boccaccio brings to bear on the literal plot the weight of allegory, its moral and doctrinal implications. In the tale of Masetto, he places in the narrative foreground an allegorical construct and shows how it dissolves as it comes into contact with the domain of worldliness. In both

---

[1] The most influential recent proponents of this critical view are Erich Auerbach, *Mimesis: The Representation of Reality in Western Literature*, trans. W. R. Trask (New York: Anchor Books, 1957), esp. pp. 177–203; and N. Sapegno, *Storia letteraria del Trecento* (Milan-Naples: Ricciardi, 1963).

cases, the procedure, taken at its simplest, issues into a corrosive burlesque of medieval techniques of allegorization. The allegory is crushed by the exigencies of the literal sense, but there is more at stake than a simple ironic process of demystification from the standpoint of "reality." The realistic impulse is only a stage, albeit a crucial one, in the endlessly ironic movement of Boccaccio's narrative: ultimately, the notion of "reality" and its mimesis—apodictic canons in recent critical endeavors—are questioned and their dangerous illusoriness is exposed. The text is unveiled as what could be called pornography, in a sense that demands some clarification.

In his essay on pornography, which he defines etymologically as the "graph of the harlot," D. H. Lawrence sets Boccaccio apart from what he takes to be the neurotic practices of nineteenth-century writing.[2] Pornography, in Lawrence's view, is the sympton of the diseased state of the body politic or more generally, "the attempt to insult sex, to do dirt on it." In this fierce polemic against the self-appointed moral guardians of society, who censor the plain representation of sex, Boccaccio's "natural fresh openness about sex" figures as the best antidote to the circle of vice and secrecy on which the worm of pornography feeds.

There is probably little doubt, as will be shown, that Boccaccio would share Lawrence's own passionate moral convictions about the need to unmask, in the name of irrepressible natural instincts, all sexual hypocrisies. But Boccaccio moves well beyond the naive myth of spontaneity that Lawrence attributes to him. He is aware, as I contend in this chapter, of the constitutive temptation of all love literature to turn into pornography, to be a "galeotto" with powers to give and arouse erotic pleasures.[3] The *Decameron* effectively provides a view to

[2] D. H. Lawrence, "Pornography and Obscenity," in *Sex, Literature, and Censorship*, ed. H. T. Moore (New York: The Viking Press, 1975), pp. 64–81.

[3] The *Decameron*, as one gathers from the Proem, is directed to women who are in need of "alleggiamento" and comfort for love's labors. By *surnaming* the text, "Galeotto," Boccaccio is clearly alluding to the erotic seduction of Paolo and Francesca by the reading of a book—*Inferno* v, 137. Boccaccio in his *Esposizioni sopra la Comedia di Dante* (ed. Giorgio Padoan in *Tutte le opere di Giovanni Boccaccio* vi [Milan: Mondadori, 1965], p. 184), refers to the book Paolo

the mechanism and poetics of pornography, and allegory plays a prominent role in it.

The point of departure for this critical-textual analysis is the Introduction to the third day. We are imaginatively located in a garden, which is a veritable *hortus conclusus*, "un giardino che tutto era da torno murato" (a garden that was walled all around, p. 236) where the storytellers retreat. Described as a space where all elements are given fixed boundaries and symmetrical arrangement, the landscape comes forth as a harmonious cluster of flowers, birds' songs, brooks and other paraphernalia of the pastoral storehouse. The overriding strain of the description is the bounty of a generous Nature, for the place swarms with the infinite variety of living things. But the natural cycle of the seasons, with its inherent hint of death and impermanence, is suspended: in this eternal springtime, the trees "(hanno) i vecchi frutti e' nuovi e i fiori ancora . . ." (have the old and the new fruits as well as their blossoms, p. 236). By the detail, Boccaccio insinuates that in spite of the natural abundance, this order of nature is wrought, that nature is an artifice miming the order of eternity. The palace that walls in the scenery, the marble fountain at the center of the lawn and the brooks which "*artificiosamente* fatti fuor di quello divenuta palese" (artifically constructed came into view out of there, p. 237) move in the direction of translating the organic and wondrous world of nature into an imaginative compression of illusion and reality, the pictorial artifice whereby substances and appearances are indistinguishable.

The enclosure, fashioned with stylized elements, resembles many other literary *loci amoeni*:[4] it recalls, for instance, other gardens that Boccaccio had described in the *Teseida, Amorosa visione* and, more fundamentally, the garden in the general Introduction to the *Decameron*.[5] In a sense, this garden is the ge-

---

and Francesco read as playing the office Gallehault played between Lancelot and Guinivere.

[4] For a literary history of the garden motif from antiquity to the Renaissance, cf. A. Bartlett Giamatti, *The Earthly Paradise and the Renaissance Epic* (Princeton: Princeton University Press, 1966).

[5] *Amorosa visione*, XLIX, 4ff.; *Teseida*, IV, 65; *Decameron*, pp. 26–27.

neric repertory of all gardens for it contains "tutta la spezieria che mai nacque in Oriente" (all the spices ever grown in the East). For all its commonplace quality, however, there is a specific *hortus conclusus* that with ironic insistence Boccaccio is recalling: the garden of *Deduit* in Guillaume de Lorris' *Roman de la Rose*.[6] After seeing the allegorical carvings on the wall, and drawn by the music that comes from within, Amant is introduced by idleness to the enclosed garden of Love. The textual parallelisms between Guillaume's and Boccaccio's descriptions are so conspicuous that they suggest more than a mere coincidence of conventional pastoral motifs. The occurrences hint, in effect, that Boccaccio is involved in a critical reading of Guillaume's poem. Let me first point out the verbal analogues.

In Boccaccio's garden, the paths are hedged by "*rosa bianchi e vermigli* e di gelsomini erano quasi chiuse" (white and red roses and jasmine, p. 236), a description that is an almost exact replica of Guillaume's phrase "videte i avoit trop bele E parvenche fresche e novele, / s'i ot *flors blanches e vermeilles* (ll. 1404–5). Boccaccio's own suggestion that the lawn seems artfully decorated—"un prato di minutissima erba e verde tanto, che quasi nera parea, *dipinto* tutto *forse di mille varietà di fiori*" (a lawn of exceedingly fine grass, so green as to seem almost black, all dotted with perhaps a thousand kind of flowers," p. 236)—closely echoes Guillaume's metaphor that the garden is "*pointe / de flors de diverses colors* / don mout estoit bone l'olors" (ll. 1408–10). The tame animals that populate the garden in the *Decameron* (rabbits, hares, does and roe-deer) roughly correspond to the list enumerated in the *Roman*.[7] More cogently, Boccaccio's underlined phrase, "*d'una parte uscir conigli, d'altra parte correr* lepri . . ." (From one side rabbits emerging, hares from the other side running, p. 237) recalls *verbatim* the underlined words in Giullaume's description of the rabbits coming out of their burrows "*Conins i avoit, qui issoient / Toute jor* hors de lor tesnieres" (ll. 1375–79). Further, Amant's astonished

---

[6] *Le Roman de la Rose*, ed. Langlois. The quotations are all from vol. II.
[7] Lines 1360 ff.

impression that he is in the Earthly Paradise, "Lors entrai, senz plus dire mot, / Par l'uis que Oiseuse overt m'ot, / Ou vergier, e quant je fui enz . . . sachiez che je cuidai estre / Por voir en *parevis terrestre*" (ll. 631–636) is picked up by Boccaccio, who also shows his characters spellbound by the vision and believing that if "*Paradiso* si potesse *in terra* fare" (if Paradise were constructed on earth, p. 237), it would have the enchantment of the garden they behold. Even the "trente manières" (l. 1380), a phrase by which Guillaume summarily encompasses the variety of animals, become "venti maniere" (twenty kinds, p. 237) as Boccaccio refers to the birds singing.

I readily grant that no single textual parallel, taken in isolation, is particularly compelling, for each element is uniformly part of stock material. Yet, taken cumulatively, they suggest a deliberate pattern of allusions; the case is strengthened by the fact that Boccaccio adapts the conceptual frame of Guillaume's garden in order to establish some vital counterpoints to, and to argue against, the broader implications of the *Roman*. For Guillaume, the artfulness of the garden is a sign of the perversity of the place where rationality is befuddled by cupidinous love. Amant's quest for the rose is a sexual quest and as such it mocks the allegory of the spiritual pilgrimage for, like Adam in the Earthly Paradise, Amant fails.[8] The fountain of Narcissus to which he comes reveals his erotic quest to be an experience of self-love and makes the garden the place where, as the story of Narcissus' self-fascination exemplifies, love and death mingle.[9]

Boccaccio's introduction to the third day is, like Guil-

[8] A recent allegorical reading of the *Roman de la Rose* is provided by John V. Fleming, *The Roman de la Rose. A Study in Allegory and Iconography* (Princeton: Princeton University Press, 1969). For an entirely different perspective, see Daniel Poirion, *Le Roman de la Rose* (Paris: Hatier, 1973). Cf. also the remarks by C. S. Lewis, *The Allegory of Love* (London: Oxford University Press, 1953), pp. 115–156. Very suggestive is the recent paper by Thomas D. Hill, "Narcissus, Pygmalion, and the Castration of Saturn: Two Mythographic Themes in the *Roman de la Rose*," *Studies in Philology*, 71 (1974), pp. 404–426. See also the recent doctoral dissertation by David Hult, *In Quest of the Rose* (Cornell Dissertation, 1977).

[9] For a general treatment of the Narcissus myth in medieval literature, cf.

laume's poem, a subtle mockery of the religious quest for Eden. The opening sentence of the description 'L'aurora già di vermiglia cominciava, appressandosi il sole, a divenir rancia, quando la domenica . . .'' (Dawn was already beginning to change from vermilion to orange with the approach of the sun, when on Sunday . . . , p. 235) is a poignant paraphrase of Dante's *Purgatorio.*[10] The leisurely journey of the *brigata* alludes to and mocks Dante's painful askesis from Purgatory to the Garden of Eden. But for the *brigata* this is not, as it is for Dante, Easter Sunday, nor will there be for it a stern moral voice—as there is for the pilgrim—to dissipate the esthetic relief provided by Casella's song. Boccaccio's mockery, actually, is twofold. He spoofs Dante's allegory of the spiritual pilgrimage, his ascent to Eden, and, in so doing, he follows Guillaume's own parody of the Earthly Paradise. But Boccaccio also mocks the naturalistic thrust of Guillaume's poem. Far from being Amant's erotic quest, the *brigata*'s journey aims at a gratuitous, purely esthetic evasion into the artifice of nature. If Guillaume exposes the deceptive lures of the garden and obliquely denounces the fallacy of art because art—like the ambiguous mirror of Narcissus—makes things appear both as they are and are not, Boccaccio capitalizes on this very ambiguity. His garden is neither Dante's allegory of Eden nor is it Amant's garden of literal, fleshly delights. It is the imaginative domain where the allegory and the letter are alluded to and equally superseded, where the young people of the *brigata* indulge in esthetic pastimes and are drawn into the artifice: they dance, play, read romances and tell stories. Within this illusory context, their stories evoke a world of sexuality which superficially appear to be an ironic counterpoint to the garden of the introduction but, in a real sense, they end up by exposing the dangers of the esthetic imagination.

The explicit impulse of the tale of Masetto (III, 1), which im-

Frederick Goldin, *The Mirror of Narcissus in the Courtly Lyric* (Ithaca: Cornell University Press, 1967).

[10] ''. . . sì che le bianche e le vermiglie guance, / là do'i' era, de la bella Aurora / per troppa etate divenivan rance'' (*Purgatorio* II, 7–9).

mediately follows this contrived picture of nature, is to shed without compunction all artifices. Filostrato, the narrator, seems to make merry wreckage of artificial morality as he upbraids both the false belief that nuns by taking a vow have renounced their sexual appetites and the pious assumption that to love them is to perpetrate a sin against nature. Filostrato objects that nature is not a fixed moral order; he buoyantly asserts that everyone is free to live as he pleases and justifies the love of nuns on account of their idleness and solitude. Solitude, as the circumstance favorable to love, is one of the many pointed allusions, as we shall see shortly, to the *De arte honeste amandi*. Idleness, a crucial category in Boccaccio's fiction, is not the *otium* which allows the humanists to indulge in scholarly pursuits.[11] It leads, rather—as in the case of Amant—to the garden of sexual delights.[12]

The tale of Masetto begins, cogently enough, as a parody of the allegory of Eden. The monastery where Masetto enters, ostensibly as a gardener but with the secret purpose of seducing the nuns, is conveniently glossed as the *hortus deliciarum* where the mystical marriage of Christ and the Virgins is celebrated.[13] Christ is the "virginum Sponsus" according to the mystical exegeis that Bernard of Clairvaux gives of the *Canticle of Canticles*.[14] The allegory of marriage is obliquely suggested in the text and becomes the object of overt fun. In the closing lines, Masetto's sexual feat is viewed as cuckolding Christ: "così trattava Cristo chi gli poneva le corna sopra 'l

---

[11] The motif is extensively examined by Michael O'Loughlin, *The Garlands of Repose: The Literary Celebration of Civic and Retired Leisure* (Chicago: University of Chicago Press, 1978).

[12] The classical link between idleness and sexuality is to be found in Ovid's *Remedia amoris*, 139: ". . . otia si tollas, periere cupidinis arcus."

[13] The motif of the monastery as Paradise on earth is much too frequent in patristic exegesis. See, among others, Peter Damian, *PL* 144, col. 837; Alphonsus of Salerno, *PL* 147, col. 1238B; Bernard of Clairvaux, *PL* 183, col. 1484. For additional bibliography, see R. E. Kaske, "Langland and the *Paradisus Claustralis*," *Modern Language Notes*, 72 (1957), pp. 481–483; see also Morton W. Bloomfield, "*Piers Plowman* and the Three Grades of Chastity," *Anglia*, 76 (1958), p. 229, n. 1.

[14] *PL* 183, col. 1369.

cappello" (. . . so did Christ treat anybody who placed a pair
of horns on his crown, p. 246). Boccaccio clearly reverses the
conventional exegeses of the *Canticle of Canticles.* While the al-
legorists spiritualize the literal erotics of the biblical garden, he
takes the allegory literally and weaves on it a series of comical
equivocations and double entendres. Thus, the sexual allusion
in Masetto's aside "io vi lavorerò sì l'orto, che mai non vi fu
così lavorato" (I will tend your garden better than it's ever
been tended before, p. 242) exploits the allegorical resonance
from the interpretation of the *Canticle* by St. Bernard who
speaks of "virginitas flos horti."[15] And even Masetto's own
role as a husbandman is the parodic literal inversion of the allegory of Christ as the spiritual husbandsman who redeems
and changes the wilderness into a paradise.[16] In this process of
reducing the allegory to its literal counterpart, Masetto, as he
puts his devilish plan to work, acts as the metaphorical serpent
of Eden corrupting the mystical garden of the *Canticle*—itself
a typological reenactment of prelapsarian innocence—into the
garden of the fall.

The allegory of the fall is in turn questioned by another subtle reference. The sexuality of the monastery, we are told, is
not barren and, actually, Masetto and the nuns are "blessed"
with a large number of children. By the detail, Boccaccio
seems to exploit the potential whimsicality of the casuistic debate in which the Fathers of the Church were long engaged.[17]
Discussing the morality of sexual intercourse, the fathers distinguished between the prelapsarian and postlapsarian sexuality. In the Garden of Eden—they surmised—sexuality must
have been carried out without the lustful shame which accom-
panies the act in the fallen world. Procreation, they concluded,
is the moral end which redeems sexuality as it is practiced since

[15] *PL* 183, col. 1430.

[16] A general treatment of the motif is to be found in G. H. Williams, *Wilderness and Paradise in Christian Thought* (New York: Harper, 1962).

[17] See on this Jerome, *Adversus Iovinianum, PL* 23, cols. 218ff. See also Peter
Riga's comment on Genesis 1:22 in his *Aurora,* ed. Paul E. Beichner, C.S.
Publications in Medieval Studies, 19 (Notre Dame, Ind.: 1965), 1, 32. More
importantly, cf. St. Augustine, *De genesi contra Manicheos, PL* 34, col. 187.

the fall.[18] But Masetto's lovemaking is not directly *causa prolis* and his sexual aim is unencumbered by moral sophistries. Masetto acts as if he were in the Garden of Eden, and as Boccaccio alludes to the fertility of the union, he flagrantly pokes fun at—and dismisses—the pertinence of the patristic distinctions.

The metaphor of the mystical marriage in the garden—though extensively mocked—provides the rationale for the articulation of the tale and binds together its disparate dramatic elements. Boccaccio, in effect, grafts onto it a series of verbal allusions drawn from the *De arte honeste amandi*.[19] Andreas' system of adulterous love, of course, depends on marriage and is unimaginable outside of it. As Boccaccio casts Masetto cuckolding Christ, he signals that this story is to be read within the bounds of the courtly love system. Masetto's feigned muteness, as has been remarked, observes a basic requirement of courtly love.[20] Secrecy, the injunction that love cannot be divulged—as the nuns quickly realize—is seemingly assured by Masetto's muteness: "costui perché egli pur volesse, egli nol potrebbe né saprebbe ridire" (if he wanted to, he wouldn't be able to tell anybody about it, p. 243). At the same time, by highlighting Masetto's trick, Boccaccio parodies still another principle of Andreas' doctrine. For Andreas, a successful way of acquiring love is "copiosa sermonis facundia."[21] He ostensibly dismisses this means of gaining love, yet his own text is, ironically, a repository of speeches which the lover should use to seduce the woman. By Masetto's muteness, Boccaccio implies that sexual seduction needs no language. This ironic twist is effected on another requirement of

[18] St. Augustine, *De civitate dei*, XIV, 22, in *Corpus Christianorum Series Latina* 48 (Turnhout: Brepols, 1955). See also John T. Noonan, Jr., *Contraception: A History of Its Treatment by the Catholic Theologians and Canonists* (Cambridge, Mass.: Harvard University Press, 1965).

[19] Andreas Capellanus, *De amore libri tres*, ed. E. Trojel (Munich: Eidos Verlag, 1964). The Italian translation, to which I refer in this discussion, is in the edition of *De amore libri tres*, ed. Salvatore Battaglia (Rome: Perrella, 1947).

[20] Howard Limoli, "Boccaccio's Masetto (*Decameron*, III, 1) and Andreas Capellanus," *Romanische Forshungen*, 77 (1965), pp. 281–292.

[21] *De amore*, I, 6.

the art of love. Andreas rebukes readiness in granting what the lover seeks. Masetto does precisely the opposite: "senza farsi troppo invitare quel fece che ella volle" (without needing too much coaxing, he did what she wanted him to do, p. 244).

The ironic inversion of Andreas' doctrine is paramount in the tale. In the chapter on the love of nuns, the chaplain suggests that he who indulges in their love "ab omnibus meretur contemni et est tanquam *detestabilis belua fugiendus*"[22] or, as a fourteenth-century Italian adaptation of *De arte* renders it "come *odievole bestia è da fuggire*."[23] In Boccaccio's novella, Masetto sets out deliberately to seek the nuns' love and it is the nuns who approach Masetto in order to "provare che *bestia fosse l'uomo*" (find out what kind of animal man is, p. 244). Under the same rubric "de amore monacharum," Andreas enjoins Walter "unquam poteris opera Veneris evitare nefanda scelera sinistra committens."[24] Boccaccio picks up the precept and turns it against the moralists who object to the love of nuns "come se contra natura un grandissimo e *scelerato male fosse stato commesso*" (as if some enormous and evil crime against nature had been committed, p. 239). Further, under the heading of "de amore rusticorum," Andreas vetoes their love and as the Italian version has it "adunque basti loro la continua fatica di *lavorare i campi* e gli sollazzi della zappa e del marrone."[25] The proposition is given a pointed refutation by the very experience of Masetto and, more precisely, by a phrase that seems to be a calculated polemic against Andreas' veto and those who believe that "*la zappa et la vanga . . . tolgano del tutto a' lavoratori della terra* i concupiscibili appetiti" (digging and hoeing . . . remove from those who work on the land all lustful desires, p. 239).

It would appear from this sustained parody of *De arte honeste amandi* either that Boccaccio writes against the subtle ironies that punctuate Andreas' handbook of love or that, blind to these ironies, he mistakes the chaplain's pornographic text for a moralistic construction which he sets out to dismantle. If this

[22] *De amore*, II, 8.
[24] *De amore*, II, 8.
[23] *De amore*, ed. Battaglia, II, 8, p. 257.
[25] *De amore*, ed. Battaglia, II, 11, p. 273.

were the case, it could be argued that Andreas' system of courtly love, much like the allegory of the mystical marriage in the garden, is decried by an all too urgent sense of the power of sexuality.[26] Within this perspective, it could also be argued that the tale of Masetto serves as a deliberate shattering of the esthetic garden of the Introduction to the third day. But Boccaccio creates a vastly more complex irony through the juxtaposition. As the two gardens stand in sharp contrast to each other, they mirror and parody each other. Masetto's "edenic" delights debunk the artifices of the introductory garden; the tale of Masetto, however, is a *story told* within the bounds of that artifice; it is drawn within an illusory frame. The fictional frame undercuts the substantiality of the literal sense in Masetto's story and it is for Boccaccio a way of bringing into the open the imaginary quality of the sexual experience. Significantly enough, Masetto's tale is told by Filostrato, the emblem of the frustrated lover as he defines himself at the close of the third day.[27] Masetto's successful adventures jar with the narrator's unhappy loves and the ensuing disparity makes the story a pure fantasy, Filostrato's imaginary self-projection. This narcissistic underpinning belies the notion that the tale is simply a mimesis of reality; it emerges, on the contrary, as a reflection on the constitutive properties of pornographic literature, the literature, that is, in which sexuality is suspended as a self-contained vagary of the imagination. But why would Boccaccio indulge in a polemic gesture against *De arte honeste amandi* which is a veritable specimen of pornographic literature? Can it be that he is deliberately misreading this text as an ironic means of hiding a more profound complicity with it?

The explicit burden of *De arte* is to expose the techniques of

---

[26] Aldo S. Scaglione, *Nature and Love in the Late Middle Ages* (Berkeley and Los Angeles: University of California Press, 1963), esp. pp. 73ff.

[27] "Amorose donne, per la mia disaventura, poscia che io ben da mal conobbi, sempre per la bellezza d'alcuna di voi stato sono a Amor subgetto, né l'essere umile né l'essere ubidente né il seguirlo in ciò che per me s'è conosciuto alla seconda in tutti i suoi costumi m'è valuto, che io prima per altro abbandonato e poi non sia sempre di male in peggio andato; e così credo che io andrò di qui alla morte" (*Decameron*, pp. 339–340).

erotic seduction so that Walter may know how to avoid them. The moralistic caveat and the retraction by which Andreas disavows the erotic thrust of his book are too bland to be taken seriously—as some critics have done—or to dispel the lingering suspicion that the very palinode is the target of the chaplain's irony.[28] The critical debate directed to establish whether Andreas' overall "intentions" are moralistic or not is doomed to be fruitless if it must end up by choosing one such reading to the exclusion of the other. In effect, there is no antagonism between the moral and the erotic elements in the treatise. It is actually the moral cover that, by veiling the directly lewd statements, makes Andreas' text pornographic. The moral justification is essential to pornography because it provides a necessary alibi, an obliqueness which is pleasurable in so far as it obscures what it seeks to reveal.

The pornographic quality of *De arte* is sharply suggested by Dante. In the canto of the lecherous sinners in *Inferno*, Francesca's speech is replete with allusions from Andreas Capellanus:[29] for Dante, this text is as much a "galeotto," a dangerous erotic mediator, as is the romance of Lancelot which muddles Francesca's imagination, leads her into narcissistic identification with the love heroine and engenders her fall into sinfulness.[30] Boccaccio, however, does not share Dante's hard indictment of pornographic literature: he even twists Dante's *ethos* as he subtitles the *Decameron*—echoing the same canto v of *Inferno*—"galeotto" and overtly acknowledges it to be a surrogate of love, a book written to be enjoyed.[31]

Like Andreas who obscures the eroticism of his manual with moralizations, Boccaccio shrouds the sexual facts with verbal puns which allude to sexuality and at the same time elude it.

[28] D. W. Robertson, *Preface to Chaucer* (Princeton: Princeton University Press, 1963), pp. 393–448.

[29] Gianfranco Contini, "Dante come personaggio-poeta della *Commedia*," in *Varianti e altra linguistica* (Turin: Einaudi, 1970), pp. 346–347 particularly.

[30] For a discussion of this issue see my *Dante, Poet of the Desert: History and Allegory in the Divine Comedy* (Princeton: Princeton University Press, 1979), pp. 165–170.

[31] See on this chapter 2, nn. 16 and 17.

Thus, Masetto is said to plan cultivating the nuns' "orto;" Filippo Balducci's son is strongly attracted by "papere."[32] Dioneo's novella at the close of the third day, more poignantly, exploits the ambiguities which inhere in the language of sexuality and that of the practice of spiritual askesis. The story, as every reader of the *Decameron* remembers, takes place in the desolation of the "diserto di Tebaida" (the desert of Thebaid, p. 333) and it involves Alibech, a very young woman who wants to learn how God can best be served, and Rustico who lives as a hermit in the desert. Alibech's youth and beauty act on Rustico as the hermit's steady obsession and thereby defeat his monastic discipline.

There is a subtle irony in Boccaccio's use of the word "discipline." Etymologically the word suggests the monk's ascetic exercise, the stiff spiritual training he daily subjects himself to in order to repel the temptations in what is a fierce *psychomachia*.[33] By an ironic reversal, Rustico (one wonders if this is not a faint echo of Andreas' *de amore rusticorum*) takes on the role of a "migliore maestro" (a more capable teacher, p. 333), one who is thought of as fit to guide Alibech in her apprenticeship. The reversal is not an isolated occurrence. Even the detail, for instance, that the makeshift bed, on which Alibech will spend her first night in Rustico's cell, is made of "frondi di palma" (palm leaves, p. 333) belongs to the same rhetorical scheme. The seemingly offhand specification of the foliage is primarily, no doubt, an element of local color, a reference to the vegetation in the quasi-tropical region where the action develops. But the palm leaf is also a symbol of triumph: in a context in which Rustico first surrenders to the urgings of the flesh and

---

[32] It is of interest to point out that the discussion of Filippo Balducci's geese takes place in the context of Boccaccio's own reflection on what constitutes stylistic decorousness in the stories of the third day. More importantly, since the question at stake is how to name reality "properly," one should recollect the section of the *Roman de la Rose*, ll. 7080 ff., devoted to this issue. See the discussion of the question in chapter 5 below.

[33] For a general bibliography on the tradition of temptation, see D. R. Howard, *The Three Temptations: Medieval Man in Search of the World* (Princeton: Princeton University Press, 1966).

later gives up when he cannot satisfy Alibech's abundant sexual appetite, the irony of the emblem is transparent. The irony is heightened, one might add, by another symbolic value with which the palm tree is invested. In patristic exegesis, the process by which the Christian *viator* moves from the realm of fleshly delights to the pleasures of the Heavenly Jerusalem is figured through the palm tree.[34] In the novella, by a pointed reversal, the palm leaves are the bed on which Rustico moves from prayer to carnal pleasures. To complicate the pattern further, by the end what seemed for the monk to be carnal delights become for him a veritable hellish punishment.

These reversals turn out to be the playful center of the narrative and are even part of the special structural role the novella occupies in the economy of the day. It is quite clear, to begin with, that Dioneo, by telling at the end of the day the story of an anchorite in the desert who is unable to satisfy the sexual advance of a novice, pokes fun at Filostrato's first story of one man, Masetto, who in the garden manages to look after the needs of nine nuns. More specifically, key phrases in Dioneo's tale such as "la resurrezion della carne" (the resurrection of the flesh, p. 334), "la superbia del capo" (the pride of the head, p. 335), and "rimettere il diavolo in inferno" (put the devil back into Hell, p. 336) rhetorically organize the text by their overt movement from their original spiritual sense to a physical context, as well as by their concealing the sexual act in the guise of moral allegory. The humor of the story issues from the strident and close union of the spiritual and physical activities, from the ease with which the two registers are "exchanged." The humor, which is a cardinal ingredient of the narrative, stems from the confusion of the two semantic fields, a confusion which humor, paradoxically, also sanctions.

[34] Gregory the Great writes: "But on the other hand by the character of palm trees the progressive life of the righteous is represented, who are never strong in earthly pursuits, and weak in heavenly ones, but exhibit themselves devoted to God with a farther and wider extension than that they remember to have been to the world" (*Morals on the Book of Job*, Library of Fathers of the Holy Catholic Church [Oxford, 1844–50], II, 437–438).

The technique of indirection—the strategy of *not* naming sexuality directly—is deployed systematically in the *Decameron* and not just to observe a principle of esthetic decorum. In the *Conclusione dell'autore*, Boccaccio attempts to rescue his novelle from the charges of immorality by claiming that the objectionable words he uses such as " 'foro' e 'caviglia' e 'mortaio' e 'pestello' e 'salsiccia' . . ." ('hole' and 'rat' and 'mortar' and 'pestle' and 'crumpet' . . .) p. 960 are not obscene in themselves and that his tales are no more harmful than the Scriptures have been to some readers.[35]

The apology implies that all writings, sacred and profane alike, are morally neutral allegories and openly claims that the responsibility for interpreting the stories lies with the reader. The notion that Scripture and the *Decameron* have in common a dangerous ambiguity—they can edify or corrupt the reader—retrospectively illuminates the perverse poetics at work in the tale of Masetto. Pornography in the story parodies the allegory. But the allegorization of the *Canticle of Canticles* or Andreas' allegory of education, far from being simply dismissed as abstract moralizations, are implicitly unveiled as pornography because the erotic story they tell is contrabanded as a moral myth. By the same token, the opposite is also true: pornography is an allegory for like allegory it needs a cover. In allegory, the ambiguities are provided by the husk that envelopes the moral kernel; in the present figuration of pornography, morality is the chaff hiding the erotic fruit. This bold view is the precise reversal of the theory of allegory Boccaccio elaborates and underwrites in his *Genealogy of the Gentile Gods*.[36] In this mythographic encyclopedia the allegorical veil

---

[35] An analogue to this issue is to be found in the *Roman de la Rose*, ll. 7137ff.: "Custom is very powerful, and, if I know it well, many a thing is displeasing when new that it becomes beautiful by custom. Every woman who goes around naming them calls them I don't know what: purses, harness, things, or prickles, as if they were thorns. But when they are well joined to them and feel them, they do not consider them piercing; then they name them as they are accustomed to do" (*The Romance of the Rose*, trans. Dahlberg, p. 136).

[36] Under the heading, "It is rather useful than damnable to compose sto-

which clothes the naked truth is said to challenge the subtle reader to exercise his understanding, whereas the unskilled one is captivated by the pleasures of the surface. Pornography, instead, makes the pleasure of the surface the narrative's own aim, while the naked truth is always bypassed.

By this unusual complicity between allegory and pornography, Boccaccio lays open the esthetic basis of pornography. Like the garden to which the storytellers retreat, pornography is a locus where the distinction between reality and imagination is blurred, the metaphor whereby literature is in the process of becoming sexuality and sexuality becomes a book. In this steady movement of dislocation pornography is always irreducibly "other," a version of formal allegory, one which in effect is devoid of any substantial, intrinsic moral content and by which sexuality is dodged even as it is at the same time kept as an alluring mirage. This constant oscillation suggests, further, that the imaginary pleasures engendered by the reading of the "galeotto" are essentially hollow: there is always a split at the heart of the pornographic text, for desires are aroused and are simultaneously frustrated. Filostrato, in a real sense, is the true pornographer.

But does Boccaccio ever break out of this bind? Does he ever gain an undistorted perspective of moral order in the *Decameron*? To answer these questions we must turn to the novella of Griselda which ostensibly presents itself as an allegory of order. In the tales of the tenth day, actually, there seems to be a radical shift away from the dramatic substance of the previous days. The jests and bawdiness commonly associated with the *Decameron* give way now to exemplary moral tales. It is as if Boccaccio were intent on sealing his narrative with the reassuring intimation that all contrasts are resolved and a desirable moral order is finally established. In this sense, the *Decameron* mimes, at least on the surface, the trajectory of the comical plot as it moves from its bleak beginnings (the plague) to its climax with the cathartic vision of a happy ending.

---

ries," Boccaccio vindicates the moral sense, which ". . . is revealed from under the veil of fiction" (*Boccaccio on Poetry*, trans. Osgood, pp. 47ff.).

The specific moral substance of the last tales, however, is somewhat ambiguous. The sixth story, for instance, dramatizes a process of moral conversion. Within the framework of the chivalric tradition, it features the *fol amor* of the old King Charles of Anjou for the young Guinivere and for her twin sister Iseult. The king ultimately acknowledges the madness of his desire and turns into the girls' benefactor. But the bulk of the story lies in the account of how the king, who has just experienced a victory on the battlefield, is in turn defeated by love. The time is one of leisure in Neri's delightful garden, where food and delicate wines are served according to a model of "ordine"—which is to be understood here as Boccaccio's own ideal of elegant ritual and gracious living.[37] The pleasant conviviality is interrupted by the arrival of two young girls, the sight of whom causes astonishment in the king. The girls enter a pond to catch fish, some of which they throw on the table where the king is seated.

For all its playfulness, the fishing scene is a metaphoric displacement of the king's erotic fascination with the two young women, whom he cannot distinguish from each other. As the text moves to recount the king's passion, Boccaccio gives an arresting dramatization of Andreas' etymological definition of love. "Love," Andreas writes, "gets its name (*amor*) from the word for hook (*amus*), which means 'to capture' or 'to be captured,' for he who is in love is captured in the chains of desire and wishes to capture someone else with his hook. Just as a skillful fisherman tries to attract fishes by his bait and to capture them on his crooked hook, so the man who is a captive of love tries to attract another person by his allurements and exerts all his efforts to unite two different hearts with an intangible bond, or if they are already united he tries to keep them so forever."[38]

[37] ". . . comandò che servissero secondo l'ordine posto da messer Neri. Le vivande vi vennero dilicate, e i vini vi furono ottimi e preziosi, e l'ordine bello e laudevole molto senza alcun sentore e senza noia: il che il re commendò molto" (*Decameron*, pp. 884–885). One could point out Boccaccio's use of alliteration and the assonant "comandò-commendò" as a way of conveying the sense of harmony of the scene.

[38] *De amore*, I, 3 (*The Art of Courtly Love*, trans. Parry, p. 31).

Captive of this passion, the king is tempted to take the two girls away from their father, but is persuaded not to do so by Count Guido. His arguments span the morality of courtly love (it does not become an old man to fall in love with young women); the questions of political self-interest (Manfredi's defeat was a consequence of the violence his soldiers perpetrated on women); and finally, what could be called the king's own narcissism: the reasoning is that it is a great glory to defeat Manfredi, it is a greater one to triumph over one's own baser appetites.

The count's words effect the king's moral conversion, and his generosity in supplying the girls with splendid dowries is unequivocal. The reference to Guinivere's and Iseult's marriages supplants the picture of sexual temptation; it further suggests that marriage, by which most of the last novelle are brought to a close, is the exemplary metaphor of order and reconciliation in the *Decameron*. In this view of marriage Boccaccio is of course exploiting a standard Christian motif. If the fall is the sin by which man has lost the order of Eden (and the delightful garden here is its faint echo), marriage is the sacrament that reflects and reenacts the plenitude of the prelapsarian condition. The final tale of Griselda, which we shall examine in some detail, tests directly the allegory of order and plots the incongruities within it.

Readers of the story have traditionally been baffled and frankly disappointed by what they have taken to be its exaggerated moralism and lack of verisimilitude. Luigi Russo is an exception, however, to this general view.[39] He interprets the novella as a case of "oratorical" literature in the sense that in it Boccaccio willfully contemplates an ideal world which he superimposes on his genuinely comical vein. Instead of pursuing further this central intuition, Russo ultimately shares the general opinion that the narrative is uninspired and impaired by the abstract idealizations. By and large, the critical reaction has been such that one is led to infer that modern critics have

[39] Luigi Russo, *Letture critiche del Decameron* (Bari: Laterza, 1967), pp. 315–328.

hardly departed from Petrarch's reading of the story. In his celebrated translation, it will be remembered, Petrarch makes of the ordeals of Griselda and the cruel arbitrariness of Gualtieri the allegory of the soul tested by God. Petrarch recounts it, as he says, not to arouse the ladies to imitate Griselda but to urge all men to be steadfast to God when he tries us just as this poor woman was steadfast to her temporal lord.[40] Petrarch's allegory is a veritable "translation" because it deliberately transforms into a pietistic tract and considerably simplifies the ironic complexities of Boccaccio's story. The allegory which Petrarch explicitly brings out has as its paradigm the biblical account of God testing the patience of Job. This paradigm, in fact, is already present in Boccaccio's version.

The ordeals of Griselda, to begin with, are symmetrically encompassed between two correlated actions. As she emerges from her father's hut to be introduced to Gualtieri's retainers, she is stripped of her clothes: "(Gualtieri) la fece spogliare ignuda; e fattisi quegli vestimenti che fatti aveva fare, prestamente la fece vestire e calzare e sopra i suoi capelli . . . le fece mettere una corona" (Gualtieri caused her to be stripped naked: and calling for those clothes which he had had specially made, and quickly got her to put them on and made her put a crown . . . on her hair, p. 945). Toward the end of the novella, Gualtieri humiliates Griselda by sending her back to her father stripped of all ornaments: "scalza e senza alcuna cosa in capo" (barefoot and without anything on her head, p. 950). We might point out that in formal terms the language of clothing and nakedness, traditionally charged with allegorical resonances, heightens the allegorical thrust of the events narrated.[41] More to the point, the two actions broadly hint at

[40] The texts are available in D. D. Griffith, *The Origin of the Griselda Story* (Seattle: University of Washington Publications in Language and Literature, 1931). Cf. also the remarks by A. L. Kellogg, "The Evolution of the Clerk's Tale," *Chaucer, Langland, Arthur* (New Brunswick, N.J.: Rutgers University Press, 1972), pp. 276–329.

[41] The *locus classicus* for this formulation is St. Paul, *First Letter to the Corinthians* 15:53. Another instance is Macrobius, *Commentarium in Somnium Scipionis*, ed. J. H. Willis (Leipzig, 1970), I, 2, 11, p. 6.

Job's own suffering, his patient acceptance that he has come naked from his mother's womb and naked returns to it. What is even more important is the fact that the description of the two moments echoes Job's lament "spoliavit me gloria mea, et abstulit coronam de capite meo."[42] Griselda's response as she endures her grief at losing her children: "*signor mio*, pensa di *contentar te* e di sodisfare *al piacer* tuo" (My lord look to your own comfort, see that you fulfill your wishes, p. 948), recalls Job's own grief and prayer at the loss of his children: "Dominus dedit, Dominus abstulit; *sicut Domino placuit*, ita factum est."[43] Even Job's humility at the tragic horrors that fall on him, "in omnibus his non peccavit Job labiies suis, neque stultum quid contra Deum locutus est,"[44] finds a thematic counterpart in Griselda's conduct as she bears her burden without cursing: "I subditi . . . alla donna avevan grandissima compassione. La quale . . . mai altro non disse se non che quello ne piaceva a lei che a colui che generati gli avea . . ." (His subjects . . . felt great compassion for the woman. She never said anything else but that their father's pleasure was good enough for her, pp. 948–949).

These biblical echoes comprise the allegory of the novella which is overtly suggested by another dramatic element. As Gualtieri, at the end of the story, restores Griselda to her proper place in the household, he concedes that his wife's ordeals were part of a plan and purpose which he knew from the beginning: "Griselda, tempo è omai che tu senta frutto della tua lunga pazienza, e che coloro li quali me hanno reputato crudele e iniquo e bestiale conoscano che ciò che io faceva a antiveduto fine operava . . ." (Griselda, the time has come for you to reap the reward of your long patience, and for those who considered me a cruel and bestial tyrant to know that whatever I had done was done of set purpose . . . , p. 953). Gualtieri, in reality, casts himself as God. Like God, who in his omniscience governs the design of history, Gualtieri claims that he has manipulated the plot of the story. This claim ac-

---

[42] *Job* 19:9   [43] *Job* 1:21   [44] *Job* 1:22

counts for a series of ambiguities which disrupt the allegorical pattern of the story.

Precisely to the extent that Gualtieri arrogates to himself literally what is God's unique lordship over human events, he ends by playing the role that in Job's tragedy is that of the tempter. Ironically, he wishes to test Griselda's pride, but is blind to his own pride in his playing to be God. In effect, the "matta bestialità" (mad bestiality, p. 942), as Dioneo defines Gualtieri's conduct, casts him as God's inverted image. The phrase, to be sure, is a direct recall of Dante's description of the moral structure of Hell where it defines one of the three dispositions to sin.[45] Boccaccio's gloss on canto XI of *Inferno* sheds light on Gualtieri's self-contradictory roles in the tale: "E adunque questa bestialità similmente vizio dell'anima opposto, secondo che piace ad Aristotile nel VII dell'Etica, alla divina sapienza."[46]

Gualtieri's double role does not result simply in an ironic shattering of his illusion that he is God to all his subjects and his wife; the contradiction, rather, is crucial to the whole tale and, in a real sense, is its very substance. Gualtieri's own madness, for instance, thwarts the typology of Eden which is suggested by the marriage metaphor. Man's fall from Eden, as we have previously said, has abrogated rationality by subjecting it to the disorder of the appetites. The sacrament of marriage, on the contrary, aims at correcting the perversion produced by the fall; it is a redemptive experience because it unifies and reorders the twin faculties of the soul (intellect and will) and reestablishes the edenic condition whereby reason holds sway over the lower appetites,[47] just as in marriage, according to St.

---

[45] "Non ti rimembra di quelle parole / con le quai la tua Etica pertratta / le tre disposizion che 'l ciel non vole, / incontenenza, malizia e la matta / bestialitade? . . ." (*Inferno* XI, 79–83).

[46] *Esposizioni sopra la Comedia*, p. 551.

[47] The formulation for this spiritual hierarchy was best put forth by St. Augustine, *De Trinitate*, XII, xiii, p. 551 (in *Corpus Christianorum Series Latina* 50 [Turnhout: Brepols, 1968]).

Paul, man holds sway over the woman.[48] Gualtieri's madness, however, forfeits the Pauline notion of the hierarchy to be enacted by marriage and from the point of view of Griselda this sacramental Eden is literally a hell.

Unlike Petrarch, who exploits the story for a univocal fable of moral edification, Boccaccio delineates the allegory and at the same time undercuts it. He does not aim, by so doing, at a simple mockery of allegorical abstractions in order to vindicate the value of the reality of experience. By the strategy of contradictions and inversions, Boccaccio actually represents the radical rupture between the allegory of order and its human, literal counterpart. By showing the contradiction within the metaphor of marriage, he splits open the very rock upon which the possibilities of order are founded and recognizes that human existence and its allegorical formulations collide with and contradict each other; what may be fully significanat in God's plan appears as a mass of unaccountable and senseless quirks in the world of man. In this rupture, the allegory and the letter function each as a critical perspective on the other and both together map out the rift at the core of the myth of order.

The doubleness in the midst of the sacrament of unity is consciously deployed in the novella. From one point of view, the novella is structured as a veritable *psychomachia*, a moral battle of vice and virtue. Boccaccio's gloss on "bestialità" as "vizio dell'anima," on the one hand, and Griselda's continuously acknowledged virtue, on the other, strongly hint that the spiritual battle is a real, though somewhat submerged, motif. The conflict is introduced in Dioneo's opening remark as he addresses the "mansuete mie donne" (my gentle women, p. 942), an epithet which obliquely alludes to Griselda's *mansuetudo*, and announces that he is about to recount a story of "matta bestialità." The primary battle is between *mansuetudo* and *bestialitas* and the moral link between them was formulated by Thomas Aquinas.

In the seventh book of the *Nichomachean Ethics*, Aristotle

---

[48] *Ephesians* 5:21ff.

identifies *bestialitas* as a kind of madness, the occurrence of cruelty, folly, and tyranny in exaggerated forms.[49] In his commentary on the *Ethics*, Thomas Aquinas links bestiality to intemperance ("Et inde est quod vitia intemperantiae maximam turpitudinem habent, quia per ea homo bestiis assimilatur").[50] But it is in the *Summa theologiae* that he explicitly classifies *bestialitas* as a sin against the virtue of temperance. In answer to the question whether or not temperance is a virtue, St. Thomas writes that man naturally seeks a delight which is appropriate to him and that ". . . temperantia non contrariatur inclinationi naturae humanae, sed convenit cum ea. Contrariatur tamen inclinationi naturae bestialis non subiectae rationi."[51] And in the definition of the virtues in the *secunda secundae* of his *Summa*, more cogently, Aquinas proposes a scheme by which *mansuetudo* is a part of temperance, the quality of bridling one's own excesses ("clementia autem et mansuetudo similiter in quadem refrenatione consistunt . . . et secundum hoc ponuntur partes temperantiae").[52]

Even Griselda's endurance of her misfortunes is explainable within the framework of the *psychomachia*: as she bears her afflictions "con fermo viso" and "con forte animo" (with a show of bravery and strength of mind, pp. 949, 951), she displays a spiritual fortitude which consists, as Aquinas says, in the possession of firmness, ". . . secundum quod important

[49] Aristotle, *The Nichomachean Ethics*, trans. Martin Ostwald (Indianapolis-New York: The Library of Liberal Arts, 1962), VII, 5, pp. 189–191.

[50] "This is why the vices of intemperance have the greatest baseness, because by them man is like the animals" (*Commentary on the Nichomachean Ethics*, trans. C. I. Litizinger [Chicago, 1966]).

[51] The passage reads: "Clearly this is to agree and not to clash with the burden of human nature. Which is not to deny that temperance is against the grain for merely animal nature uncomplying with reason" (*Summa theologiae*, IIa IIae, 141, art. 1. The quote and translation are taken from the Blackfriars edition, 1968).

[52] The passage reads: "Clemency and gentleness likewise imply a certain restraint: as we have seen the one reduces punishment, the other softens anger. For this reason they are classified with the principal or cardinal virtue of temperance, and in this respect are treated as parts of temperance" (*Summa theologiae*, IIa IIae, 157, art. 3, r. Blackfriars trans.).

firmitatem animi in sustinendis . . . his in quibus maxime diffi-
cile est firmitatem habere."⁵³ As a virtue of the irascible appetite, fortitude is opposed to fear (*timor*): unsurprisingly, as
Gualtieri takes Griselda back, he confesses that he tested her
because he felt "gran paura" (p. 953) that she might fail him.

The *psychomachia* ends with Griselda's victory. In the moral
that Dioneo draws from the narrative, Griselda's patience is
praised and Gualtieri's fitness to rule over other men is
doubted: "che si potrà dir qui? se non che anche nelle povere
case piovono dal cielo de' divini spiriti, come nelle reali di
quegli che sarien più degni di guardar porci che d'avere sopra
uomini signoria" (What more needs to be said here, except
that celestial spirits come from Heaven even in the houses of
the poor, just as there are those in royal places who would be
better employed as swineherds than as rulers of men?, p. 954).
The rhetorical question suggests Dioneo's uneasiness over his
conclusion. In the final paragraph the uneasiness becomes outright disruption of the moral lesson he has so tentatively
voiced: "[Gualtieri] non sarebbe forse stato male investito
d'essersi abbattuto a una che quando, fuor di casa, l'avesse
fuori in camiscia cacciata, s'avesse sì a un altro fatto scuotere il
pilliccione che riuscito ne fosse una bella roba" (For perhaps it
would have served Gualtieri right if he had chanced upon a
wife, who, being driven from her house in her shirt, had found
some other man to shake her skin-coat for her, earning herself
a new dress in the process, p. 954). By the comment, which is
marked by a stylistic shift to a coarse *aequivocatio*, Dioneo
opens a breach in the moral statement of the story and, as he
alludes to a different turn that the story might have taken, he
unmakes the story he has just told. The experience of obstinate
domestic violence we have witnessed could have been replaced
by Griselda's sweet revenge had she sought, to counter her ordeal, sexual pleasures. Understood in this sense, Dioneo's last

---

⁵³ *Summa theologiae*, IIa IIae, 123, art. 2. The passage reads in its entirety:
"Secondly, courage can be taken as meaning firmness of mind in enduring or
repulsing whatever makes steadfastness outstandingly difficult; . . ." (Blackfriars trans.).

comment points to the proximity between violence and libertine pleasures, an issue fully dramatized in the seventh day of the *Decameron*, the day which is under Dioneo's rule.

But the phrase "scuotere il pilliccione" echoes "il pilliccion ti scotesse" (p. 431), which appears in another tale (IV, 10) told by Dioneo. This is the account of a surgeon from Salerno, Mazzeo della Montagna, whose marital inadequacies parallel those of Riccardo di Chinzica (II, 10). The wife's unhappiness, which is cast in unmistakable Dantesque language of the *tenzone* with Forese,[54] prompts her to choose as a lover a young libertine. One night, while the doctor is off to Amalfi, the woman arranges a rendezvous with Ruggiero, who, feeling thirsty, drinks a potion the surgeon had prepared for an operation he had to perform the next day. In a way the novella is a parody of the magic philter of romances, for the potion simply deadens Ruggiero's body. From this point the plot takes many complicated twists till the maid, to save her lady's reputation, pretends, first to the doctor and later to the judge in the courtroom, that Ruggiero was her lover and had entered her room by stealth to sleep with her. Her lie brings to a happy resolution Ruggiero's ordeal, who, finally freed, gives himself to even greater pleasure with his mistress. Their pleasures are probably intensified by the awareness of the body's fragility (the patient's leg has a gangrenous bone; Ruggiero's drowsiness is provisionally mistaken for death) or, more generally, by the relief at the dangers the two lovers avoided. More to our concern, Dioneo's phrase plunges us back to the heart of the *Decameron*'s comedy, to a story which evokes the confusion of social estates (the libertine patrician, the surgeon, the magistrate, moneylenders, maid and lady).

In a way, Dioneo's comment at the end of the last tale of the *Decameron* suggests that nothing is definitive and final in this narrative universe: the very end, conventionally seen as the

---

[54] The sentence, ". . . vero è che ella il più del tempo stava infreddata, sì come colei che nel letto era male dal maestro tenuta coperta" echoes "Di mezzo agosto la truovi infreddata:" etc. See Branca's notes, *Decameron*, p. 1255.

privileged perspective from which the moral coherence and order of the text are constituted, is disclosed as a contingent and purely formal closure. By this expedient Dioneo implies that storytelling is an endless activity and that the "right" finale lies elsewhere. When the novella of Torello is over and his turn to speak comes, Dioneo dismisses the praises showered on Messer Torello as worthless from the point of view of the "buon uomo, che aspettava la seguente notte di fare abbassare la coda ritta della fantasima" (the good man, who was looking forward to lowering the erect tail of the werewolf, p. 942). Much as he has done at the exordium of Griselda's story, he hints, as a way of closing, at a frankly erotic tale which would displace the moral sententiousness which could be extrapolated from the tale.

There is no doubt that Dioneo's comment is an ironic perversion of the traditional technique of appending a palinode to a morally ambiguous account:[55] his comment, actually, lets the pornographic dimension of the *Decameron* resurface at the point where its morality is bland and the literal and the allegorical are cut off from each other. But the erotic allusion is not simply the residue, the pleasurable alternative to the breakdown of the allegory of order. We must stress that we catch only a glimpse of the pornographic alternative, just as in the story of King Charles, when the two sisters emerge from the pool, we are allowed to see their thin white dresses clinging to their bodies as to conceal "quasi"-almost-nothing. Pornography, as has been argued, is the convergence of imagination and desire, an ever elusive mirage whose pleasures are displaced, always somewhere else. The alibi is the constitutive property of pornographic literature: its "otherness" suspends the very notion of its becoming a literal, real experience; it subverts the possibility of coercing the literal within an allegorical structure; and, more importantly, it lays open the radical instability of figurative language in the *Decameron*.

[55] The most explicit occurrence of this convention is the song to the Virgin in Petrarch's *Rime*. A more ambiguous use of the technique appears in the last stanzas of Chaucer's *Troilus and Criseyde*.

THE HEART OF LOVE

Fiammetta's tale of Tancredi and Ghismunda (IV, I) keeps exerting a powerful hold on readers of the *Decameron*, to judge from the frequency with which it is subjected to critical readings.[1] Scholarly interest in the story possibly depends on its strategic position in the text, immediately following the lengthy Introduction to the fourth day. Boccaccio, we remember, breaks the narrative sequence and launches a polemical counterattack against the censors who had objected to the "disreputable" stories of the third day. It is reasonable to infer, then, that the critics have believed that this, if any, is the moment when Boccaccio is least guarded and when, therefore, since he is ostensibly disclosing the assumptions and aims of his art, they could most easily get a grip on his moral and esthetic concerns. Yet it is not unreasonable to suspect that their fascination with this whole stretch of the text betrays a certain interpretive anxiety: because in the Introduction to the fourth day Boccaccio presents the censors, busy in prescribing norms of esthetic decorum, as figures caught in a radical misunderstanding of the purposes of his novelle, contemporary critics seem to be strangely defensive, almost sensing that in some oblique way they are implicated in the narrative.

[1] Giovanni Getto, *Vita di forme e forme di vita nel Decameron* (Turin: Petrini, 1958), pp. 95–138; Mario Baratto, *Realtà e stile nel "Decameron"* (Vicenza: Pozza, 1970), pp. 180–195; Carlo Muscetta, *Giovanni Bocaccio* (Bari: Laterza, 1972), pp. 221–225; Guido Almansi, *The Writer as Liar: Narrative Technique in the 'Decameron'* (London and Boston: Routledge and Kegan Paul, 1975), pp. 133ff.; a more recent reading is by Millicent Joy Marcus, *An Allegory of Form. Literary Self-Consciousness in the Decameron* (Saratoga, Calif.: Anma Libri, 1979), pp. 44–63.

It is perhaps because of this anxiety that, quite predictably, recent commentators have taken sides with the apparent position of the author against the censors and have underwritten the naturalistic perspective which they think sustains the *Decameron*.[2] As is known, the notion of naturalism is articulated in the Introduction through Boccaccio's own account of one Filippo Balducci, who, at the death of his wife, abandons, in the company of his only child, the "world" and its ephemeral pleasures. If at the outset the parable comes forth as another version of the *contemptus mundi* motif, with these two latter-day anchorites dwelling in a secluded mountain cave fasting and praying, it quickly shifts into an explicitlty ironic *exemplum* of the collapse of the father's ascetic ideal of continence. Many years after retreating from the world, when chastity, which for the father is a state of moral perfection, should have become the son's natural way of being, the two return to the city for some errands. Along the way the son sees what he had never seen before, some young women coming back from a wedding.[3] Caring no more for the monuments, palaces and paintings of angels the father had eagerly shown him, the son asks what those adorned "things" are called. Filippo Balducci, not wishing to arouse the young man's desires, "non le volle nominare per lo proprio nome, cioè femine, ma disse: 'Elle si chiamano papere' " (did not want to name them by their proper names, that is, women, but said: "They are called gos-

[2] The view is represented by Aldo Scaglione, *Nature and Love in the Late Middle Ages* (Berkeley and Los Angeles: University of California Press, 1963); also see the more recent R. Hastings, *Nature and Reason in the Decameron* (Manchester: University Press, 1975).

[3] ". . . per avventura si scontrarono in una brigata di belle giovani donne e ornate, che da un paio di nozze venieno: le quali come il giovane vide, così domandò il padre che cosa quelle fossero" (*Decameron*, p. 348). Branca gives numerous analogues in his notes (p. 1199). Janet Smarr, "Symmetry and Balance in the *Decameron*," *Mediaevalia*, 2 (1976), pp. 159–187, examines the links between this scene and the novella of Tancredi and Ghismunda. I would like to point out the import of the metaphor of the wedding from which the young women were seen coming. In a context of widows, widowers and forbidden remarriages, the "nozze" hint at a festivity which makes the events in the novella and the *exemplum* of Filippo Balducci even more sinister.

ling," p. 348). The son begs his father to get him one of those "goslings" to take back to their mountain retreat where he will "pop things into its bill."

The contrast between the marvels of art ("gli agnoli dipinti") and the instinctive attractiveness of real women alludes to the principle overtly proclaimed in the passage: the failure of the artifice to contain within its bounds Nature's wondrous powers, as well as the failure of that education, imparted by the father, which attempts to repress the natural compulsions of sexuality. From this point of view, the story seems to provide a gloss on the speech on nature that *La Vieille* makes to Fair Welcoming in the *Roman de la Rose*: "Nature is a very strong thing; she surpasses even training. . . . If anyone could raise a colt that had never seen a mare right to the time that it was a great charger bearing saddles and stirrups, and then afterward a mare came, you would hear him neigh immediately, and he would want to run against her if there were no one to rescue her. . . . And what I say about the black mare, . . . I say about the cow and the bull and the ewe and the ram. . . . By my soul, fair son, it is thus with every man and every woman as far as natural appetite goes."[4]

This doctrine of man's natural inclination to be free, while irrational laws restrain him from gratifying the appetites, is extended by scholars to include and explain the dramatic substance of the first story of the fourth day. Tancredi, another old father and widower, like Filippo Balducci, is confronted not by an "idiotic" son, as Balducci is, but by the keen intelligence of Ghismunda, who rebukes him for not giving her away in a second marriage and for forgetting, now that he is old, "chenti e quali e con che forza vengano le leggi della giovanezza: . . ." (the nature and power the laws of youth have, p. 360). She admits that, full of amorous longing, she is incapable of resisting the forces of nature and youth and that she has chosen a lover to satisfy her desires. If the story of Balducci remains suspended in the acknowledgment of nature's power

---

[4] *The Romance of the Rose*, trans. Dahlberg, pp. 240–241.

(we are not told whether or not the young man gets his "gosling"), the novella of Tancredi and Ghismunda gives a tragic turn to the essentially comic recognition of lusty animality which the father's law in vain attempts to restrain. This, in short, is the "naturalism" which supposedly lies at the center of Boccaccio's vision and which organizes the dramatic unfolding of both the Introduction and the first novella of the fourth day.

But the sense of the novella is not really so clear, and recently Alberto Moravia has opened our eyes, as it were, to its shadowy core by drawing attention to the incestuous desire Tancredi feels for his daughter. Starting from this insight, Guido Almansi has read the tale as an elaborate allegory of incest, making, in effect, of the father's violence a jealous lover's revenge against the rival Guiscardo.[5] In this reading, the tearing of the heart is explained as the symbolic equivalent of castration; the cavern with its aperture covered with weeds and brambles, through which Guiscardo secretly reaches Ghismunda's bedchamber, becomes the metaphoric setting by which Boccaccio figures the sexual act. All together these are viewed as elements of an allegorical pattern intimating the prince's unconfessed unnatural desire for his daughter.

At first glance, the two readings in terms of naturalism and incest are contradictory, for if one upholds the rights of nature, the other is a sharp refutation of the very assumptions of a naturalist ideology. Incest is unavoidably the stumbling block of naturalism in that, as an irresistible or unconscious passion, it announces as illusory the belief in the rationality of desire; more than that, as a metaphor of transgression, it makes nature not the symbol of order, but the locus where, once interdictions are abolished and instinctive desire ("concupiscibile desiderio") is the law, undifferentiated chaos holds sway. In such a context, fathers can lie with their daughters, or

---

[5] Alberto Moravia's suggestion was presented in his essay, "Boccaccio," included in his *L'uomo come fine e altri saggi* (Milan: Bompiani, 1964), pp. 135–158. See also Guido Almansi, *The Writer as Liar: Narrative Technique in the Decameron* (London and Boston: Routledge and Kegan Paul, 1975), pp. 133–157.

mothers with their sons, as Troilo's hymn to love's power in the *Filostrato* or Tito's lament in the eighth story of the tenth day overtly acknowledge.[6] Since incest entails a questioning of the boundaries of what is "proper," of what belongs or does not belong to oneself, it is an act that allows all metaphoric displacements and threatens with collapse the symbolic order structuring the fabric of social reality. Ironically, then, from this perspective, to consider incest as the unspoken dimension of the novella would logically lead to construing it as a plea for laws which might bridle the free movement of desire.

All of these, however, are minor quibbles. Though these two readings seem to be mutually exclusive, neither can in fact be dismissed as entirely wrong. If they were taken together, they would even appear as a version of the classical conflict between law and desire. In *Inferno* v, for instance, Dante represents through Semiramis' incest—she is the queen, "che libito fe licito in sua legge" (a line that calls attention to the sinister convergence of law and desire)—the breakdown of rational order.[7] Boccaccio, one could conceivably argue, uses the opposition between the father's law and the daughter's desire as the metaphor for the tragic impasse the novella figures. Nonetheless, what remains questionable in the two critical views is the literalism they share. In one case, in spite of Boccaccio's own *reticentia* and in a context in which the very possibility of *naming*, as we shall see, is Boccaccio's concern, the critics are all too willing to name what is the persistent darkness at the

---

[6] Tito's lament goes as follows: "Le leggi d'amore sono di maggior potenzia che alcune altre: elle rompono non che quelle della amistà ma le divine. Quante volte ha già il padre la figliuola amata, il fratello la sorella, la matrigna il figliastro? Cose più monstruose che l'uno amico amar la moglie dell'altro, già fattosi mille volte" (*Decameron*, p. 903). See also Troilo's lament, with the line, "altri, come sai, aman le suore" (*Filostrato*, ed. V. Branca in *Tutte le opere di Giovanni Boccaccio*, ɪɪ [Milan: Mondadori, 1964], ɪɪ, 20).

[7] This is the canto where the carnal sinners "che la ragion sommettono al talento" (*Inferno* v, 38) are punished. I should also stress the *political* nature of this sin: the characters listed by Dante have, almost all of them, a political role: Dido, Semiramis, Cleopatras, Helen, Paris, Achilles—the destiny of each of them is bound to the destiny of their respective cities.

core of the narrative. In the other case, the critics assume, much too easily, a transparent ideological intelligibility in the text. In the pages that follow I will show that the Introduction and first novella of the fourth day probe the relationship between the laws of passion and the power of political authority. I will also show that through these problems Boccaccio raises the issues of his own authority and of the extent to which desire can be known and represented.

A major strain of the Introduction, which is not generally taken into any serious account, deals with the censors' implied attack on the aims of a certain type of literature and, above all, the style of Boccaccio's writing. The polemic that ensues does not substantially depart from the defense of poetry in the *Genealogy of the Gentile Gods*, where Boccaccio takes on the "noisy crowd" of revilers, who see poetry as a "lascivious lie" and an "absurd craft" and who dismiss poets as "seducers of the mind," "prompters of crime" deservedly kept in poverty.[8] A noticeable difference, however, is of tone: in the *Genealogy* Boccaccio disguises himself behind the mask of an ex officio apologist of poetry's circuitous path of knowledge; in the Introduction to the fourth day the tone is airier, free of the predictable moves of an overtly apologetic text. In a way, the deliberateness with which Boccaccio mobilizes his rhetorical resources, and, indeed, the energy of his prose leave no doubt as to the importance of the issue at hand. At stake are not yet the abstract principles of literature, but the very sense of his own authority endangered by the tyranny of literal-minded censors.

With a touch of playfulness and even self-mockery, which both feign and belie detachment and by which he effectively demolishes his critics' high-minded conception that the Muses ought to dwell high on Parnassus, rather than in the "lowest brothel," Boccaccio puts forth a variety of pleas. To those who charge that he is too old to indulge in indecorous lan-

---

[8] The phrases are to be found in bk. XIV of the *Genealogy of the Gentile Gods*, chap. 5 (*Boccaccio on Poetry*, trans. Osgood, pp. 32–36).

guage, he replies that also Guido Cavalcanti, Dante and Cino da Pistoia, the poets we commonly associate with the Sweet New Style, in their old ages both strove to please the ladies and honor their beauty. To the censors' claim that the stories are not consistent with fact, he teasingly remarks that they should produce the originals and he would then emend whatever is at variance with his words; he states, pretending to authorial modesty, that his stories are written in too plain and low style to deserve the blast of the censors' eloquence or the violence with which they, as if they were hounds, tear him apart; he grants that his writing will never make him wealthy, and, finally, he maintains that he never strays from the Muses who have shown him "forse a queste cose scrivere" (perhaps how to write these things, p. 351), probably because they acknowledge the affinity between the women and themselves.

This concern with language prominently figures even in the novellette (the diminutive is Boccaccio's and it further exemplifies the rhetoric of authorial modesty which marks this section of the text). The comical focus in the story of Filippo Balducci certainly depends on our relishing Nature's triumph celebrated through the spontaneous, physical exuberance of the idiotic son and the defeat of the father's ingeniousness. But this parable of education also comes forth as a comedy of language. The father's *aequivocatio* in calling the women goslings, in hope of stifling the boy's so far only linguistic curiosity, draws attention to his naive nominalism, as well as to that of Boccaccio's critics, to their shared belief, that is, that by manipulating and tinkering with words, they can control and mask what to Boccaccio is the irreducibility of the reality of desire. Words are not the whole reality, the tale reminds us; they only bear a metonymic relation to it and, at best, they designate the father's self-interest.

As Boccaccio "plays" with his critics, the playfulness in no way diminishes the seriousness of his argument. There is, I believe, a good reason for turning seriousness into playfulness. As critics, father and son are caught in Boccaccio's joke, he is not the sovereign author who plays with all things in a serene detachment from them. He acknowledges, instead, the sovereignty of play, in the sense that, in the face of the censors' and Nature's rules, all he can do is play. The playfulness is abruptly suspended as the novella of Tancredi and Ghismunda shifts to the tragic mode. The shift is essential because it focuses on Boccaccio's narrative strategy, whereby the tragic story is part of the narrator's playful evasion which, in turn, both contains and is contained by the experience of the plague. This intersection of playfulness and tragedy does not make the story any less tragic than it is: it merely hints that tragedy is a provisional modality and not Boccaccio's generalized vision. Anyway, the story's tragic design is dramatized through a rigorous deployment of both formal and thematic trappings.

After we are told that the two lovers, having contrived to meet in Ghismunda's bedchamber, finally experience a "meravigliosa festa" together and that "con grandissimo piacere gran parte di quel giorno si dimorarono" (with greatest pleasure they spent a large part of that day together, p. 356), Boccaccio intervenes in the narrative to announce that ". . . la fortuna, invidiosa di così lungo e così gran diletto, con doloroso avvenimento la letizia de' due amanti rivolse in tristo pianto" (. . . Fortune, envious of so long and so immense a pleasure, turned the joy of the two lovers into sorrow by a sad calamity, p. 357). In subjecting their love to the unpredictable movements of Fortune, Boccaccio recognizes as illusory their idyllic world of romance. Ghismunda and Guiscardo have confined themselves to her bedchamber, which becomes an enchanted enclosure, but the spot is not secure from the treachery of Fortune and is, on the contrary, more vulnerable than ever to a tragic fall.

Unmistakably, the shift in the lovers' state from joy to grief recalls the canonical definition of tragedy. The formula is "tragicum carmen quod incipit a gaudio et terminat in luctum."[9] In the novella the formula is filtered through the lan-

---

[9] Variants of this formula are "che lieti onor tornare in tristi lutti" (*Inferno* XIII, 69) or "quod tragedia in principio est admirabilis et quieta, in fine seu exitu est fetida et horribilis" from Dante's *Letter to Cangrande*. More precisely the link between tragedy and fortune is available in Boethius' *Consolation of Phi-*

guage of *Inferno* XXVI, the canto which tells of Ulysses' journey to the boundaries of knowledge and his attempt to unlock
its gates. The phrase, "noi ci allegrammo, e tosto tornò in
pianto," sanctions the hero's quest as a tragic transgression.[10]
The echo from Dante's *Inferno* discloses, in an obvious sharp
reversal of the *sermo remissus* claimed in the Introduction, Boccaccio's retrieval of the grandeur of tragic discourse for this
love story. This open insistence on the tragic style needs a special gloss. As is well known, rhetorical conventions demand
that formal propriety be observed in the representation of reality. But style is not a mere ornament, and much less is it a mechanical question of applying the rules of rhetoric. It is, rather,
a tool by which reality is known and represented. As such, the
reference to Ulysses' tragic knowledge for the lover's experience hints that the story's concern is the probing of how desire
may be related to knowledge.[11]

The prince's palace is the tragic space for this probing.
Though the action takes place in this setting, there is no elab-
orate description of the court with its polite and refined rituals.
Nonetheless, the text conjures up, on the one hand, a

---

losophy: "quid tragoediarum clamor aliud deflet nisi indiscreto ictu fortunam
felicia regna uertentem?" (II, 2, p. 180 in the Loeb edition [Cambridge, Mass.:
Harvard University Press, 1968]).

[10] The line, which seals Ulysses' tragic fate, is *Inferno* XXVI, 136. For a discussion of the tragic quality of the canto, see my *Dante, Poet of the Desert. History and Allegory in the Divine Comedy* (Princeton: Princeton University Press,
1979), pp. 66–106. For the tragic modality in the *Decameron*, see Vittorio
Russo, "Il senso del tragico nel *Decameron*," *Filologia e letteratura*, 11 (1965),
pp. 29–83; Marga Cottino-Jones, "The Mode and Structure of Tragedy in
Boccaccio's *Decameron* (IV, 9)," *Italian Quarterly*, 11 (1967), pp. 63–88; M. J.
Marcus, "Tragedy as Trespass. The Tale of Tancredi and Ghismonda (IV, 1),"
in *An Allegory of Form*, pp. 44–63.

[11] I have in mind here for Dante's Ulysses the reading given by Bruno
Nardi, *Dante e la cultura medievale* (Bari: Laterza, 1949), pp. 153–164. But for
Boccaccio the question is clearly different. In a way, he picks up in this novella
the very problematics of the Sweet New Style, centered, as it is, on determining the relationship between love and knowledge. The thrust of the *Vita
nuova*, it can be argued, is to find out the kind of knowledge love engenders.
On this see, for now, my "The Language of Poetry in the *Vita nuova*," *Rivista
di studi italiani*, 1 (1983), pp. 3–14.

"Gothic" world of covert passions, hidden passageways, secret messages, deceptions and private revenges, of which the night is the epitome and Ghismunda the heroine. On the other hand, it features a daylight world with a visible structure of hierarchy and order, with the prince the supreme feudal lord of family and city, surrounded by courtiers and faithful vassals. In this visible world the virtue of nobility is the ideal, while treason is a heinous offense. The appearance of stability, conveyed by the metaphor of the closed and self-sufficient court, is unsettled by the passion of Ghismunda, this lonely figure of estrangement, who refuses the solaces of the court and dramatizes her slavery by choosing as her lover, Guiscardo, the father's valet.

Though the opposition between the two worlds is steadily maintained, it effectively collapses when the daughter's hidden passion falls under the prince's very eyes. One afternoon Tancredi, who would occasionally visit Ghismunda in her bedroom, while waiting for her, fell asleep on a couch hidden beneath a curtain, only to be awakened later by some noises. The action is punctuated by a language suggesting surreptitious movements (the windows in the room are shut, the prince enters unseen, falls asleep as if wishing to conceal his presence) which stress the astonishing discovery that is to follow. The sentence, "avvenne che Tancredi si svegliò e sentì e vide ciò che Guiscardo e la figliuola facevano, . . ." (it happened that Tancredi awoke and heard and saw what Guiscardo and his daughter were doing, p. 357), with its rapid sequence of verbs and conjunctions, conveys at once the quasi-oneiric quality of the father's vision as well as the hard evidence of fact.

More substantively, as Tancredi sees unseen the two lovers playing and cavorting together, there is both an assertion and an ironic reversal of the omniscient perspective he enjoys in the court. His present viewpoint gives him a knowledge that effectively sanctions his power; it also reveals to him the existence of an unsuspected world, the world of a passion he represses. The horror at his discovery is the more painful, one surmises, in that he finds out, in one stroke, the double treachery of servant and daughter. More than that, he sees his own exclusion from their pleasure and, thereby, confronts the limits of his power. In terms of plot, the discovery is the moment when a dramatic reversal occurs; the daughter's so-far hidden passion stands revealed, while the father's world enters the symbolic sway of the night. Under the cover of the night, Tancredi avenges his horror by having Guiscardo killed, his heart cut out and sent to Ghismunda.

The death of Guiscardo is preceded by his acknowledgment of his divided loyalty. The aphorism with which he replies to the prince's outrage, "Amor può troppo più che né voi né io possiamo" (Love has more power than you or I, p. 358), brings to light the thematic focus of the novella: the power of political authority as opposed to and undermined by love's tyranny. This antagonism is also suggested by the opening lines of the story: "Tancredi, prencipe di Salerno, fu signore assai umano e di benigno ingegno, se egli nell'amoroso sangue nella sua vecchiezza non s' avesse le mani bruttate . . ." (Tancredi, prince of Salerno, was a most human ruler and of kindly character, except that in his old age he stained his hands with the blood of lovers, p. 354). The proper noun, Tancredi, which is the grammatical subject, at the outset of the narrative, is a way of investing him with an attribute of sovereignty, but the claim is quickly dismantled.

The apposition, "prencipe," is, in effect, a misnomer. The reference to his giving his hands to blood casts an ironic light on the attribute and hints at the conventional contrast (which Boccaccio, in the wake of St. Thomas Aquinas and John of Salisbury deploys in his commentary on *Inferno* XII) between the benign and temperate prince and the bloody tyrant.[12] For Tancredi is a tyrant, who cannot rule over others any more

---

[12] "L'allegoria della qual favola se attentamente riguarderemo, assai bene cognosceremo che cosa sieno gli appetiti del tiranno e il tiranno, o di qualunque altro rapace uomo, ancora che tiranno chiamato non sia, e che cosa i Centauri e come essi il tiranno saettino. . . . Il nome del re è amabile, e quello del tiranno è odibile; il re sale sopra il real trono ornato degli ornamenti reali,

than he can rule over himself, or, simply, he cannot rule over others *because* he cannot rule over himself, and who makes of the arbitrariness of his will the letter of the law. Truly one can apply to him, in all its sinister ambiguity, the formula, *vis mea lex*, which later Renaissance princes would proudly arrogate to themselves.

The perspective from which Tancredi confronts his daughter with the knowledge of her deception is one which purports to uphold ideas of honor and social order which her conduct had violated:

> "*Parendomi conoscere la tua vertù e la tua onestà, mai non mi sa-rebbe potuto cadere nell'animo, quantunque mi fosse stato detto, se io co' miei occhi non l'avessi veduto, che tu di sottoporti a al-cuno uomo se tuo marito stato non fosse, avessi, non che fatto, ma pur pensato; di che io, in questo poco di rimanente di vita che la mia vecchiezza mi serba, sempre sarò dolente di ciò ricordan-domi. E or volesse Idio che, poi che a tanta disonestà conducer ti dovevi, avessi preso uomo che alla tua nobiltà decevole fosse stato; ma tra tanti che nella mia corte n'usano eleggesti Guis-cardo, giovane di vilissima condizione. . . . Di Guiscardo, il quale io feci stanotte prendere quando dello spiraglio usciva, e hollo in prigione, ho io già meco preso partito che farne; ma di te sallo Idio che io non so che farmi. Dall'una parte mi trae l'amore il quale io t'ho sempre più portato che alcun padre portasse a fi-*

---

e il tiranno occupa la signoria intorniato d'orribili armi; il re per la quiete e per la letizia de' subditi regna, e il tiranno per lo sangue e per la miseria de' subditi signoreggia; il re con ogn' ingegno e vigilanzia cerca l'acrescimento de' suoi fedeli, e il tiranno per lo disertamento altrui procura d'acrescere se medesimo; il re si riposa nel seno de' suoi amici, e il tiranno, cacciati da sé gli amici e i fratelli e' parenti, pone l'anima sua nelle mani de' masnadieri e degli scellerati uomini" (*Esposizioni sopra la Comedia di Dante*, ed. G. Padoan in *Tutte le opere di Giovanni Boccaccio VI* (Milan: Mondadori, 1965), XII (pp. 598–599). Cf. also the reference to tyrants and kings in *Decameron*, X, 7, p. 899. Even the "bes-tiality" of Gualtieri (X, 10), rightly belongs to this political tradition. Padoan in his footnotes (p. 946) mentions the tradition of Seneca and the reflections on tyrants in *De casibus*, IV. John of Salisbury's remarks are available in his *Poli-craticus*, ed. C.C.I. Webb (Oxford: Clarendon Press, 1909), bk. IV, chaps. 1–12. For St. Thomas Aquinas see *De regimine principum*, I, chaps. 1–3.

gliuola, e d'altra mi trae giustissimo sdegno preso per la tua gran follia: quegli vuole che io ti perdoni e questi vuole che io contro a mia natura incrudelisca: ma prima che io partito prenda, disidero di udire quello che a questo deie dire." E questo detto bassò il viso, piagnendo sì forte come farebbe un fanciul ben battuto.

"Thinking that I knew your virtue and honesty, it would never have occurred to me, whatever I could have heard, that you could submit to a man who was not your husband or even think of doing so. But I saw it with my own eyes and the memory of it will pain me during what remains of my old age. Moreover, since you had to come to such dishonor, would to God you had chosen a man appropriate to your nobility. But from among the many who frequent my court, you chose Guiscardo, a youth of very low class. . . . I have already made a decision about Guiscardo, whom I had arrested last night as he was coming out of the cavern and who is now in prison; but God knows what I am to do with you. On the one hand the love I have always felt for you, a greater love than any father ever felt for a daughter, pulls me in one direction; on the other hand, I feel very angry for your great folly: my love urges me to forgive you; my anger demands that I, against my own nature, punish you. But before I reach any decision, I should like to hear what you have to say about this." And so saying, he lowered his head and wept like a child who had been soundly beaten.   (p. 358)

The speech is manifestly marked by the doubleness of *psychomachia*. Along with a tone of self-pity, as the prince projects himself torn between mercy and justice (attributes of the perfect king), there is the father's disappointment at the daughter's failings.[13] The tears he sheds like a child reinforce the pathos of his old age crushed by an intolerable family experience, but, at the same time, undercut the clear-eyed, rational argu-

[13] The attributes of the perfect king are simultaneously justice and mercy. See, for instance, the line "giustizia vuole e pietà mi ritene" *Purgatorio* x, 93. Or the line ". . . per essere giusto e pio" from *Paradiso* xix, 13. See also *Policraticus*, iv, 8.

ment that as a prince he puts forth. The main indictment of Ghismunda is not so much for indulging in a sexual act, as it is political, for choosing, that is, as a lover a man of humble origin.

The opposition between "nobiltà" and "vilissima condizione," which plays out the etymology of nobilitas as *non-vilitas*,[14] evokes the prince's political values, his belief in a pattern of vertical order, in a scheme held together by the bonds of a simultaneously natural and social hierarchy. The word "sottoporti" crystallizes the prince's sense of order as a rigid system of rank. The subjection the word denotes is the subordination, given as natural, of wife to husband. In this sense it implies that a hierarchical arrangement fashions for the prince both family and society in a harmonious whole. But the context in which the word appears gives an ironic twist to the argument. Quite plainly the word refers to Ghismunda's sexual submission to Guiscardo. The double sense of the word betrays the fact that there is no inherent correspondence, as the prince would have it, between social conventions and the natural order. In a way, Boccaccio inscribes Tancredi's position within the broad lines of Andreas Capellanus' view that desire's danger lies in its power to unsettle the degrees of social order, making the master out of a servant.[15] Aware of the so-

[14] "Nobilis, non vilis, cuius et nomen et genus scitur" (Isidore of Seville, *Etym.* X, N, 184).

[15] See my remarks earlier in chapter 3 on this matter. See also this following passage as an example of how rank and social class are evoked and apparently subverted: "I know well that Love is not in the habit of differentiating men with titles of distinction, but that he obligates all equally to serve in his (that is, Love's) army, making no exception for beauty or birth and making no distinction of sex or of inequality of family, considering only this, whether anybody is fit to bear Love's armor. Love is a thing that copies Nature herself, and so lovers ought to make no more distinction between classes of men than Love himself does. Just as love inflames men of all classes, so lovers should draw no distinctions of rank, but consider only whether the man who asks for love has been wounded by love." And see also the classical counterargument: ". . . every man should stay within the limits of his own class and not seek for love in a higher one . . ." (*The Art of Courtly Love*, trans. Parry, I, chap. VI, pp. 45 and 49).

cial disruptions love engenders, Andreas constructs eros as a courtly game made of secrecy, propriety and virtue. Against Andreas, Tancredi shows the collapse of the code: the word "disonestà," with which he qualifies Ghismunda's deception, designates her violations of courtly values; the word "follia," used to define Ghismunda's blind surrender to common lust, shows the prince's perception that the madness of passion has destroyed the assumptions of the courtly world.

But it is not Ghismunda who is blind. Boccaccio intimates, rather, that the prince, more than anybody else, does not really know what he says and has no knowledge of himself. The charge of "follia" he hurls at his daughter is undoubtedly a way of asserting the rationality of his values; obliquely, however, it also hints that the scandal of "fol amor" involves him as well. It is Boccaccio's supreme irony to bring the prince's speech to a close with an echo from the *Vita nuova*. The phrase, "E questo detto bassò il viso, piagnendo sì forte come farebbe un fanciul ben battuto," recalls exactly ". . . come un pargoletto ben battuto lagrimando,"[16] which in the *Vita nuova* describes the lover's anguish at Beatrice's denial of her greetings. Later in the story, when the prince is weeping at Ghismunda's imminent death, the phrase, "L'angoscia del pianto non lasciò rispondere al Prenze; . . ." (The anguish of his sobbing prevented the prince from answering . . . , p. 351) is a resonance from "Donna pietosa e di novella etate," a song that recounts Dante's imaginary vision of Beatrice's death.[17] The use of the vocabulary from the *Vita nuova* discloses Boccaccio's strategy of suggesting how the prince's political discourse hides an erotic desire of which he is not aware.

In contrast to the mixture of delusion and vision in the

[16] "E poi che alquanto mi fue sollenato questo lagrimare, misimi ne la mia camera, là ov'io potea lamentarmi sanza essere udito; e quivi, chiamando misericordia a la donna de la cortesia, . . . m'addormentai come un pargoletto battuto lagrimando" (*Vita nuova*, XII, 2ff., ed. Fredi Chiapelli [Milan: Mursia, 1973], p. 30).

[17] "Era la voce mia sì dolorosa / e rotta sì da l'angoscia del pianto, / ch'io solo intesi il nome del mio core; . . ." (*Vita nuova*, XXIII, 19, ed. Chiappelli, p. 52).

prince's speech, Ghismunda's sharp rebuttal is ostensibly un-clouded by sentimentality or rhetoric. She impugns her father's arguments by an impressive display of mastery of language and reasoning power which far exceed his. Stating at the outset that she is resolved not to beg his clemency through tears (in itself a deliberate departure from the normal deployment of the rhetorical principle of *captatio benevolentiae*), she admits that she loves Guiscardo; that she does so not because of her womanly frailty, but because of her father's neglect and her lover's "virtù." Unable to resist the nature and "power of the laws of youth," she did not take a lover at random, but assumes full responsibility, retorting firmly to the father's charge of madness and blindness, for her action: "con dilibe-rato consiglio elessi innanzi a ogni altro e con avveduto pen-siergo a me lo 'ntrodussi e con savia perseveranza di me e di lui lungamente goduta sono del mio disio" (with deliberate judg-ment I chose him over all others and with careful planning I brought him to me, and with the commitment of us both I have long been enjoying my pleasures, p. 361). From this as-sertion of her wise and deliberate choice she moves on to what to her are the absurdities of her father's speech on rank and no-bility, which she counters with her own social-moral convic-tions.

For Ghismunda the worth of man is not an inherent, natural property, nor, as the implication of Tancredi's statement seems to be, does the stability of the world depend on the duty of each person to keep his place. Rehashing arguments derived from no single source, but having identifiable strands in au-thoritative texts by Boethius, Andreas, Dante and the Stilno-vists, she states that the worth of man is not a fixed attribute conferred by nature, but a moral distinction to be earned.[18] Men descend from the same stock and are created with "iguali

[18] "Dove è da sapere che oppinione di questi erranti è che uomo prima vil-lano mai gentile uomo dicer non si possa; nè uomo che figlio sia di villano si-milemente dicere mai non si possa gentile . . ." (*Convivio*, ed. G. Busnelli e G. Vandelli, 2nd ed., ed. A. E. Quaglio, 2 vols. [Florence: Le Monnier, 1964], IV, xiv, 15, and notes).

forze, con iguali potenze, con iguali vertù . . ." (with equal capacities, equal powers and with equal virtues, p. 361). In the wake of Dante and the poets of the Sweet New Style, who consistently redefine aristocratic values, she claims that it is excellence of character and gentleness of heart which set a distinction of nobility among men.

It is clear from the foregoing that the prince's narrow doctrine of a literal, fixed nobility collides with Ghismunda's assessment of moral worth. The real point of the exchange, however, is that we are witnessing an uncompromising confrontation without a possible dialogue or agreement. Father and daughter are two parallel figures of loneliness, who can never meet and whose display of reason ends up being its own self-mockery. Yet the distance between them is not as absolute as they themselves probably believe. The fact of the matter is that for Boccaccio they are both deeply deluded. The father, as we have already seen, is deluded in his sense of mastery and self-mastery, blind, like Filippo Balducci or the censors, to the irrepressible impulses of sexuality, and his reason disguises a passion he may or may not know. Ghismunda's delusion, however, is less evident but no less insiduous.

Her repeated and proud claim throughout the story, and Boccaccio's own language heightens the impression, is her autonomy and freedom to choose. It is she who decides, after carefully observing the conduct and manner of the other courtiers, on the lover; she who arranges the tryst with him and displays self-control and mastery of rhetoric in the exchange with Tancredi. Yet her speech is replete with language of the current *auctoritates*; more importantly, as she vindicates the strength of her love, "Egli è il vero che io ho amato e amo Guiscardo, e quanto io viverò, che sarà poco, l'amerò, e se appresso la morte s'ama, non mi rimarrò d'amarlo" (It is true that I loved Guiscardo and that I love him still. I shall love him as long as I shall live, which will be little. And if it is possible to love after death, I shall never cease to love him, p. 360), the lines resonate with the formulaic fixity of love poetry (love and death, love beyond death), while the alliterative, incantatory sounds may even echo Francesca's anaphoras on love in *Inferno* v, the canto where the lovers, who have inverted the order of reason and will, are punished. [19] And just as in the case of her incestuous affair with her brother-in-law, Francesca's sense of spontaneous passion is forfeited by the love conventions through which she speaks, so in Ghismunda's experience, her claim of autonomy turns out to be service, in the words of the valet Ghiscardo, to love's mastery and its poetry. [20]

That Ghismunda's imagination is thoroughly possessed by literature comes to the fore in the morbid scene when she receives from her father the chalice with the lover's heart in it. Before drinking her potion, she addresses the heart:

> *"Ahi! dolcissimo albergo di tutti i miei piaceri, maladetta sia la crudeltà di colui che con gli occhi della fronte or mi ti fa vedere! Assai m'era con quegli della mente riguardarti a ciascuna ora. Tu hai il tuo corso fornito, . . . Io son certa che ella è ancora quincentro e riguarda i luoghi de' suoi diletti e de' miei e, come colei che ancora son certa che m'ama, aspetta la mia dalla quale sommamente è amata."*

Ah sweetest vessel of all my joys, cursed by the cruelty of him who makes me see you with the eyes of my body. It was enough already to gaze at you with those of the mind all the time. Your life has already run its course, . . . I am

---

[19] Luigi Russo, *Letture critiche del Decameron* (Bari: Laterza, 1977), pp. 156–162, builds his argument about the oratorical quality of Ghismunda's speech by its juxtaposition to Dante's representation of Francesca.

[20] A grammatical-rhetorical brief analysis of *Inferno* v is by Natalino Sapegno, ed., *La Divina Commedia* (Milan and Naples: Ricciardi, 1967), pp. 64–65. He points out how the grammatical subject in Francesca's speech does not coincide with the real subject of her actions. The notion that Francesca is possessed by literature is examined by Renato Poggioli, "Paolo and Francesca," in *Dante: A Collection of Critical Essays*, ed. John Freccero (Englewood Cliffs, N.J.: Prentice-Hall Inc., 1965), pp. 61–77. See also A. C. Charity, *Events and Their Afterlife: Dialectics of Christian Typology in the Bible and Dante* (Cambridge: Cambridge University Press, 1966), pp. 214–217. For the general problem, see René Girard, *Deceit, Desire and the Novel*, trans. Yvonne Frecceró (Baltimore: The Johns Hopkins Press, 1965).

certain that his soul is still here within you, and still gazes
at the scenes of our common delights, and as I am certain
that his soul still loves me, she waits for my soul which
loves her deeply.   (p. 364)

The plain sense of the apostrophe is the desirability of death
in order to rejoin her dead lover. But in spite of the heroic
composure in the face of death, as critics have occasionally described her stance (which also is bound to strike one as somewhat melodramatic), Ghismunda is lost in a delirious experience which yokes together hallucination and physical reality.
As she looks at the physical heart, she charges it with the illusory attributes and conceits of love poetry, and revives, in effect, a dead metaphor. In his jealous anger the father tears out
Guiscardo's heart, lays bare and disfigures, that is to say, the
root of all love literature, which in the heart finds the metaphoric source of nobility, virtue and love, and, thus, mistakes
the metaphor for a literal reality. Ghismunda, in the extremity
of her passion, reverses the process. She mistakes the literal,
dead heart for a living metaphor. Like her father, she is now at
the threshold where the differences between life and death, the
metaphorical and the literal, have vanished and are no longer
recognizable. For all her convictions firmly rooted in reason,
she strays to a dazed imaginary world comparable to that of
her father's darkened judgments.

   What brings her close to her father, however, is her suicide,
an act which ostensibly asserts her final mastery over her own
life. No doubt, there is a stoical nobility in this gesture by
which she refuses to make her world a stage for hazard's or her
father's tyranny. But if suicide is a way of imparting her own
will and sense to her life, it also irrevocably discloses the illusion of choice and self-mastery, for, ironically, what appears
to be freedom turns out to be madness and bondage to death.
Since suicide is itself a form of violence, it actually puts Ghismunda in the same realm where are the critics who in their
rabid fury dismember the body of Boccaccio's text, Filippo
Balducci who educates his son against the laws of nature, and
Tancredi who mutilates Guiscardo's heart.

I would suggest that all these forms of violence, taken together, echo the middle ground in the moral system of Dante's
Hell. In the *Divine Comedy* the river of boiling blood, in which
the souls are punished, is the area where the laws of the natural
order are deranged by violence or "matta bestialità." More
specifically, it is the area where the violence of educators is
coupled to that of tyrants, homicides and suicides. The mythological hybrids presiding over this ditch of Hell, Minotaur,
Centaurs and Harpies are figures which dramatize the doubleness of man precariously poised between reason's sovereignty
and a brutish rage which disrupts that sovereignty. In Dante's
moral topography, moreover, the breast is the locus where
their "two natures are yoked together,"[21] while the heart is the
emblem of blood and violence. There is no doubt that Tancredi would belong to this place where tyranny must groan,
alongside the one who ". . . fesse in grembo a Dio/lo cor che
'n Tamisi ancor si cola."[22]

The heart, I would further suggest, is the enigmatic emblem
around which all the characters converge and, at the same
time, pull apart. It is only too well known how for poets such
as Guinizzelli and Cino, in the wake of Galenic doctrines, the
heart is the locus of spiritual refinement of the vital spirits, as
well as the place where the imagination makes its impressions
available to the intellectual faculty.[23] The myths of these poets,
along with those of Dante (who literally figures in the *Vita
nuova*, in the horrifying vision that elicited Cavalcanti's re-

[21] "E 'l mio buon duca, che già li era'l petto, / dove le due nature son con-
sorti, . . ." (*Inferno* XIII, 83–84).

[22] "Clove, in God's bosom, the heart which on the Thames still drips with
blood" (*Inferno* XIII, 119–120).

[23] One would only have to recall "Al cor gentil rempaira sempre amore,"
or the sonnet by Cino, "Io fui 'n su l'alto e 'n sul beato monte," etc. More
generally, see Bruno Nardi, "L'amore e i medici medievali," in *Studi in onore
di Angelo Monteverdi* (Modena: Società Tipografica Editrice Modenese, 1959),
II, pp. 517–542; see also A. E. Quaglio, "Prima fortuna della glossa Garbiana
a "Donna me prega" del Cavalcanti," *Giornale storico della letteratura italiana*,
141 (1964), pp. 336–368. See also the general synopsis of the question in Mau-
rice Valency, *In Praise of Love* (New York: The Macmillan Co., 1961), pp.
205-255.

sponse, how the heart feeds love, and who writes celebrated aphorisms on love and the gentle heart)[24] stand behind Ghismunda's theories and actions.

Unlike the poets of the Sweet New Style, who believe that desire can be organized into knowledge and that love can even lead to the knowledge of God, Boccaccio shows how love lapses into madness and violence. He also shows, with astonishing skill, how the violence of the father, in turn, is a metaphoric displacement of love. In short, he probes the tragic paradox of the heart, at once the seat of love and of violence, which steadily overlap and slide into each other. It is this radical ambiguity of the heart that unsettles the possibility of a univocal, literal reading of the novella. More than that, it marks the rupture between knowledge and desire as the essence of the tragic plot the story tells. To the censors who believe that the writer's responsibility is to name reality "properly," either according to a fixed hierarchy of style or a principle of decorum, Boccaccio replies with the comical attempt of Filippo Balducci who uses words as an illusory and futile mask of reality. Against the censors, he also evokes a world where hierarchies collapse and founding metaphors, such as the heart, yield equivocal meanings which make all efforts at reliable knowledge and mastery simply flounder.

That the heart is the chamber of contradictory and shifty impulses is dramatized even more explicitly in the novella of the eaten heart (IV, 9). The tale takes place in Provence, a geography which is as real as it is part of a literary myth, and in-

---

[24] Cf. the sonnet "A ciascun' alma presa e gentile core / . . . Allegro mi sembrava Amor tenendo / meo core in mano, e ne le braccia avea / madonna involta in un drappo dormendo. / Poi la svegliava, e d'esto core ardendo / lei paventosa umilmente pascea: appresso gir lo ne vedea piangendo." Cf. also the other sonnet "Amor e'l cor gentil sono una cosa, / sì come il saggio in suo dittare pone," from *Vita nuova*, respectively chapters 3 and 20. The foregoing and the preceding notes emphasize the erotic, medical and intellectual issues debated around the heart. I should also mention the theological-symbolic debates traced recently by Jean Leclerq, "Le Sacre-Coeur dans la tradition bénédictine au moyen âge," in *Cor Jesu*, ed. Augustinus Bea et al. (Rome: Casa editrice Herder, 1959), II, pp. 3–28.

volves the friendship of two neighboring knights, Guiglielmo
Rossiglione and Guiglielmo Guardastagno. In spite of the
bonds of friendship between the two men, a passion develops
between Guardastagno and Rossiglione's wife. Though the
text explicitly states that this is a conflict between friendship
and love, it also intimates in an oblique yet unmistakable way
the presence of a different rationale. In effect, the friendship
between the two men, the proximity of their castles, their
equal rank, common first name and the other traits they share
(they are, we are told, equally valiant, wear the same uniform
and colors, go jousting together in the same tournaments) pre-
figure as an inevitable occurrence Guardastagno's passion for
Rossiglione's wife. Since the two men share so much, Guardastagno's loving his friend's woman appears to be a logical
extension of all their other identical pursuits, a way of achieving a fuller identity.[25]

The woman's name is never mentioned, as if Boccaccio
meant to stress that this triangle is essentially a story of dou-
bles, two men who resemble each other in the idyllic world of
play, but whose likeness is illusory and quickly disintegrates in
a tragic difference. From this point of view, the primary aim
of the narrative is to gauge the irreducible distance between
two contiguous terms, "amistà" and "amore," which have the
same etymological derivation, from *hamus*, hook, but which,
ironically, cannot themselves be held together, so to speak, in
the same knot.[26] Tancredi and Ghismunda, for all the closeness

[25] Clearly what I am alluding to is what has come to be known as the logic
of triangular, mimetic desire, which has been probed, in medieval terms, by
Denis de Rougemont, *Love in the Western World*, trans. Montgomery Belgion
(Greenwich, Conn.: Fawcett Publications, 1966); see especially pp. 27–58.
The issue has been treated in modern literature in René Girard, *Deceit, Desire,
and the Novel*, pp. 1–52.

[26] "Love gets its name (*amor*) from the word for hook (*amus*), which means
'to capture' or 'to be captured,' for he who is in love is captured in the chains
of desire and wishes to capture someone else with his hook" (*The Art of
Courtly Love*, trans. Parry, p. 31). See also the dramatic use of this etymology
in chapter 4, n. 38 above. For the etymology of *amicus*, see Isidore of Seville:
"Amicus, per derivationem, quasi animi custos. Dictus autem proprie: amator
turpitudinis, quia amore torquetur libidinis: amicusa hamo, id est, a catena
caritatis; unde et hami quod teneant" (*Etym.*, X, A, 4).

of their bonds, think they are worlds apart but are, nonetheless, caught in a specular self-reflection, of which their shared widowhood is the signal. In contrast to that experience, the self-mirroring of the two knights, of which friendship is the symbol, hides a desire for a difference which violence seals. Aware of his friend's betrayal, Rossiglione ambushes Guardastagno, tears his heart out and, pretending it is a boar's, serves it for dinner to his wife, who, finally being told the truth, jumps to her death.

The horror of the sequence, intensified by the counterpoint between the chivalrous pastimes of courtly life and the grim reality of violence, is possibly a faint recapitulatiton of the general outline of Dante's moral plan in Hell, arranged, as it is, in incontinence, violence and fraud. This tripartite division of sin collapses in Boccaccio's representation, where all the passions entail each other in a ghastly symmetry. Rossiglione's love turns to hatred, Guardastagno's treachery is countered by Rossiglione's treacherous violence, while the lovers' passion brings about their violent deaths. The world of love is supplanted by one of hatred, but when characters are most divided, they are drawn into a circle of violence wherein they end up most resembling each other.

From this standpoint there is a special dramatic aptness in Rossiglione's gesture of offering his wife the lover's heart as if it were a boar's. The violence against the heart is here, too, first of all, a disfiguration of love's myths. At the same time, the symbolic property of the boar, *aper*, for encyclopedists such as Isidore of Seville, Neckham and Cantimpré, is *saevitia* and *feritas*.[27] Ostensibly the substitution Rossiglione feigns is his way of suggesting that Guardastagno's is not a loving heart but a savage one. In spite of Rossiglione's intent, however, the emblem of the boar discloses his own savagery. As friends, Rossiglione and Guardastagno were linked by bonds of reciprocity; as enemies, the form of this reciprocity is still ob-

---

[27] "Aper a feritate vocatus, ablata F littera et subrogata P." *Etym.*, XII, i, 27. For Alexander Neckam, see *De naturis rerum*, ed. Thomas Wright, Rolls Series, 34 (London, 1863). Thomas Cantimpré, *Liber de natura rerum*, ed. H. Boese, I (Berlin-New York: W. De Gruyter, 1973).

served: one's violent revenge comes forth as the exact response to what he perceives as the other's violence, and the boar's heart is the metaphor around which they meet.

Yet to the wife the lover's heart is a "nobil vivanda" (noble food, p. 421) which, as in the scene of the *Vita nuova* alluded to earlier, nourishes her love. What was offered as a punishment turns out to be the very opposite: the wife commits suicide and in her death she is to be forever with her lover. Just as in the case of Tancredi, Ghismunda and Guiscardo, here, too, central to the characters' intricate actions, is the heart with its dark and simultaneously dazzling potential to join and divide the two friends and divide and join the two lovers. More than that, the novella's total pattern dramatizes, as in the first story, how love and violence implicate each other in a ceaseless movement of substitution whereby every action a character performs leads to consequences that he cannot control, and the denomination of an entity, such as the heart or the figures of the narrative, has contradictory properties and shifty significance.

In such a context where questions of definitions, difference and identity are unstable and precarious, the act of naming emerges as a fact of appropriation. To explain what is meant by this statement, I must briefly examine the Ovidian story of Pyramus and Thisbe to which there are some oblique allusions in the novella of Tancredi and Ghismunda. Ovid's text is first recalled when Ghismunda remembers the secret passageway to her bedchamber, "ma Amore, agli occhi del quale niuna cosa è sì segreta che non pervenga . . ." (But for love nothing is so secret that it won't be noticed by his eyes, p. 356). The phrase echoes the discovery of the chink in the wall ("Quid non sentit Amor?") through which the two Ovidian lovers communicate with each other.[28] Another somewhat generic parallel with the classical fable occurs at the end of the story when we are told that Ghismunda and Guiscardo, like the two lovers in the *Metamorphoses*, are buried in the same urn.[29] Even the overall situation of the Latin account, the love of two

---

[28] *Metamorphoses*, IV, 68.

[29] ". . . una requiescit urna" (*Metamorphoses*, IV, 166).

young people forbidden by their parents, which Boccaccio fully elaborated in his *Concerning Famous Women*, is in part reenacted in the novella of Ghismunda.[30] Above all, it is the implication of Ovid's story that might shed some light on Boccaccio's handling of the relationship between language and desire.

The exordium of the narrative, "Pyramus et Thisbe, iu-venum pulcherrimus alter, / altera, quas Oriens habuit prae-lata puellis, / contiguas tenuere domos . . . ," announces Ovid's main concern.[31] The parallelism and even the graphic position of the two pronouns display the proximity and sepa-ration to which the two young lovers are doomed. This is, in effect, the double focus of the romance: they live contiguously but are barred by a wall their houses have in common; their nearness engenders love, but they are kept apart by their par-ents' prohibition; through the chink in the wall each of them throws kisses that can never reach the other side. Yet, impelled by desire, the two agree to elope at night and choose Ninus' tomb as their meeting place. The irony is transparent, for as they name Ninus' tomb the lovers unwittingly make the place of death the point of destination of their desire. The irony is the more powerful in that no other mention of this tomb will reappear in the text. The lovers' insight into their mortality, conveyed by the image of Ninus' tomb, is replaced by the im-ages of the fountain and the tree, which are near there, as their point of reference. On the surface these are emblems of life, nonetheless there Pyramus and Thisbe find their death.

One sense of Ovid's parable is clear: desire misconstrues signs and is doomed to mistake one thing for another. Thus, when Pyramus, coming on the scene at the appointed time, sees a torn veil stained with blood, he quickly infers that

[30] *Concerning Famous Women*, trans. G. A. Guarino (London: Allen and Un-win, 1964), XII, pp. 25–27. For the text see Guarino's useful introduction.

[31] The lines read: "Pyramus and Thisbe—he, the most beautiful youth, and she, loveliest maid of all the East—dwelt in houses side by side" (*Metamor-phoses*, IV, 55–57; trans. F. J. Miller [Cambridge, Mass.: Harvard University Press, 1977], p. 183).

Thisbe had died and kills himself. The two lovers escape the enmity of their households under the cover of the night, which is evoked as propitious to their adventure ("per amica silentia lunae"). But the night is the time of dangers and the outside world is one of lairs inhabited by prowling beasts, where the lovers will miss each other. They were immured before eloping and in the end are immured in their common grave.

The novella of Tancredi and Ghismunda is also punctuated by spatial metaphorics (palace, bedchamber, prison, cup and grave) which bespeak the progressive contraction of the world of the lovers. But unlike Ovid, who writes a fable wherein words miss their mark and desire does not become reality, Boccaccio writes stories, to which he refers by the Ovidian formula "senza titolo," in which there is not simply such a quandary.[32] More precisely, in the novella of Tancredi and Ghismunda the problem is given a different twist. When at the end of their exchange Ghismunda promises to kill herself, the father doubts that she would resolve to translate her words into action (". . . non credette per ciò in tutto lei sì fortemente disposta a quello che le parole sue sonavano, come diceva; . . .") (he did not believe that she was so firmly set to do what her words said . . . p. 362). His doubt, as we know, is a miscalculation, for the daughter carries out her threats. But the miscalculation betrays his conviction that only he, as the prince, has the power to change words into deeds. The prince is not alone in entertaining this conviction. Filippo Balducci calls women "goslings" in the attempt to control his idiot son's desire. The censors attack Boccaccio's authority and try to control his language. Boccaccio may well have suspected that in some way censors and tyrants succeed in their wish.

The story of Tancredi comes to a climax with his burying

---

[32] ". . . le presenti novellette . . . , le quali non solamente in fiorentin volgare e in prosa scritte per me sono e senza titolo, ma ancora in istilo umilissimo e rimesso quanto il più si possono" (*Decameron*, p. 345). See the Proem to the *Esposizioni sopra la Comedia di Dante*, ed. G. Padoan in *Tutte le opere di Giovanni Boccaccio*, VI (Milan: Mondadori, 1965) for a technical use of "titolo" (p. 3). See also the following passage: ". . . compose (Ovidio) uno (libro), partito in tre, il quale alcun chiamano *Liber amorum*, altri il chiamano *Sine titulo*: e può l'un

the remains of Ghismunda and Guiscardo in the same urn in the presence of all the people. After the experience that had threatened the differences through which the social fabric is organized, the tragic action gives way to reconciliation and by the tomb symbolic order is finally restored. But the tomb is a double-edged metaphor: it is both a simulacrum of the eternal love of Ghismunda and Guiscardo, and it is the emblem of the persistence of political authority, ready to change the death it inflicts into its own survival. Boccaccio's authorial modesty, then, in this section of the text is not merely an ironic pose: it is the acknowledgement of the political, literal manipulations to which the complexity of the symbolic order is unavoidably vulnerable.[33]

But the text also tells a different story, that there can be no deliberate collusion between the ideologists and this writer. What Boccaccio knows, and both the censors and his characters do not, is that all efforts at total controlling power stumble against the unpredictable turns of events. He intimates this much as he identifies in "Fortuna invidiosa" the agency that shapes the story's tragic movement.[34] The epithet, "invidiosa," alludes to the traditional figuration of blindfolded fortune.[35] "Invidia" is also the term used in the Introduction to designate the censors' envy as well as their blindness, accord-

---

titolo e l'altro avere, per ciò che d'alcuna altra cosa non parla che di suoi ina-moramenti . . ." (*Esposizioni*, IV L., p. 200).

[33] The awareness of how complex are the ties linking literature and politics is manifest in Boccaccio's *Trattatello in laude di Dante*, ed. Pier Giorgio Ricci in *Tutte le opere di Giovanni Boccaccio*, III (Milan: Mondadori, 1974), pp. 437–538, for the careful changes between the two redactions.

[34] "Ma la fortuna, invidiosa di così lungo e di così gran diletto, con doloroso avvenimento la letizia de' due amanti rivolse in tristo pianto" (*Decameron*, p. 357).

[35] For the motif of *Fortuna caeca*, represented blindfolded at the wheel, see Howard R. Patch, *The Goddess Fortuna in Medieval Literature* (Cambridge, Mass.: Harvard University Press, 1927). See also F. P. Pickering, *Literature and Art in the Middle Ages* (Coral Gables: University of Miami Press, 1970). The blindness of Fortune usually finds a correspondence in the blindness of love. See E. Panofsky, "Blind Cupid," in *Studies in Iconology: Humanistic Themes in the Art of the Renaissance* (New York: Harper & Row, 1962), pp. 95–128. In Boccaccio's novella the move is to make love the power that sees.

ing to a current etymology of the word from *non video*. [36] These discrete hints of blindness reverse the dominant metaphoric pattern of the novella in which love, far from being "caecus," opens the lovers' eyes, the prince's power comes forth as a function of vision (with the suggestion that surveillance is the essential ingredient of political practice), Ghismunda is "avveduta." In this world of Fortune's randomness everyone's vision is impaired by blind spots. Claims of omniscient perspective by critics, lovers, prince or author are, thus, deflated by Boccaccio's text. Each of us can only afford transversal perspectives, limited viewpoints and partial truths, and the writer, who by necessity conceals himself behind the masks of multiple narrators, such as Fiammetta, has just recounted the parable of a common predicament we all too easily wish were not there.

[36] The etymology of *invidia* from *non video* is played out by Dante in *Purgatorio* XIII, where the envious penitents are represented with their eyelids sewn closed.

6

THE COMEDY OF LOVE

The two preceding chapters have focused, respectively, on the imagination of sexuality and the errors (in the full sense of the word) of desire. The questions raised there are very likely to be at odds with the more conventional image of Boccaccio's bawdy humor, which, in a rather descriptive fashion, I intend to examine in this chapter. The terms within which the comic laughter of the *Decameron* can begin to be understood are provided by Boccaccio himself in the polemical piece at the very end of the text. In the piece he dismisses his critics' standards of *gravitas*; he denies that he is heavy and says, first, that he wants to be "lieve"—lighthearted—and then he adds that the friars' sermons, which are "piene di motti e di ciance e di scede" (full of nonsense, chatter and silliness, p. 963) fit his *novelle*, meant, as they are, to dispel women's melancholy. The paragraph also announces the therapeutic power of laughter: the verb "guerire"—healing—appears in a context in which Jeremiah's lamentations and the Magdalene's regrets are recalled.[1]

[1] "Né dubito punto che non sien di quelle ancor che diranno le cose dette esser troppe, piene di motti e di ciance, e mal convenirsi a un uomo pesato e grave aver così fattamente scritto. A queste son io tenuto di render grazie e rendo, per ciò che da buon zelo movendosi tenere sono della mia fama. Ma così alla loro opposizion vo' rispondere. Io confesso d'esser pesato e molte volte de' miei dì essere stato; e per ciò, parlando a quelle che pesato non m'hanno, affermo che io non son grave, anzi son io sì lieve, che io sto a galla nell'acqua; e considerato che le prediche fatte da' frati per rimorder delle lor colpe gli uomini, il più oggi piene di motti e di ciance e di scede, estimai che quegli medesimi non stesser male nelle mie novelle, scritte per cacciar la malinconia delle femine. Tuttavia, se troppo per questo ridessero, il lamento di

The irreverence in the recalling of the Magdalene is transparent: by naming the repentant whore, Boccaccio seems to imply that behind the rigorism of his critics there may be stories of lust, just as behind the Magdalene's moral regeneration there is a long legend of promiscuous pleasures. As argued in chapter 4, what one might expect to be a palinode to make amends for a lax morality in fact is a piece which deploys an equivocal rhetoric whereby both the moral and the erotic are adumbrated. Above and beyond this comical equivocation, however, the polemic is a miniature of a fundamental mechanism of Boccaccio's comedy, one that mixes body and language, or more precisely, focuses on what can be called the body's language. Thus, the adjective "lieve" can be taken as a principle of style and, possibly, as an echo of the definition one finds, for instance, in Geoffrey de Vinsauf, ". . . omnia sint levia . . . res levis, et leve verbum."[2] But the word, as well as its antithetical "pesato"—heavy—has obvious overtones of sexuality. This overtone comes forth explicitly in the successive paragraph when Boccaccio denies having a poisonous tongue for writing the truth about friars. A lady neighbor of his, Boccaccio adds, told him that he has the sweetest tongue in the whole world. Even the satire against the friars combines attacks on their sermons with remarks on their bodily smells.[3]

Germia, la passione del Salvatore e il ramarichio della Magdalena ne le potrà agevolmente guerire" (*Conclusione, Decameron*, p. 963).

[2] Geoffrey de Vinsauf, *Poetria nova in les arts poétiques du XIIe et du XIIIe siécle*, ed. E. Faral (Paris: Librairie H. Champion, 1924). The whole passage reads: "Hac ratione levis signatur sermo jocosus: / Ex animi levitate jocus procedit. Et est res / Immatura jocus et amica virentibus annis; / Et leve quid jocus est, cui se jocundior aetas / Applicat ex facili. Res tertia sit levis. Erog / Omnia sint levia. Sibi consonat undique totum / Si levis est animus, et res levis, et leve verbum" (ll. 1910–1916).

[3] "E chi starà in pensiero che ancor di quelle non si truovino che diranno che io abbia mala lingua e velenosa, per ciò che in alcun luogo scrivo il ver de' frati? A queste che così diranno si vuol perdonare, per ciò che non è da credere che altro che giusta cagione le muova, per ciò che i frati son buone persone e fuggono il disagio per l'amor di Dio e macinano a raccolta e nol ridicono; e se non che di tutti un poco vien del caprino, troppo sarebbe più piacevole il piato loro" (*Decameron*, pp. 963–964).

The insistence on the body as the place of comedy is not un-usual. While it is true that Dante envisions a disembodied laughter, the laughter of the "angelici ludi,"[4] the tradition of French *fabliaux* and the Italian "poeti giocosi," as historians re-fer to them, constitutes the sure background for Boccaccio's comedy. The *sermo jocosus* of this tradition enacts an anti-Pla-tonic strain, in that the body, its physical messages and calls, not the world of ideas, is the central concern. Accordingly, the motifs of the "poeti giocosi," such as Cecco Angiolieri and Folgore da San Gimignano, are gambling, drinking, women, food, tavern, the sort of imaginative world that Dante himself conjures in the so-called comedy of the devils.[5] This type of comedy is deployed in the seventh day, the day that is under the reign of Dioneo.

The day's narrative opens with a compressed description of the *brigata* revisiting the lovely spot of the day earlier, the se-cluded Valley of the Ladies, so placed as to seem shut out from all the world. However real its topography, the landscape, with the picture of the White Dawn banishing the stars of the night except for the still glowing Lucifer, or the birds singing as if rejoicing at the coming of the young women and young men, is designed to evoke more a stylized version of the Gar-den of Eden than the physicality and concreteness of the earth.[6]

---

[4] *Paradiso* XXVIII, 126.

[5] Cecco Angiulieri is the protagonist of *Decameron* IX, 4, in a story which seems to pull together the various motifs of his poetry: hatred for his father's avarice, the life in the tavern, gambling and pennilessness. For the poetry of Cecco and Folgore, see *Sonetti burleschi e realistici dei primi due secoli*, ed. Aldo F. Massera, 2 vols. (Bari: Laterza, 1920). For a delineation of the esthetic prin-ciples of this poetic tradition and rich bibliography, see Mario Marti, *Cultura e stile nei poeti giocosi del tempo di Dante* (Pisa: Nistri-Lischi, 1953), pp. 1–40 and 83–129. The so-called "commedia dei diavoli" in *Inferno* XXI and XXII, which will be discussed in the next chapter (see notes 29 and 30), with its metaphors of cooking, tavern, jousting, anality, etc, is, it can be shown, Dante's critical adoption of the rhetoric of the jocose poets to the devils' tricks.

[6] "Ogni stella era già delle parti d'oriente fuggita, se non quella sola la qual noi chiamiamo Lucifero che ancora luceva nella biancheggiante aurora, . . . nè era ancora lor paruto alcuna volta tanto gaiamente cantar gli usignuoli e gli al-tri uccelli, quanto quella mattina pareva; da' canti de' quali accompagnati in-fino nella Valle delle Donne n'andarono, dove da molti più ricevuti, parve loro

The emphasis of the passage falls both on the harmony linking man and nature, and on the happy bond existing between man and man in this landscape. Boccaccio goes out of his way to intimate that order sustains the world of the storytellers: we are told, thus, that the steward arranges the place where the *brigata* will spend the day by following faithfully his masters' instructions. At the same time, here Nature has no secret and unintelligible voice; rather, Nature has a language and her voice is translated into the language of men as the birds sing for the *brigata*'s delight and accompany the *brigata*'s own song. In an oblique allusion to the poetic agons conventionally featured in the pastoral world, the *brigata* even bursts into singing so as not to be outdone by the birds. The contest is no hint, as it is, say, in the Vergilian eclogues, of a latent rivalry which troubles the idyllic quality of the place, for this valley echoes the different sounds, "alle quali tutti gli uccelli, quasi non volessono esser vinti, dolci e nuove note aggiugnevano" (to which all the birds, as if they did not want to be outsung, added new and sweet songs, p. 585).

If the phrasing of the description draws fields, animals and men within the common, binding language of the song, its underlying concern is to suggest that this imaginative plenitude is shaped by a transcendent principle of love. The reference to the morning star, Lucifer, also known as Venus, at the very beginning of the Introduction to this day, projects this idyllic space as a garden of love; it even acknowledges the role of Dioneo, whose name means the child of Dione, mother of Venus, and under whose sovereignty the stories of the seventh day unfold.[7] The topic he announces as the organizing focus for this day's tales are the tricks that women have played on

---

che essi della loro venuta si rallegrassero . . . E poi che col buon vino e co' confetti ebbero il digiun rotto, acciò che di canto non fossero dagli uccelli avanzati, cominciarono a cantare e la valle insieme con essoloro, sempre quelle medesime canzoni dicendo che essi dicevano; alle quali tutti gli uccelli, quasi non volessono esser vinti, dolci e nuove note aggiugnevano" (*Decameron*, Introduction to seventh day, p. 585).

[7] For Dione as the mother of Venus, see Aeneid III, 19ff.; *Paradiso* VIII, 7, etc.

their husbands, either in the cause of love or for motives of self-preservation.[8]

The theme of the day could not have been started with more beguiling accuracy. After the imaginative experience of the beauty of the scenery, we are disengaged from it as the narrative plunges into the realm of dangers and actualities, the world of marriage where treachery and dissimulation prevail, one in which bonds are in disarray with wives laying traps, concealing signs, making up evidence, and with husbands hovering like spies but ending by seeing only what they are deliberately shown or what they want to believe.

There is a clear discrepancy between the harmony of the natural landscape and the stories of intrigues and snares within marriage, and this discrepancy may even be taken as an intimation that marriage falls short of being the sacramental reenactment, as the biblical typology of marriage has it, of Edenic unity. But Boccaccio's main concern in the seventh day is not gauging the gap between ideal constructions and the reality of private purposes and schemes. The theme purports, rather, to tell the strategies of simulation which wives use against their husbands either to gain love or to avert violence. The term, "amore," in the title page, is best understood as sexual pleasure and it is a principle which is overtly the point of departure and arrival of all the stories of the day. Laughter arises primarily from the cluster of libertine pleasures, violence, which is on the verge of breaking out, and from the disguises deployed both to contain violence and to gratify one's desires. This chapter and the next explore the implications of this cluster of questions; here, more specifically, I shall examine the motif of deception that is at the heart of the mechanism of laughter in the *Decameron*. These issues are not raised in the text in a logical pattern and, clearly, not in a serious vein. The stories, in effect, pretend to be nothing more than variations of the same

[8] ". . . Incomincia la settima (giornata), nella quale, sotto il reggimento di Dioneo, si ragiona delle beffe, le quali o per amore o per salvamento di loro le donne hanno già fatte a' suoi mariti, senza essersene avveduti o sí" (*Decameron*, p. 583).

theme, amusing jokes of inconsequential deceptions, for which Boccaccio retrieves the conventional wares of low comedy. Petulant husbands, resentful and resourceful wives, bodily urges, puns, plays or equivocation, parodies of rituals and sacred language, mixtures of various stylistic codes and other motifs are deployed to brush aside all intellectual artifices and to figure the raw and simple force of sexual impulses.

Yet this comical-naturalistic perspective, which is loudly celebrated on this day as well as elsewhere in the *Decameron* in the belief that sexuality is a spontaneous, natural reality, always entails masks of deception. No doubt, sexuality dons disguises primarily as a tactic for its gratification. The panegyric to Love, with which Lauretta prefaces the story she is about to tell (VII, 4), underscores, however, her sense that love is intimately allied to and even inspires duplicities:

> *"O Amore, chenti e quali sono le tue forze, chenti i consigli e chenti gli avvedimenti! Qual filosofo, quale artista mai avrebbe potuto o potrebbe mostrare quegli accorgimenti, quegli avvedimenti, quegli dimostramenti che fai tu subitamente a chi seguita le tue orme? Certo la dottrina di qualunque altro è tarda a rispetto della tua, sì come assai bene comprendere si può nelle cose davanti mostrate; alle quali, amorose donne, io una n'agiugnerò d'una semplicetta donna adoperata, tale che io non so chi altri se l'avesse potuta mostrare che Amore."*

O Love, how many and how great are your powers, how many your counsels and your insights! What philosopher, what artist could ever have displayed the prudence, the caution, the arguments that you quickly bestow on those who follow in your footsteps? Certainly every other doctrine is slow with respect to your own, as can very well be seen from the cases shown earlier; to these, loving ladies, I shall add the story of such a trick used by a simple woman, that I do not know who else could have shown it to her if not Love. (p. 606)

Quite appropriately, this *laudatio* is spoken by Lauretta whose name, as every reader of Petrarch's *Canzoniere* knows, is etymologically related to *laus*.[9] More to the point, the brunt of her hymn is an explicit redefinition not of love's essence but of its power. In a flagrant inversion of the literary resonance of her name, suggested by a very Petrarchan pun when she is crowned by Dioneo with a laurel wreath at the end of the seventh day, she discards Petrarch's view of love as the locus of anguished, equivocal passions, either, that is, as the *eros* which pulls man up the Platonic ladder of truth, or as sinful idolatry. Readymade doctrines are useless for Lauretta, for love cloaks itself in a variety of mutable shapes so as to be both irreducible to the fixed formulas of the philosophers and uncontainable within the boundaries of the artists' representations. Against the generalized, abstract theories, which are inadequate because they are the product of thought only, she conjures up a view of love that needs no preexisting intelligence, such as the one the *Vita nuova*, for instance, calls for. Preexisting intelligence is of no use to her because it is love itself which mobilizes the mind, leads to guile and instigates to lie. Within this perspective, the vocabulary of prudence and insight which punctuates the passage ("chenti gli avvediment," "quegli avvedimenti") may even be taken as a somewhat oblique reversal of the foundation of the Sweet New Style, the doctrine whereby vision engenders love, which, in turn, produces moral knowledge. For Lauretta love is an irresistible impulse which inspires, more than knowledge, craftiness and stratagems and in which moral concerns are suppressed.

Lauretta's notion of deception in love finds its extension in most of the stories of this day which insistently return to this motif. The only exception to this pattern is Dioneo's tale at the

---

[9] The etymology is actually Isidore's, who writes "Laurus a verbo laudis dicta; hac enim cum laudibus victorum capita coronabantur. Apud antiquos autem laudea nominabatur; postea D littera sublata et subrogata R dicta est laurus; . . ." (*Etym.*, XVII, vii, 2). Petrarch's puns—"laurea," "laude," "Laura," etc.—abound in the *Canzoniere*. See, for instance, "Quando io movo i sospiri . . ." which is sonnet V in the *Canzoniere* (ed. Gianfranco Contini [Turin: Einaudi, 1964], p. 7). See also the overt pun in Dioneo's speech at the *Conclusione* of the seventh day: " 'Madonna, io vi corono di voi medesima reina della nostra brigata" (*Decameron*, p. 662).

close of the day, which seems designed to surprise our expectations. On all other days Dioneo has refused to tell stories that would be bound by the rules the other storytellers agree upon: claiming and enjoying the freedom to speak last, he has consistently played out the role of the caustic and charming libertine, who mocks convention-bound figures, laughs at all attempts at seriousness, parodies other tales and outrageously taunts any idea of suffering in love. On the day under his reign he again chooses not to observe the law he himself has prescribed: he intended, he says, to forego his privilege and submit to the same rule as the others, but the subject has been so extensively discussed that he cannot think of anything to say on this topic that would stand comparison with the stories already told. By this elegant *captatio benevolentiae* he falls back on his customary privilege to infringe his own law. This is in part a predictable gesture, for as the child of Venus, he can only be a figure of transgression, always outside of any law, as if to intimate that which will become the glittering truth of the day and the point of the story he will tell, that love can never be hedged in and that when love is domesticated it still devises to be outside of the boundaries of the law.

What is surprising about the tale is that it is not even about clever wives and their tricks, but a "serious," quasi-philosophical parable about two friends from Siena, Tingoccio and Meuccio, who, hearing in the sermons at church about the suffering or blessedness to be experienced in the afterlife, make an agreement. They promise each other that whoever of them dies first will return from the world of the dead to reveal to the other what the souls really do in the beyond. The belief in the afterlife, where rewards and punishments are assigned according to the souls' moral merits, does not restrain Tingoccio from having an adulterous affair with a woman of great beauty, Monna Mita. The tale provisionally brackets the friends' arrangement and proceeds, instead, to relate the circumstances of the adultery. Tingoccio, who has become the sponsor for the christening of the woman's child, falls in love with her and, exploiting the opportunity he has to call on her, manages to seduce her. Because of the zeal he puts in the sexual pleasures he contracts a fever and in a space of a few days he dies.

The third night after his death Tingoccio fulfills his promise and appears to Meuccio in a dream to inform him that in his afterlife he is being punished for the sins he has committed and to ask that prayers and masses be offered on his behalf. Just as the shade is about to vanish, Meuccio inquires whether he is being punished for making love to his godchild's mother. Tingoccio replies that he has found out from other sinners in the beyond that there is nothing special "down there" about the mother of a godchild.

The tale is, among other things, a burlesque of visionary literature and its accounts of the dark terrors with which the imagination of life after death is possessed. It also aims at defining the place of sexuality in the scheme of values and, as such, it is Dioneo's effort to impart a rationale to the subject matter he has imposed on the other storytellers. The substance of his parable is that adulterous love, not even mentioned as a sin whether or not it is consummated with the mother of one's godchild, can be viewed as free from moral anxieties. The doctrine, it might be added, recalls Andreas Capellanus' own vision of the posthumous bliss granted to adulterous lovers.[10]

There is, however, a strain in Dioneo's narrative that both opposes and complements his pronouncements. In this day of bodily pleasures and activities, Tingoccio's death stresses, ironically, the painful limit of the body, its vulnerability to infirmity and death. This sense of physical frailty is no real hindrance to sexual pleasures; on the contrary, it can give poignancy to their pursuits and, appropriately, Meuccio, after his dream vision, regrets having in the past spared from his attention several ladies such as Monna Mita. At the same time, we cannot be blind to the fact that, for all the humor in the metaphoric displacement which represents sexuality as a dig-

[10] The area of "Delightfulness" is reserved to lovers, that of "Aridity" to those who had no pity on the soldiers of Love (*The Art of Courtly Love*, trans. Parry, I, vi, 5th dialogue, pp. 74–81).

ging of the soil, death is the limit against which libertine pleasures stumble.

Dioneo's perspective on the limits of the body is flagrantly
reversed by Filostrato's tale (VII, 2). His novella, which we
would have expected rather from Dioneo, evokes for us the
world of low comedy, the ordinary and even homely reality of
Naples, where Peronella, the beautiful wife of a poor brick-
layer, has arranged to let into her house her lover, Giannello,
right after her husband goes to work in the morning. The plan
runs smoothly till one morning the husband comes back home
while the lovers are together. Peronella, on the spur of the moment, decides to hide Giannello in a tub, then opens the door
and berates her husband as a worthless good-for-nothing. The
husband explains that he is not working that day because it is
a holiday and has returned home to sell, to a man willing to
pay five silver ducats, the tub that has been cluttering the
house. The events seem to take a hopeless turn, but Peronella's
quick wit gets her out of trouble. She tells her husband to send
away his customer because that very morning she had sold the
tub, for more money than he was getting, to a man who at that
moment was inspecting it.

Peronella's explanations to her husband are also aimed at her
lover, who having followed the exchange, agrees to buy the
tub on condition, he says, that the sediments coating the inside
be removed. The husband lights a lamp and lowers himself
into the tub to scrape it, while Peronella leans over to instruct
him where to clean. The wife's instructions to the husband become instructions also to the lover, who, in the meantime, has
decided to satisfy his sexual desires in the manner that in the
open fields "gli sfrenati cavalli e d'amor caldi le cavalle di Par-
tia assaliscono" (the unbridled horses, hot with love, mount
the Parthian mares, p. 597). No sooner is the scraping of the
tub completed than the urge is satisfied, and, after handing the
seven ducats to the husband, Giannello gets him to carry the
tub to his house.

The burden of the novella, which echoes an episode from
Apuleis' *Golden Ass*, is to dramatize the perception of the ele-

mental and uncontrollable power of sexuality. The plot is organized as a series of symmetries: the naiveté of the husband is set against the wife's shrewdness; the husband's work is juxtaposed to Giannello's and Peronella's sexual activity; the closed space of the tub is countered by the metaphoric "open fields" of the unchecked passion; the scraping of the tub is the overt metaphoric parallel of love-making. Peronella stands at the center of these symbolic oppositions and her power lies in her ability to satisfy the two men's needs: the husband's deal and profit and the lover's pleasures.

This sense of comic order comes to rest with the reassurance that the dangers impending on the adulteress have been averted.[11] But there is more to it. The reference to the unbridled steeds of passion, which is a conventional, and especially Ovidian, emblem of sexual incontinence, makes the point that the impulses of sexuality are too wild to be accommodated within the bounds of the family.[12] The simile, for all the fantasy of animal, hyperbolic vigor it conveys, is also incongruous because it works as a way of removing the domestic, local scene to a far-away, mythic place. By the move, the known confines of the household are quickly shattered and the implication is that at the center of one's own familiar world there is a powerful, unknown strangeness which is located, so to speak, in the body itself.

The value of the epithet, in the phrase, "sfrenati cavalli," is made poignant by Filostrato's reference to "raffrenamento"

[11] On the stories of the seventh day the most valuable bibliographical items are Thomas Greene, "Forms of Accomodation in the *Decameron*," *Italica*, 45 (1968), pp. 297–313; for a structural analysis see Cesare Segre, "Funzioni, opposizioni e simmetrie nella Giornata VII del *Decameron*" in *Studi sul Boccaccio*, 6 (1971), pp. 81–108. More generally see also Tzvetan Todorov, *Grammaire du Decameron* (The Hague and Paris: Mouton, 1969). See also Alfredo Bonadeo, "Marriage and Adultery in the *Decameron*," *Philological Quarterly*, 60 (1981), pp. 287–303.

[12] *Ars Amatoria*, I, 209ff. Cf. Franco Fido, "Silenzi e cavalli nell'eros del 'Decameron,'" *Belfagor*, 38 (1983), pp. 79–84. For the motif of the binding of love, see L. C. Clubb, "Boccaccio and the boundaries of love," *Italica*, 37 (1960), pp. 188–196.

(bridling) in the preamble to this tale: "Chi dubita dunque che ciò che oggi intorno a questa materia diremo, essendo risaputo dagli uomini, non fosse lor grandissima cagione di raffrenamento al beffarvi, conoscendo che voi similmente, volendo, ne sapreste beffare?" (Who can doubt, then, that when men learn what we have to say about these matters today, they will find a good reason to refrain from deceiving you, since they will know that you could also deceive them, if you wish, p. 593). The statement is ostensibly a technique of ingratiating the ladies; yet, from all we know of Filostrato's resentment against women, the statement also implies that men and women will go on forever deceiving one another. From this standpoint, the story dramatizes how the practice of deception safeguards both order and pleasure within the family.

The story Lauretta tells (VII, 4) explores further this issue.[13] On the surface the tale exemplifies the main insight of Lauretta's own hymn to love. Love is ever the wise counsellor of women in love, and, in fact, love counsels a woman of great beauty, called Monna Ghita, in the art of manipulating the appearance of reality. The story takes place, as we are told at the very onset, in Arezzo, where Tofano, the husband, grows unreasonably jealous of Ghita. Humiliated by his jealousy, Ghita decides to avenge herself by having an affair with a young man who has been casting amorous glances in her direction. When their acquaintance has reached a point where it only remains for them to meet, she carefully devises a way of doing it. Knowing that one of her husband's bad habits is a fondness for drink, she begins to encourage and commend him for it, till he drinks himself into a stupor. Once she sees he is drunk, she puts him to bed and goes to meet her lover.

Ghita has been doing this for quite some time, when Tofano notices that while she encourages him to drink, she herself never drinks at all. Suspecting that his wife is getting him drunk in order to have freedom to do what she pleases while he is asleep, he decides one day only to pretend drunkenness.

[13] For the story, see also the remarks by Giovanni Getto, "Le novelle dello scambio di illusione e realtà," in *Vita di forme e forme di vita* (Turin: Petrini, 1958), pp. 164ff.

As on previous occasions, Ghita puts him to sleep and makes her way to her lover's house where she stays for half the night.

No sooner has Ghita left the house than her husband bolts the door from the inside and waits for her to come back. When she finally returns, finding herself locked out, she whispers to Tofano to let her in, explaining that she has not been doing anything wrong, as he supposes, but has simply been keeping vigil with a neighbor. Seeing that there is no point in pleading further with him Ghita threatens to hurl herself into a well, rather than face dishonor. The threat leaves Tofano unaffected, and Ghita is forced to devise a new trick. She drops an enormous stone into the depths and the thump convinces the husband that she has thrown herself into the well: he rushes out, while Ghita, who has been hiding near the door, steps inside and bolts it. Tofano, outwitted, tries in vain to open the door, while Ghita now shouts, for the benefit of the neighbors who, awakened by the racket, have appeared at the windows, that she cannot put up any longer with a husband who returns home drunk and abuses her. Tofano tries to explain what has actually happened; but, first, the neighbors revile him for slandering his wife, and later, the wife's kinsfolk give him a fierce beating and take Ghita back with them. Eventually through the good offices of some common friends Ghita returns to Tofano, after he promises never to be jealous again and after giving her permission to take all her pleasures, provided that she be discreet enough not to let him find out.

In spite of Lauretta's claim, it would probably be more appropriate to call this, more than a love story, the story of an ordinary and verisimilar domestic crisis in which the central concern is authority or power within the family. We know from a host of other novelle that authority, as chapter 5 has argued, far from having a known and fixed determination, is a variable value. In this novella, the Pauline injunction that women obey the authority of their husbands is overtly transgressed.[14] Authority is here power, and power comes forth

---

[14] "Wives, be subject to your husbands, as to the Lord; for the husband is the head of the wife, even as Christ is the head of the Church" (*Letter to the Ephesians* 5:22–23. See also chapter 2, n. 14).

primarily as a question of perspective. In effect, the dramatic energy of the story springs from the various movements of the characters as they attempt to gain a privileged viewpoint from which each of them can organize the reality in which each is engulfed. The neighbors, who watch the noisy commotion from the windows of their houses, dramatically exemplify what can be said to constitute the legitimacy of perspective, which the novella, however, seeks to put into question. Thus Ghita is, at first, outside, where love is; her effort is to get inside and by her guile she succeeds; Tofano is inside and when he goes outside he is the loser, for to be outside is a transgression, while the inside is the safe locus of stability.

It can be said, within this context, that the *Decameron* is a consistent and trenchant ironization of the very notion of a fixed vantage point. A quick glance at the episode of the enchanted pear tree (VII, 9) bears this out: the perspective of the pear tree, from which the young Pirro claims to see his master Nicostrato making shamelessly love to his wife Lidia, is a transparent strategy by which Pirro can enjoy Lidia under her husband's very eyes and make the old man believe that what he actually can see from any point whatsoever in the garden is a marvelous delusion made possible by the magic powers of the tree. More generally, the multiplicity of narrative voices in the *Decameron* shows that there is never a single world, our own, and that the world is by necessity forever multiplied in a variety of fragmentary and partial visions.

But Ghita knows that vision is enlarged by the spot one occupies, even if this vision is no vision at all, and is best called an ability to fashion and distort the plain evidence of the world. As a matter of fact, the novella probes the ease with which evidence can be tampered and also it obliquely brings to the surface the fact that we see what we like or what we hear, either because the deeds are done in the dead of the night, or because they correspond to our own safe illusions of order, as Ghita's neighbors do, or because lamps, like the one lighting the inside of the tub in Peronella's household, show nothing or almost nothing. It should be remarked that most of the stories told on this seventh day take place at night, the dramatic time, that is, when the security of daylight knowledge no longer exists, if it can be said to exist even then, and when visibility is eclipsed. But knowledge is never secure, and Tofano's jealousy, which triggers the events of Lauretta's story, is a vehicle to question evidence.

Boccacio's understanding of jealousy in a way revises Andreas Capellanus' theories. In the *De arte honeste amandi*, Andreas distinguishes between jealousy in love, which to him is a legitimate passion ("Qui non zelat, amare non potest," as one of the rules states), and jealousy in marriage, which he condemns, for a husband cannot suspect his wife without the thought that such conduct on her part is shameful.[15] In a sense, the story maps out this shame. But the story moves beyond the determination of what a right conduct in marriage can be and makes jealousy the metaphor that discloses the suspicion that appearances are deceptive, that the messages we hear and the evidence we see are subject to being misread. No doubt, by this jealousy Tofano displays his desire to possess and control Ghita; but by it he also shows a distrust of appearances, a refusal to take the world at face value: surfaces, he suspiciously believes, lie and the wife's kindness must conceal secret motives and hidden worlds which exclude him. For all the rich imaginings that jealousy inspires in the jealous man, he is deceived from the start for he either sees deceptions where there are not any yet, or discovers that he has been betrayed before he had any inkling of the betrayal.

To be sure, Tofano attempts to unmask Ghita's tricks by re-

---

[15] "Love increases, likewise, if one of the lovers feels real jealousy, which is called, in fact, the nurse of love. Even if he does not suffer from real jealousy, but from a shameful suspicion, still by virtue of this his love always increases and grows more powerful . . ." (*The Act of Courtly Love*, trans. Parry, II, iii, p. 153). The passage should be compared with the earlier one (I, vi, 7th dialogue): ". . . jealousy between lovers is commended by every man who is experienced in love, while between husband and wife it is condemned throughout the world; . . . Now jealousy is a true emotion whereby we greatly fear that the substance of our love may be weakened by some defect in serving the desires of our beloved, . . ." (trans. Parry, p. 102).

counting to the neighbors what really happened. He fails in his effort because he is blind to the fact that the perception of reality is contrived, that every literal truth is made up, produced by the persuasiveness of the stories one tells or hears, and that the persuasiveness is sanctioned by the privileged vantage point one occupies in the space where the spectacle is played out. More importantly, his telling the factual truth makes him the object of his wife's kinsfolk's violence. Finally, out of fondness for Ghita, he gives up the will to establish the truth altogether: earlier in the story the stupor of intoxication, a vestige of romances' love philters turned upside down, blinded Tofano; now, because of violence and his own love for his wife, a new stupor sets in. He allows himself to be deceived, asking only that the deception be discreetly masked.

This is not, of course, the only tale in the seventh day where deception is at first suspected and opposed and is in the end accepted. A host of novelle are variations of this pattern. Thus Fiammetta follows up Lauretta's tale with her account of a husband (VII, 5), a rich merchant whose jealousy impels him to act like a powerful jailor, isolating and sequestering his wife from any contacts with the outside world. But the wife cannot be immured. In what is a comic trivialization of Pyramus' and Thisbe's passion, we are told how she discovers a crack in the wall of the house through which she arranges to meet her young lover. The husband even disguises himself as a priest in order to spy on her and capture imagined secrets by hearing her confession, but the wife eludes his surveillance, till he, who had worn the mantle of jealousy when it was unnecessary, casts it off completely now that his need for it is paramount.

When Filomena's turn to speak comes (VII, 7), she recounts the adventure of Lodovico, who, upon hearing of the unrivaled beauty of a lady from Bologna, Beatrice, is drawn to Bologna from Paris, where he lives, out of longing to see her. If the initial pretext of the narrative vaguely recalls the tradition of the *peregrinatio amoris*, or the *amor de lohn*, the outcome of Lodovico's quest undercuts the implications of the tradition:

in the novella, dislocation is not the inevitable, perennial condition of desire, as it is for, say, Jaufré Rudel or Petrarch; on the contrary, unabashed sexual pleasure crowns Lodovico's longing.

Vittore Branca's notes provide the complex array of analogues for this novella, but there is one text that I would like to isolate for a brief examination.[16] This is a *fabliau*, "La bourgeoise d'Orléans ou de la femme qui fit battre son mari."[17] In it the husband lays a trap for his wife, whom he suspects is carrying on an affair with a student, by pretending to go on a trip, but returns at night disguised as the wife's lover. The woman recognizes the husband, but feigns to believe that he is the lover and asks him to wait till she is free to be with him. She then tells her servants that she has been pestered by one of the students and asks them to give him a beating. When this is done, the husband is firmly convinced of his wife's chastity.

The plot of Boccaccio's novella differs on a number of details from the *fabliau*: the husband, for instance, dresses as a woman in order to test the servant's loyalty; the servant gives him a beating in the belief that it was Beatrice to whom he had proposed, he says, only to test her fidelity to her husband. There is another important way in which Boccaccio departs from the *fabliau*: whereas the *fabliau* evokes the experience of a merchant, Boccaccio sets the events in a patrician household. This difference cannot be accounted for in simply sociological

[16] *Decameron*, p. 1386. For the tradition of the *fabliaux*, I should mention Per Nykrog, *Les Fabliaux: Etude d'histoire littéraire et de stylistique médiévale* (Geneva: Droz, 1973) for an updated bibliography. See also Jean V. Alter, *Les Origines de la satire anti-bourgeoise en France* (Geneva: Droz, 1966); Joseph Bedier, *Les Fabliaux*, 6th ed. (Paris: Champion, 1964); *The Humor of the Fabliaux: A Collection of Critical Essays*, eds. Thomas D. Cook and Benjamin L. Honeycutt (Columbia, Missouri: University of Missouri Press, 1974). See also Alexandre Leupin, "Le sexe dans la langue: la dévoration. Sur Du C., fabliau du XIIIe siècle, de Gautier Le Leu," *Poétique*, 45 (1981), pp. 91–110; and the forthcoming study by Howard Block, *The Scandal of the Fabliaux* (Chicago: Chicago University Press, 1986).

[17] *Fabliaux ou contes du XIIe et du XIIIe Siècle*, ed. P.J.B. Le Grand d'Aussy (Paris: E. Onfrey, 1779), III, pp. 411ff.

terms, for the *Decameron*, as is known, is peopled with the new breed of heroes, the merchants, and one would expect Boccaccio to place his material within their world. Lodovico, however, deliberately rejects the mercantile world in favor of his father's noble lineage.

The shift from the comic domain of the *fabliaux* to the aristocratic palace enables Boccaccio to mingle the values of the *fabliau* with those of the world of courtly love. Many are the references to the courtly tradition: the knights returning from the Holy Sepulcher, Egano's pastimes of hawking and chess games, the high birth of the characters and, finally, the secret passions Lodovico harbors for Beatrice till he asks the lady to allow him to be in her service. The mixture of the literary materials from tradition makes it impossible to assign the novella uniformly to the genre of the French *fabliaux*. In effect, it can be argued that Boccaccio uses the perspective of the *fabliaux* to expose the violence that the code of courtly love and its elegant etiquette seek to mask; by the same token, the ceremonies and high ideals promoted by the *De arte honeste amandi* are also drawn within the concrete, earthy boundaries of the *fabliaux*.

From Boccaccio's standpoint these two rhetorical modalities, which in a sense correspond to two antithetical levels of style, the high and the low style for the representation, respectively, of high and low social classes, share, for all the differences in their assumptions, a common ground. They are both forms of deception and tools of comic representation, which Boccaccio overtly understands as playfulness. The metaphor of play appears at the crucial middle of the narrative: Lodovico, under the guise of the servant Anichino, is asked by Beatrice to "giucare a scacchi" (play a game of chess, p. 629). Anichino, wishing to make the woman he loves happy, plays his pieces so skillfully as to allow her to beat him. When the lady's attendants, who have been watching the game, leave them alone, Anichino reveals his love to Beatrice.

It is possible to view the connection of the chess game and the disclosure of love, which is a frequent device in medieval chivalric romances, as nothing more than another deployment of a conventional narrative technique.[18] But we cannot ignore the implications that the metaphoric yoking of love and play entails. For Boccaccio is asking of us, primarily, to equate the rituals of passion with the rigorous, geometric moves of the chess game. At the same time, since the game is for Anichino an occasion to make Beatrice happy by simulating defeat, it can be construed as a strategy of dissemblance contrasted to the truth of the love passion, with the suggestion that the power and spontaneity of love exceeds the artificiality of play.

The implied contrast between love and play is blurred, however, by the fact that the love between Anichino and Beatrice is all around an act of deception. More pointedly, Boccaccio deflates the notion of the spontaneity of their love by the digression on the "sweet blood of Bologna," as soon as Beatrice yields to Anichino: "O singular dolcezza del sangue bolognese! quanto se' tu sempre stata da commendare in così fatti casi! Mai di lagrime né di sospir fosti vaga, e continuamente a' prieghi pieghevole e agli amorosi disiderii arrendevol fosti:" (Ah, the singular sweetness of the blood of Bologna! How commendable you have been in such affairs! You were never fond of tears and sighs, but you were always moved by entreaties and would always yield to a lover's yearnings, p. 630). The repeated apostrophe to the Bolognese blood comically transforms the private story of the two lovers into a general law of nature. It also makes of the seduction scene a rhetorical exercise and the mirror reflection of the metaphor of play.

The link between love and play is brought into sharp focus in the *fabliau*, "Le Revenant," which Boccaccio, as has been suggested, adapts for the first novella of the seventh day, told by Emilia.[19] I would like to look, even if summarily, at this *fa-*

---

[18] The idea of allowing the woman one desires to win has analogues in Ovid, *The Art of Love*, II, 203ff.: "If she be gaming, and throwing with her hand the ivory dice, do your throw amiss and move your throws amiss; or if it is the large dice you are throwing, let no forfeit follow if she loses . . ." (trans. J. H. Mozley [Cambridge: Harvard University Press, 1969], pp. 79–81). See Branca, *Decameron*, p. 1383, for further bibliography.

[19] A. C. Lee, *The Decameron: Its Sources and Analogues* (London: D. Nutt, 1909), p. 185.

bliau, not so much to assess the degree of Boccaccio's autonomy of derivativeness from it, but to explore the metaphoric
tension between play and desire.

The story in its general outline goes as follows: a knight is in
love with a married lady, who states that she will consent to
love only a man who is capable of courageous and noble deeds.
To prove his worth, the knight proposes to hold a tournament
at the gates of the lady's castle, and while she watches the spectacle from her windows, he will challenge her husband.
Clearly, her viewpoint, dramatized by her being up in the castle, asserts the woman's sovereignty, but with an ironic twist:
husband and lover stage a duel for her benefit, but at the same
time, she is the object that one of them will possess. This notwithstanding, the lady agrees to the knight's plan in the
knowledge that should the husband be the loser, the winner is
her lover. The tournament is interrupted when by chance another knight is killed. The intrusion of chance violence into the
joust does not trouble the narrative sequence of the *fabliau*:
rather, it will be subsumed into the lover's strategy of seduction. Having won the contest, the lover also wins the lady,
who promises to receive him into her bedroom as soon as the
husband falls asleep. But it is the lover who, exhausted by the
fighting of the day, is asleep when the lady comes to ask him
in. Offended by what she takes to be a sign of his indifference
to her, the lady instructs her maid to wake him up and show
him out. The lover thinks of an expedient to gain her back: he
strips his clothes off and pretending to be the knight killed that
day, he enters the bedroom to beg the lady's pardon. The husband, duped by the stratagem, intercedes on behalf of the
knight, and the lady, disarmed by the lover's ruse, surrenders
to him.

The *fabliau* is at best an analogue of the novella of Gianni
Lotteringhi (VII, 1), the weaver who spends his evenings singing in the church choir, while his wife, the beautiful Tessa, arranges to have a young man, Federigo, keep her company
overnight in her country house.[20] To avoid being found out

---

[20] An examination of the semiotic issues of the novella, to which I have little
to add, is by Millicent J. Marcus, *An Allegory of Form. Literary Self-Conscious-*

the two lovers devise a secret code whereby she can signal to Federigo whether or not he can come to the house. The plan works for a long time, but one night, when the tryst has been arranged, the husband unexpectedly shows up. Tessa, enraged at his coming, gets her maid to carry large quantities of food into the garden for Federigo to eat, but forgets to tell her to inform Federigo that her husband is at home.

After a joyless supper Gianni and Tessa go to bed from where they hear a tapping at the door. When the knock is heard a second time, Tessa pretends to wake up and explains that for the past few nights a phantom has been haunting the house and has frightened her. Gianni reassures Tessa by telling her that he has recited the *Te lucis* and the *Intemerata*. The irony in the allusion to the two hymns is flagrant: the antiphon, "O Intemerata et in Aeternum Benedicta," a prayer to the Virgin without blemish to preserve the soul from the temptations of the flesh, is pointedly turned around, and at the same time fulfilled, in this story where the parodic double focus is the pursuit of carnal delights for the wife and of abstinence for the husband. The hymn, "Te lucis ante terminum," which calls on God for the guardianship of the angels so that "procul recedant . . . noctium phantasmata," triggers Tessa's suggestion that they exorcise the ghost by a prayer which is a transparent double entendre: "Fantasima, fantasima che di notte vai, a coda ritta ci venisti, a coda ritta te n'andrai; va nell'orto, a piè del pesco grosso troverai unto bisunto e cento cacherelli della gallina mia: . . ." (Ghost, ghost who goes by night, you came here with your tail up, keep it up and go: go to the garden and at the foot of a large peach you'll find capons' oily grease and a hundred eggs of my chicken: . . . , p. 590). The play of words recalls Frate Cipolla's sermon which mimed the

---

ness in the Decameron (Saratoga, Calif.: Anma Libri, 1979), especially pp. 93–109. See also Franco Fido, "Rhetoric and Semantics in the *Decameron*," *Yale Italian Studies*, 2 (1978), pp. 1–12. Noteworthy are the remarks by Giuseppe Billanovich, *Restauri boccacceschi* (Rome: Ed. di storia e letteratura, 1947), pp. 112–119. For the language of incantation, see Marga Cottino-Jones, "Magic and Superstition in Boccaccio's *Decameron*," *Italian Quarterly*, 18 (1975), pp. 5–32.

popular corruption of devotional language; here the exorcism is a coded bodily message.

The difference between the *fabliau* and this novella are too many, and too obvious, to be overlooked, yet the French text contains at least one insight that Boccaccio adapts. The *fabliau*, in effect, gives the question of deception in love a crucial twist. Deception no longer appears a term referring to women's fakery and betrayals. What their betrayal reveals, however, to the deceived ones as well as to us is that in every corner of the house, behind every door of either castle or villa, in every object there may be the occult presence of an elusive something or someone else. Gianni Lotteringhi thinks it is the supernatural; Nicostrato, the magic of the pear tree; the knight in the *fabliau*, the shadowy apparition from the beyond—they all share in the jealous man's suspicion that the familiar and ordinary experience is not what it seems to be. In "Le Revenant" this generalized dissemblance is equated with the world of play.

The tournament, with its simulation of war, transforms the assumption of concrete realism, which according to a critical commonplace informs the genre, into a space of artifice. Even the love passion is drawn, just as was Filomena's novella, within the sphere of the pageant. Pierre d'Angel, more precisely, dramatizes the metaphoric similarity between the two by deploying the rhetoric of the tournament for the love passion (the lady, for instance, admires the lover's "strategy" and is "disarmed" by his guile).[21] But this play is not empty ceremony or make-believe: the chance event of a knight's death betrays how earnestly men are caught in the game they play. Play is breached by the intrusion of chance and death. In this sense, play is the emblem of dissemblance and of the precariousness of dissemblance.

This notion of play is extended by Boccaccio into the domain of rhetoric. I would like to turn to the tale of a Friar Rinaldo (VII, 3) in order to map out this imaginative extension in

[21] "Le Revenant," in *Fabliaux ou contes du XIIe et du XIIIe siecle*, I, See pp. 317ff.

the *Decameron*. This is the story of a man, Rinaldo, who has fallen in love with the beautiful wife of a neighbor, and who, to find the pretext to converse with her in private, offers himself to become the godfather of the child the woman is expecting. The familiarity, albeit spiritual, which is thus established gives Rinaldo the opportunity to see her and to make clear to her his passion, which the woman resists. Not long afterward, Rinaldo becomes a friar and puts aside the cravings he has for her, but only for a while. The lady finally yields and—without arousing suspicion, for his sponsorship of the child makes it easy for him to visit her—they meet at her house. One day, while they are in her bedroom and the child is with them, the husband returns home. The woman has a sudden inspiration: she tells Rinaldo to get dressed and listen to what she says to her husband. What she says is that the child had fainted and that Friar Rinaldo, who happened to come there, was casting a spell on the worms that the child had in his body, thus saving him from sure death. Friar Rinaldo puts on his clothes and comes out with the child in his arms, who now has been restored to health.

The purpose of the tale is to launch a satiric attack against friars, who, we are told, alien to frugality and fasting, walk clad in elegant clothes and are incontinent to the point that gout is their distinctive disease. From this perspective it should be remarked that the friar's very name alludes to the fox, Reynard of the French romances, who is the symbol of treacherous Franciscans.[22] The failure of Rinaldo's conversion is widened in the novella to cover the general corruption of the fraternal orders.[23] They are all a scandal to the world, for ". . . Essi non si vergognano d'apparir grassi, d'apparir coloriti nel

---

[22] *Roman du Renart*, ed. D. M. Meon, 4 vols. (Paris: Treuttel and Wurtz, 1826), IV, pp. 125–461; Ernst Martin, *Le Roman de Renart* (Strassbourg: K. J. Trubner, 1882). See also *The Exempla or Illustrative Stories from the Sermones Vulgares*, Folklore Society Publication V, 26, ed. T. F. Crane (London: D. Nutt, 1890), p. 125.

[23] The overt antifraternal satire is to be found in Jean De Meun, *Le Roman de la Rose*, ed. Langlois, vol. III, ll. 10931ff.

viso, d'apparir morbidi ne' vestimenti e in tutte le cose loro,
. . . lasciamo stare d'aver le lor celle piene d'alberelli di latto-
vari e d'unguenti colmi, di scatole di vari confetti piene, . . . in
tanto che non celle di frati ma botteghe di speziali o d'unguen-
tarii appaiono . . ." (They are not ashamed to appear fat, to
appear flushed-face and effeminate in their clothings and all
their dealings, . . . furthermore their cells are stuffed with jars
full of electuaries and unguents, with boxes full of various
confections . . . so much so that they do not seem to be friars'
cells but shops of apothecaries and druggists . . . , p. 600).

The sharp attack against the friars' degeneracy (which
echoes the one in III, 7) may be the expression of a moral passion, but it is also the manipulation of a well-defined intellectual tradition. For the cell, be it the infirmary of Cassino, St.
Gall or Chartres, is the place where historically medicine abandons its age-old dependence on incantations and superstitious
charms as means for curing the sick and acquires the status of
an empirical science.[24] Actually medicine, as practiced in these
religious communities, is the more valued because there they
know how to distinguish, as Fulbert of Chartres puts it, between "earthly medicine," which explores the power of herbs
and similar substances, and "heavenly medicine," alone capable of raising the dead from the sepulcher.[25]

---

[24] For the practice of supernatural healing via relics and charms, see, for instance, Gregory of Tours, *De miraculis Sancti Martini, PL* 71, col. 525. See also
Gregory the Great, *Miracula Sancti Benedicti, PL* 66, col. 134. More generally,
cf. L. Thorndike, *A History of Magic and Experimental Science* (New York: The
Macmillan Co., 1923), I, esp. pp. 590 ff. See also n. 40, chapter 8. It is part of
the historical record that the revival of empirical medicine in Europe started in
monasteries, and the infirmary established by St. Benedict of Nursia in the
first half of the sixth century is credited with this revolutionary accomplish-
ment. See *The Rule of St. Benedict (PL* 66, col. 36): "Infirmorum cura ante omnia et super omnia adhibenda est. . . . See also Cassiodorus, "De Monachis
Curam Infirmorum Habentibus . . ." in *De institutione divinarum litterarum, PL*
70, col. 31.

[25] "Duas esse medicinas Christiani novimus, una quidem de terrenis, de su-
pernis alteram; quarum ut diversos ortus, sic et efficaciam. Medici terreni lon-
gam per experientiam, surculorum didicerunt vires, et similium quae per-
mutant qualitates humanorum corporum . . . Hoc testatur ille vir Hippocrates
qui fuit hoc de coelo sublimatus vir Aesculapius, quibus nemo ventilatur ma-

In the novella the cells have been deformed into apothecary shops; the friars have reverted to empty incantatory formulas while they simulate administering to, and bringing back from the dead, bodies which, in reality, are perfectly sound. Finally, far from being physicians of the soul, the friars have turned into cosmeticians and all spiritual duties are openly breached. If medicine is a forgotten and betrayed art, equally betrayed is the art of rhetoric. There is no doubt that Friar Rinaldo, with his unreal transformations, deceitful appearances and cultivation of externals (such as the work of dressmakers and cosmeticians) is the embodiment of the rhetorician. In a sense, Elissa's apostrophe, with its focus on deception, is the means of heightening the vulgarity of the friar's dissemblance. Nonetheless, he comes forth as a rhetorician who pretends to have the magic art to cast spells, who knows the art of ". . . fare delle canzoni e de' sonetti e delle ballate e a cantare, e tutto pieno d'altre cose a queste simili" (Composing songs and sonnets and ballads, singing, and many other similar things, p. 600).

By placing the friar at the imaginative crossroads between medicine and rhetoric, Boccaccio seems to allude to the Platonic alliance between the two *technes*, which take, as shown in chapter 1, as the object of their concern, respectively, the care of the body and of the soul, and of which dressmaking and cosmesis are spurious counterfeits. The two arts are now tools for the body's pleasure and of the art of gratifying that pleasure. More specifically, Rinaldo's rhetoric has the power, because of its simulated logic, to seduce the lady. The links between sexuality and rhetorical manipulations, it might be added, cannot startle us, for it is clear that Boccaccio is reviving, and giving a concrete cast to, the commonplace, spelled out, for instance, in Dante's *Convivio*, that Venus is both the planet of love and of rhetoric.[26] This connection accounts for

---

jor esser medicus. At supernae medicinae Christus auctor emicat, qui curare sola potest jussione morbidos, et ad vitam de sepulcro revocare mortuos . . . (*Hymnus seu prosa de Sancto Pantaleone, PL* 141, col. 341).

[26] *Convivio*, eds. G. Busnelli and G. Vandelli, 2nd ed. A. E. Quaglio (Florence: Le Monnier, 1964), II, xiii, 13–14: "E lo cielo di Venere si può com-

the insight, which is central to the stories of the seventh day, that disguise is the essence of love, and that the instinctive bodily desires are caught in a play of equivocations which mask concerns such as power, violence and authority.

These comical equivocations, which are the result of either deliberate or chance manipulation of the physical signs surrounding the experiences of the various characters, point to a condition whereby anything can be taken for anything else in a dizzying freeplay of the imagination. The metaphors of play and rhetoric, as has been argued in the foregoing pages of this chapter, dramatize this precariousness of the symbolic order. The potential boundary for this sort of radical symbolic confusion is madness, but Boccaccio shies away from it. In the novella of Madonna Isabella (VII, 6), madness makes an appearance, but it is a strategy of simulation. This is a story of a woman who is visited in close succession by two lovers and they are all surprised by the unexpected return of her husband. It is by feigning madness that one of the visitors, Ser Lambertuccio, with a dagger in his hand, runs forth from the house, and the husband can be safely duped. This simulation of madness, like magic, enchantment, drunkenness, jealousy and chance are all metaphoric variations of the insight that the world of sense is always on the verge of sliding into non-sense. Comedy is the hinge of these two intimately related possibilities.

The storytellers, with their firm reasonableness and intelligence, seem to know the boundaries between facts and fictions, truth and simulation, and the next chapter will probe further this issue. It must be said, however, that as they construct an imaginative world at the edge of facts and as they tell tales, as they do on this seventh day, which explicitly focus on

parare a la Rettorica per due proprietadi: l'una si è la chiarezza del suo aspetto, che è soavissima a vedere più che altra stella; l'altra si è la sua apparenza, or da mane or da sera. E queste due proprietadi sono ne la Rettorica." In this connection one should mention the historical material which also concerns Boccaccio provided by C. Vasoli, *La dialettica e la retorica dell'Umanesimo* (Milan: Feltrinelli, 1968), pp. 12ff. See also G. Sinicropi, "Il segno linguistico nel *Decameron,*" *Studi sul Boccaccio,* 9 (1975–76), pp. 169–224.

the split between words and deeds, the storytellers dramatize for themselves the predicament in which their characters often find themselves.[27] When the seven women go to the Valley of the Ladies, for instance, for a swim and then return to tell the young men, who had been busy playing a game of dice, Dioneo remarks, "E come? . . . cominciate voi prima a far de' fatti che a dir delle parole?" (What? . . . do you begin by putting the facts before the words? p. 580). Dioneo, as his question implies, perceives that he, the trickster, has been tricked.

More to the point, by the end of the seventh day, Dioneo shifts his own ground: to while away the time to their delight until the hour of supper, some members of the company wade in the waters of the lake, others roam off among the trees. Dioneo and Fiammetta sing a love duet about Palamon and Arcite. The detail, seemingly offhand, is not gratuitous. Through the detail, the trivial images of food, pulled teeth, spit, worms, sexual intercourse, laughter, etc.—the wares of low comedy and of the seventh day—are abandoned in favor of the recollection of Boccaccio's own epic story, the *Teseida*. The allusion marks Dioneo's reversal of the story he has just told, the story of two friends, Tingoccio and Meuccio, who dialogue across the barrier of death, while the *Teseida* tells of a friendship betrayed by love. It also tells of a love which, as it uses war as one of its strategies, is as deep as its imagination can make it. The reversal, finally, also shows that for Boccaccio the trivial and comic elements of literature belong in the same figurative space as high literature, that the rhetorical hierarchy of high and low styles and genres is illusory, for they all provide versions of the same simulations. It may well be that variation is the point of the seventh day and its stories, which endlessly repeat each other and which also differ from each other. It is by varying from each other that they all converge on the same insight that the comic truth of love is at one with its betrayal.

[27] On the representation of the Valley of the Ladies, see Marshall Brown, "In the Valley of the Ladies," *Italian Quarterly*, 18 (1979), pp. 33–52. See also Thomas C. Stillinger, "The Language of Gardens: Boccaccio's *Valle delle Donne*," *Traditio*, 39 (1983), pp. 301–321.

GAMES OF LAUGHTER

The fifth novella of the eighth day features Maso del Saggio who goes to the local law court in the belief that a friend he is looking for may be idling his hours away watching the lawyers' performances and squabbles. As soon as Maso catches a glimpse of the judge who appears "più tosto un magnano che altro a vedere" (more like a coppersmith than anything else, p. 698), he abandons the search for his friend and decides to play a trick on the judge.[1] He feigns a complaint against an imaginary thief and vociferously pleads his case in order to fix upon himself the general attention. In the meantime, an accomplice of his who has secretly crawled beneath the bench where the judge sits, pulls his pants off.

By these simple touches Boccaccio has drawn the classic pattern of the *beffa*—literally a joke, a comic situation—to which we shall repeatedly return. The foolish magistrate, like all fools in the *Decameron*, is mercilessly flouted by the trickster, and by the mockery the very principle of inviolability of the law is subverted.[2] But what on the surface may seem to be merely a somewhat anarchic pleasure of undermining pretenses, of literally divesting the figurehead of his semblance of authority, hides important implications for some comic motifs in the *Decameron*. The oblique target of the *beffa* is the notion that there can ever be a detached perspective snugly sheltering the judge: Maso's trick actually shatters that distance

---

[1] This tale of "giudici e notari" (p. 698) logically belongs to the discussion of the theme of law which is taken up in the next chapter. Here I choose to emphasize the satire of the profession.

[2] For an important perspective on the trickster, cf. Karl Kereny's introduction to Paul Radin, *The Trickster* (London: Routledge and Kegan Paul, 1956).

and, through the resulting inversion, the man who sits ostensibly outside the events to judge them is turned into a principal while the spectators take his place. The comical shifts of focus are constant in the *beffa*, and because of them any fresh attempt on the part of the critic to fix the comedy of the *Decameron* with stable definitions may turn out to be a hazard, a way of falling into the author's unconscionable trap and being caught, like the judge, in the spirals of laughter.

But critics have traditionally practiced a calculated prudence when engaged in a definition of Boccaccio's laughter. They have generally eluded the problem or, what amounts to the same thing, have reduced the comical sense of the *Decameron* to a caricature of the social order. Auerbach, to mention a critic who has most powerfully probed the ideological subversiveness of this text, echoes De Sanctis' detached Hegelian stance in his view of Boccaccio's "light entertainment" as the radical perspective from which he is enabled to dismantle the moral relics of medieval Christianity.[3]

Auerbach's critical statement is certainly not wrong; if anything, it is partial or, more precisely, evasive. The evasiveness may be the proper response to the problem of laughter, which, according to an age-old commonplace, eludes all definitions. In any discussion on laughter, the obvious point of reference is tragedy, and it, by comparison, seems all too accountable. We acknowledge rather clearly, for instance, the grief and terror which shape the tragic vision, or at least accept their mystery as the inevitable ingredient of a dangerously alien world. But laughter, for all our familiarity with it, remains impenetrable, and as soon as we ask the question "why do we laugh," we reach a deadlock.

De Sanctis, to be sure, knows why we do not laugh with the *Decameron*. To him, the *Decameron* represents "un mondo della commedia (cui) manca quell'altro sentimento del comico che nelle sue forme umanistiche e capricciose gli darà l'Ariosto."[4]

---

[3] Erich Auerbach, *Mimesis: The Representation of Reality in Western Literature*, trans. Willard R. Trask (New York: Anchor Books, 1957), pp. 197–203.

[4] Francesco De Sanctis, *Storia della letteratura italiana*, ed. Niccoló Gallo (Turin: Einaudi, 1958), I, p. 383.

Its precise meaning notwithstanding, De Sanctis' insight is capital for it captures, as we plan to show, Boccaccio's singular impasse. The *Decameron* is a book of consolation for impending death; but it is also an elegy for comedy and a systematic retrenching into the production of games, *beffe*, which might be called emblematic of the loss if the emblem were not in itself a problem for Boccaccio.

Maso's trick on the judge seems to originate spontaneously and erupt unpremeditated into the ordinary business of life, transforming its texture into a playground, a theatrical space where Maso impersonates both the role of the defendant and the lawyer's cavils. By so doing, he brings into the open the inherent theatricality of the situation, in which a crowd was already idly watching the debates and the judge was as deceptive as the thieves whose cases he tried.[5] In effect, Maso's own trick (and the implication of this statement will be evident later on) is a weapon in that it appropriates the spectacle; more cogently to our concern, it discloses the mimetic quality of the text. Mimesis is conventionally seen as the rational, Aristotelean principle of imitating the fragmentation of reality. This traditional definition is encompassed, in a fundamental way, within a view of mimesis as impersonation—the actor's specific craft, the deceptive emblem of the play which sustains the world of the *Decameron*.

It is through this shifty metaphor that Boccaccio persistently and obliquely raises the question "why do we laugh" every time the *brigata* laughs at each funny story. For there is a sense in which the *brigata*'s laughter is willed just as the choice of the comical perspective in the *Decameron* is deliberate. The general Introduction to the tales bears an unmistakable tragic focus: the city of Florence is infected by the plague; laws and familial bonds are shattered; medical science cannot purge the city of its evil. No sooner, however, has Boccaccio conjured

---

[5] "E come spesso avviene che, bene che i cittadini non abbiano a fare cosa del mondo a Palagio, pur talvolta vi vanno, avvenne che Maso del Saggio una mattina, cercando d'un suo amico, v'andò; e venutogli guardato là dove questo messer Nicola sedeva, parendogli che fosse un nuovo uccellone, tutto il venne considerando" (*Decameron*, pp. 698–699).

this tragic horror than he turns his back to it. The catharsis can occur by moving to a *locus amoenus*, the playground where the burdens of life are lifted by the *brigata*'s indulgence in dances, games and storytelling. Here the young people even tell tragic stories which possibly betray the symbolic hold that death has over their imagination and suggest that laughter is flanked by a fear of death. How the thought of death and comedy will encroach upon each other's borders remains to be seen. The *brigata*, nonetheless, seems untroubled by darker visions and its somber stories, untypical of the mood of the *Decameron*, are part and parcel of the world of play.

The company's play cannot be dismissed a priori as a simple experience of non-sense: it aspires, rather, to be a utopia, a totally inverted image of the chaotic world left behind. And ostensibly, by moving to a marginal rest spot, the company constructs a realm of fantasy which suspends the purposive structure of ordinary life and envelopes it within the form of the ritual.[6] The conclusion to the seventh day and the brief introduction to the eighth—a day on which this chapter largely focuses—emphasizes this point.

The *brigata*, we are told, resumes storytelling on a Sunday after observing a suspension of two days in memory of Christ's death. As Boccaccio specifies the Sunday, he seems to stress the sense of time off, the holy-day spirit which shapes

---

[6] This strategy has been explored earlier in chaps. 1 and 2, where the power, paradoxically, of the *marginal* perspective is studied. There are two general works that I would like to recall for the benefit of the reader as cogent to the point I am making. One is by Johan Huizinga, *Homo Ludens: A Study of the Play Element in Culture* (London: Routledge and Kegan Paul, 1949). For a philosophical approach to the question of play, see Eugen Fink, *Spiel als Weltsymbol* (Stuttgard: W. Kohlhammer, 1960). For additional bibliography, see above Introduction, n. 2. I would also like to point out a passage from *The Art of Courtly Love* on the sense of "time off" (bk. vi, and dialogue): "But where can one find greater effrontery than in a man who for the space of a whole week devotes all his efforts to the various gains of business and then on the seventh day, his day of rest, tries to enjoy the gifts of love and to dishonor Love's commands and confound the distinctions of classes established among men of old?" (trans. Parry, p. 46). In Boccaccio's text there is an inversion of the situation envisaged by the woman in the dialogue with the man of the middle class.

the *Decameron*. The juxtaposition of religious ritual and storytelling, however, deserves a special comment. It may be taken to be a sign of Boccaccio's confused morality, the surd coherence of piety and worldliness. But in their contiguity the two experiences stand in an ironic self-reflection: as each is cut loose from the other, the ritual purification is emptied of any content, and storytelling, in turn, is drawn within the boundaries of pure ritual. Yet the characters' own sense of utopia, of the imagination entirely self-enclosed, is not very sure of itself. As they tell stories of *beffe*, symbolically sitting by the fountain, they are, in effect, engaged in an act of self-reflexiveness in which their desire for an imaginative utopia is asserted and its possibility is questioned. It is as if by the *beffe*, to anticipate, they localize their imagination and in the process utopia is lost.

Fundamental to the motif of the *beffa*, a prank by which a schemer is unmasked and repaid in kind, is a paradigm of exchange, the quid pro quo; and as such it mimes both the law of the market, a recurrent motif in the *Decameron*, and the narrative structure of the text. Stories are recalled and exchanged by the *brigata* and this circuit of exchange simultaneously depends on, and constitutes the bond of, community between narrators and listeners.

The law of exchange and its mobile structure is the explicit theme of the *beffa* in the first story of the eighth day. Gulfardo, a German mercenary soldier, falls in love with Ambrogia, a merchant's wife, and asks her to be "del suo amore cortese" (gracious to his love, p. 671). Ambrogia will comply with his request on two conditions, first that secrecy, a basic requirement of the courtly love transparently evoked in the story, be maintained; secondly that he pay her two hundred florins. If the point of departure of the novella is the metaphoric exchange, conventional in medieval love literature, from *ars bellandi to ars amandi*, the metaphoric movement is undermined by the very emblem of exchange, money.[7]

Ambrogia's demand transgresses the code of "courtly" love: what for Gulfardo is a purely gratuitous giving is to her

----

[7] The *topos* of love and war, commonly used by Petrarch, for instance,

a transaction, an occasion of barter. Deeply humiliated by her commerce (meretricious love can find no place in Andreas Capellanus' system), Gulfardo turns his love to hatred and contrives his *beffa*.[8] He borrows the two hundred florins from her husband, gives it to her but later tells her husband that, having had no need of the money, he handed it back to Ambrogia.

From the point of view of Neifile, the storyteller, Gulfardo's *beffa* is an expedient of retributive justice, the just counterpart for Ambrogia's greed.[9] Her demand, it would seem, violates the free exchange of love, draws it within the law of the marketplace, while the *beffa* punishes her wrongdoing. Neifile's pattern, however, is at odds with a more fundamental motif of the novella. What Gulfardo reacts against is precisely a threat to his very identity. The price which has been fixed gives a fixed value to him and to his desire; more importantly as Ambrogia asks for money she turns into a mercenary, deals with him on his own terms. The *beffa* Gulfardo devises is the weapon by which he establishes a difference: he casts Ambrogia as a worthless item and himself as her intellectual superior.[10]

---

among others, is studied by Denis de Rougemont, *Love in the Western World*, trans. Montgomery Belgion (Greenwich, Conn.: Fawcett Publications, 1966), pp. 257–286.

[8] The question has been examined earlier in chapter 3. I shall add here the passage by Andreas Capellanus, *The Art of Courtly Love* (bk. 1, chap. 9): "Now let us see whether real love can be got with money or any other gift. Real love comes only from the affection of the heart and is granted out of pure grace and genuine liberality, and this most precious gift of love cannot be paid for at any set price or be cheapened by a matter of money. If any woman is so possessed with a feeling of avarice as to give herself to a lover for the sake of pay, let no one consider her a lover, but rather a counterfeiter of love, who ought to join those shameful women in the brothel. Indeed the wantonness of such women is more polluted than the passion of harlots who play their trade openly, for they do what one expects them to, and they deceive no one since their intentions are perfectly obvious" (trans. Parry, p. 144). See also bk. 1, chap. 12 (Parry, p. 150) for a further dismissal of the "love of prostitutes."

[9] "Avvegna che, chi volesse più propriamente parlare, quello che io dir debbo *non si direbbe beffa anzi si direbbe merito*: . . ." (*Decameron*, p. 670; italics mine).

[10] A recent statement on comedy in terms of identity and difference has been

There are, thus, two perspectives on the *beffa*: on the one hand, the storyteller assigns to it a value of retributive justice against the law of the market which has disrupted the fairyland of courtly love. On the other hand, Gulfardo sees in it the means by which a hierarchy of intelligence is asserted. The double perspective designates the interest, the movement of appropriation which is inherent to the *beffa*. The very notion of free entertainment that underlies the *brigata*'s escape is undercut by the investment that each character and the storyteller have at stake and because of this the *beffa* enters the world of commerce.

This motif carries thematic weight throughout the *Decameron*, where money lenders and crafty merchants are the characters that to some extent eclipse the medieval romances of lovers and heroes. The merchants are the true tricksters who manipulate events and are in full possession of rationality. Critics, unsurprisingly, have always noted how keenly Boccaccio looks into men's affairs and their ability to deal with the dangers that lurk behind all transactions.[11] It would be easy to remark that the critics, flattered in their own sense of intellectual self-importance, are like merchants fixing a value on their own superior wisdom. Yet, by the *beffa* the world of rationality and self-possession, ostensibly celebrated in the *Decameron*, is subjected to a fierce critique and Boccaccio has a way of insinuating that the fool, dispossessed of value, is always somehow right. We must turn to the story of Calandrino's quest for the heliotrope (VIII, 3) in order to explore this structure.

The primary trait of Calandrino is to be forever the same, unchanged by his experiences and, like the masks of the *commedia dell'arte*, eminently predictable.[12] By the quest of the he-

---

provided by René Girard, "Perilous Balance: A Comic Hypothesis," *Modern Language Notes*, 87 (1972), pp. 811–826. See also C. L. Barber, *Shakespeare's Festive Comedy* (Princeton: Princeton University Press, 1959).

[11] Vittore Branca, *Boccaccio medievale* (Florence: Sansoni, 1956), pp. 71–99. See also Guido Pugliese, "*Decameron*, II, 3: un caso di contingenza causale," *Esperienze letterarie* 5 (1980), 4, pp. 29–41.

[12] Ireneo Sanesi, *La Commedia* (Milan: Vallardi, 1935), II, pp. 1–109. For an

liotrope, he seeks an absolute autonomy and pursues his own fantasy to become transcendent and invisible, and gain the invulnerable standpoint from which he can govern and control the world. His steady reappearance as a fool in the *Decameron*, however, shows that he is doomed to be visible and that his desire is shattered. His recurrence, no doubt, is the core of the comical: as the two painters Bruno and Buffalmacco endlessly contrive plots by which Calandrino is forced into his space of self identity, we know that nothing irrevocable happens to him. At the same time, Bruno's and Buffalmacco's repeated *beffe* at his expense bespeak the pleasure inherent in the impulse to repeat: the *beffa* is the weapon to master even if it may betray the masters' insecurity in the presence of Calandrino's foolishness.

For he is very much a fool: not the fool in motley who cloaks himself in simulated inferiority to best ridicule his masters, the clown such as those one finds on the Elizabethan stage. Calandrino's foolishness is banal and his banality is profoundly disturbing. For in the measure in which he is a fool, he asserts the value of the imagination and at the same time sanctions its inevitable failure to create vital resemblances.

As the novella opens, Calandrino—himself a painter—is looking at the paintings and *bas-relief* of the tabernacle which has recently been erected above the high altar in the church of San Giovanni. While he is enthralled by the artifice, Maso contrives a trick against him. He pretends to confide to a friend, loudly enough so that Calandrino may hear, the secret of the land of Cockayne, the place where vines are tied with sausages and mountains are made of Parmesan cheese.[13] Calandrino, the maker of images to which he is provisionally bound, is quickly ensnared by the tale and takes Maso at his word. But he is not a Don Quixote who will wander over the vastness of the world to test and find the reality of his fiction. The horn of

updating of the questions of the *commedia dell'arte*, see also Roberto Tessari, *La Commedia dell'arte nel seicento* (Florence: Olschki, 1969).

[13] A history of this utopian motif from antiquity down is provided by Arthur O. Lovejoy and George Boas, *Primitivism and Related Ideas in Antiquity* (New York: Octagon Books, 1973).

plenty Maso evokes is distant and out of reach, and Calandrino will settle on the heliotrope, the fabulous stone which, according to the lapidaries, gives the bearer invisibility and which he thinks he can find along the banks of the Mugnone river.[14] The heliotrope, as the wise Maso of course knows, does not exist: it is only a name, literally the "utopian" center of gravity of the novella and around this absence, this word without content, the vault of the story is built.

It could be argued that in the measure in which Calandrino believes he can find the magic stone along the local river, the myth of utopia has already collapsed. Yet the implied contraction of his vision also suggests that Calandrino lives in a world of confused unreality where all that is familiar is at the same time strange, the near-at-hand mysterious. He is, after all, a foreigner displaced in Florence, and to him Florence is the realm of the marvelous where the impossible quest can occur.

The quest marks both a logical extension and a radical departure from the world of painting. If painting is the fictional space of semblances, the quester seeks reality and sheer invisibility.[15] But there is a special dramatic force in Boccaccio's detail at the beginning of the story where Calandrino is gazing at the "dipinture e gl'intagli del tabernacolo" (the paintings and carvings of the tabernacle, p. 682). In the liturgy of the Church the tabernacle is God's dwelling, the place where the invisible Godhead is given a sacramental visibility. In patristic exegesis, more cogently, the tabernacle is uniformly glossed as "aedificatio terrenae felicitatis" because it symbolizes the promise of the messianic millennium.[16] At the same time, the tabernacle

---

[14] The specific virtue of the heliotrope is described by Marbodus, *Liber de gemmis*, PL 171, col. 1757; Pliny, *Natural History*, x, xxxvii, p. 165. Cf. also *Inferno* xxiv, 93.

[15] The link between appearance and identity is featured in vi, 5. See the discussion of it in chapter 8 below, when Giotto figures.

[16] The definition is given by Garnerius de S. Victore, *Gregorianum*, PL 193, col. 396. It is also echoed in *Allegoriae in universam sacram scripturam*, PL 112, col. 1062. The work, which Migne attributed to Rabanus Maurus, is now doubtfully attributed to Garner of Rochefort or Adam Scotus. Cf. also Adam Scotus, *De tripartito tabernaculo*, PL 198, col. 746. The biblical place where the tabernacle is alluded to as a prefiguration of the paradisiac order on earth is

is the typological sign of the transfiguration, the event of the manifestation of the Messiah and the prophecy that like Moses and Christ on Mount Tabor the faithful will experience the glory of divinity and attain to the knowledge of the invisible realm.[17]

From one point of view, Calandrino's adventure is a brilliant parody of the traditional spiritual associations with which the emblem of the tabernacle is burdened. The promise of the millennium is inverted into the quest for earthly pleasures; the mystery of the transfiguration is comically turned into a mad desire to be invisible so that he can rob the banks of their riches. But above and beyond these parodic reversals of the biblical and Christian motif, something very serious takes place. Calandrino, in effect, attempts to charge with an immediate reality both the world of symbolic constructs and Maso's fable. Whatever is just a pure image is valueless to him. The myth of formal, esthetic self-enclosure, in which even the *Decameron* ostensibly partakes, is dismissed by Calandrino's sublime artlessness. And as he tries to seduce both Bruno and Buffalmacco into joining him in his search for the heliotrope, he trivializes the import of their paintings:

"Compagni, quando voi vogliate credermi, noi possiamo divenire i più ricchi uomini di Firenze: per ciò che io ho inteso da uomo degno di fede che in Mugnone si truova una pietra, la quale chi la porta sopra non è veduto da niuna altra persona; . . . Noi la troverem per certo, per ciò che io la conosco; e trovata che noi l'avremo, che avrem noi a far altro se non . . . andare alle tavole

---

Isaiah 32:18 and Haymo's brilliant gloss on the verse in Isaiah, *PL* 116, col. 876. The motif of the feast of the tabernacles is studied with great care by Jean Danielou, *Bible et liturgie* (Paris: Les Editions du Cerf, 1958), pp. 449–469.

[17] The scene of the Transfiguration is described by Matthew 17:1; Mark 9:2; Luke 9:28. The typological link between the feast of the tabernacles and the Transfiguration is established by the apostle Peter's proposal to build the tents for Moses and Eliajah. 2 Peter, 1:18, puts forward the view of the Transfiguration as the prophetic sign of the Parousia. Cf. also Origines, *Homelies sur l'Exode*, trans. P. Fortier, intr. and notes H. De Lubac (Paris: Editions du Cerf, 1947), sec. XII, pp. 244–255. Noteworthy are the documented remarks by Danielou, *Bible et liturgie*, pp. 457–461 especially.

de' cambiatori, le quali sapete che stanno sempre cariche di grossi
e di fiorini, e torcene quanti noi ne vorremo? Niuno ci vedrà; e
così potremo arricchire subitamente, senza avere tutto dí a
schiccherare le mura a modo che fa la lumaca"

Believe me, friends, we can become the richest men in
Florence, for I have heard from a man who is to be believed that along the Mugnone there is a certain kind of
stone, and when you carry it you become invisible; . . .
We'll find it without a doubt, because I know what it
looks like; and once we have found it, all we have to do is
. . . go to the money changers, whose counters, as you
know, are always loaded with groats and florins, and help
ourselves to as much as we want. No one will see us; and
so we'll be able to get rich quick, without having to
whiten walls all the time like a lot of snails.   (p. 684)

It is at this point that the *beffa* reaches its climax. On a Sunday before sunrise, Bruno and Buffalmacco pretend to join
him on his venture but secretly engineer a spectacle whereby
the city of Florence is a stage on which Calandrino, believing
himself unseen, is the visible occasion for general laughter.
Calandrino never reaches the object of his search for the point
where the word and its reality coincide is nonexistent, truly
utopian. Nevertheless, the illusion that he has found the stone
is to him an exhilarating experience: he is provisionally freed
from the tyranny of the others' gaze, unaware that his illusion
of being autonomous, to put it in the terms of the profound
insight of the *commedia dell'arte*, masks the fact that he is more
than ever an automaton.

Nor does the final fall from his fantasy, when on reaching
home he is seen by his wife, bring any sobering self-awareness
to him. In the best misogynistic tradition, he attributes the loss
of the stone's virtue to his wife and fiercely beats her.[18] This is

---

[18] The myth of the woman as the devil ("questo diavolo di questa femina
maladetta mi si parò dinanzi e ebbemi veduto, per ciò che, come voi sapete, le
femine fanno perder la vertù a ogni cosa: . . . *Decameron*, VIII, 3, p. 690) echoes
a solid patristic tradition about the woman as Eve, on account of whom man,
like Calandrino in the novella, loses Paradise. Cf. Tertullian: "Tu es diaboli

possibly for Boccaccio a way of saying that there is no deception which is ever quite as powerful as self-deception: more
cogently, this is his expedient for releasing Bruno's and Buffalmacco's hoax into the domain of the inessential.

For their trick is dwarfed by Calandrino. Ostensibly, they
occupy a world of sense, of orderly and meaningful patterns.
They are makers of images who can tell fiction from reality
and reason from unreason, and who know that the heliotrope
is an arbitrary sign without any reference outside of itself. Calandrino, by contrast, is involved in a quest over the trails of
the imagination. This imagination is not to be understood as
the esthetic faculty that duplicates the world or funnels its experiences into a stable picture. It marks, rather, a purely visionary venture which blurs the line of separation between illusion and reality.[19] On Sunday, the *dies solis*, he seeks the
heliotrope, literally the conjunction with the sun.[20]

---

ianua, . . . tu es quae suasisti . . . tu imaginem dei, hominem Adam, facile elisisti." (*Du cultu feminarum*, I, I, in *Corpus Christianorum, Series Latina*,
LXX, pp. 59–60). See also Jerome, *Adversus Iovinianum*, PL 23, cols. 211–338.
For a general sketch of the tradition, see F. L. Utley, *The Crooked Rib* (Colum-
bus: Ohio State University Press, 1944). See also Katharine M. Rogers, *The
Troublesome Helpmate: A History of Misogyny in Literature* (Seattle: University
of Washington Press, 1966).

[19] This notion of the imagination can be found in Dante's *Purgatorio* XVII,
13ff. In this central canto of the *Divine Comedy*, Dante suggests how the imaginative faculty, far from duplicating the world of reality or originating from
the perception of outside events, *steals* us away from the experience of familiar
reality. Cf. the still important survey by M. W. Bundy, *The Theory of the
Imagination in Classical and Medieval Thought*, University of Illinois Studies in
Language and Literature, no. 12, 2–3 (Urbana: University of Illinois Press,
1927). A valuable reading of this novella, even if in terms entirely different
from mine, has been given by Luigi Russo, *Letture critiche del Decameron* (Bari:
Laterza, 1977), pp. 245–274; Mario Baratto, *Realtà e stile nel Decameron* (Vicenza: Pozza, 1970), pp. 309–318. See also the remarks by Marga Cottino-
Jones, "Magic and Superstition in Boccaccio's *Decameron*," *Italian Quarterly*,
18 (1975), pp. 5–32; and by Millicent Joy Marcus, *An Allegory of Form* (Saratoga, Calif.: Anma Libri, 1979), pp. 79–92.

[20] It may be of interest to remark that Calandrino's quest takes place on a
Sunday and that the story is told on the eighth day, also a Sunday, as if Boccaccio were obliquely hinting that Calandrino's hope for a utopia is the specular and distorted reflection of the storytellers' *locus amoenus*. The motif of

This impossible hope depends on his act of faith that objects must exist because words for them exist and this, in a real sense, is his folly to which the text twice has oblique but certain allusions. The first time, when the two friends feign not to see Calandrino, Buffalmacco says: "Chi sarebbe stato sì *stolto* che avesse creduto che in Mugnone si dovesse trovare una così virtuosa pietra, altri che noi?" (Who in his right mind, other than we, would ever have believed all that talk about finding such a powerful stone along the Mugnone? p. 687). The second time madness is Calandrino's direct attribute: as he is seen by his wife, "*niquitoso* corse verso la moglie, e presala per le treccie la si gittò a piedi" (Like a madman he rushed toward his wife and catching her by the tresses hurled her to the ground, p. 688). As a fool and madman, he lives in a world of pure exchange in the sense that everything can be mistaken for everything else, and a word, literally nothing, can give access to the whole world.[21] By mistaking what are only words for reality, Calandrino ultimately obliterates the value of words. Asked by Buffalmacco the name of the stone they would be looking for, he simply replies: "Che abbiam noi a far del nome, poi che sappiamo la vertù? A me parrebbe che noi andassomo a cercare senza più" (What do we care about the name, when we know its power? I think we should go looking for it without wasting any more time, p. 685).

Calandrino's foolishness is his chief liability but also his strongest asset. As he is visible, he opens our eyes to a world which is too small, to a vision which is too narrow; and his story is a veritable romance of which he is the mad hero. He travels the distance that separates words from things, trying to fill that gap and knowing that the value of fictions does not lie

---

Sunday as the *dies solis* and as the typological eighth day (the day of the spiritual recreation of which Boccaccio gives its frivolous counterpart) is explored by Danielou, *Bible et liturgie*, pp. 328–387. Cf. also Jean Danielou, "La Typologie millenariste de la semaine dans le Christianisme primitive," *Vigiliae Christianae*, 2 (1948), pp. 1–16.

[21] For this notion of foolishness and madness see Michel Foucault, *Histoire de la folie* (Paris: Librairie Plon, 1961).

in their self-enclosures; as such, he is the boundary line within which Bruno and Buffalmacco are contained. In a way, even Boccaccio himself can be said to be contained within Calandrino's imaginative powers, in the same manner in which, say, Cervantes is contained by Don Quixote. In both cases the writer is confined to elaborate parables about characters who are not bound by any laws of logic or reality: in contrast to the freedom of their own characters, these writers will at best take refuge in the safety of ironic distance or what could be called a mixture of fascination and skepticism toward the dreams of the characters. In this sense, Calandrino is something of a threat to the ironies of the artists who give up, a priori as it were, the possibility of finding utopia and accept its irrevocable absence within the world.

Calandrino's wondrous imagination surfaces also in the third story of the ninth day. The narrative focuses once again on Bruno's and Buffalmacco's extraordinary invention that Calandrino is pregnant so that Calandrino, in order to get well without giving birth, will have to make available some of the money he had just inherited. With the help of Master Simon, the trick works out fine. And yet, while we can't but admire the two painters' craftiness, we are equally struck by Calandrino's belief that he can experience the marvelous adventure of crossing the boundaries of natural difference, that biology itself is not a fixed system. Calandrino's stupidity makes everybody roar with laughter, but stupidity is an *imaginative* value against which the tricksters' intelligent, ironic plans unavoidably stumble. What is, then, involved in our laughter either in this story or in the one about the heliotrope?

For the storytellers join Bruno and Buffalmacco and the Florentine public in laughing at Calandrino. But as they laugh with "gran piacere" (p. 691), they betray their uneasiness over their own utopian quest, over their belief that by moving to the *locus amoenus* they have found the hiding place from the convulsion of the times. Their laughter seems to draw attention to the fact that their own utopia—far from being a self-enclosed totality—is a play, a put-on like Bruno's and Buffalmacco's tricks; and for all their frivolity, the games of laughter are a necessary retrenching from madness.

Madness, to be sure, constantly menaces the stability of the world in the *Decameron*. Witness, for instance, the story of Cimone (v, 1). Cast as an epyllion, the tale focuses on Cimone's redemption from beast (the significance given his name by Boccaccio) to man through the love for Ifigenia. Cimone sees Ifigenia asleep—discovers, that is to say, his own spiritual lethargy—and inflamed by love for her wakes up to virtue. The stilnovistic dream that love ennobles man is flagrantly parodied as Cimone's newly acquired virtue turns into a veritable madness of love. The narrative (one is reminded of *Othello*) takes place in Cyprus, the island of the mad Venus, and Cimone's love succeeds only after generating mighty wars.[22] This story of madness is controlled by the frame of order, is part of the experience of storytelling; yet, as an object of persistent fascination, madness is the border line of fiction, the temptation that threatens to erode the edifice of order and occasions, just as Calandrino does to Bruno and Buffalmacco, the world of representation.

We must turn to another novella (VIII, 9) where Bruno and Buffalmacco once again come forth as the zany fabricators of the *beffa* in order to probe further the question of the value of the trick. The joke this time is contrived against a foolish physician, Master Simon, with the ostensible purpose of unmasking his pretenses of learning: from the outset, in fact, Simon is introduced as dressed in scarlet robes and "con un gran batalo, dottor di medicine, secondo che egli medesimo diceva" (with a fine-looking hood, and calling himself doctor of medicine, p. 744).

The carefree life of both Bruno and Buffalmacco arouses his curiosity and he decides to befriend them to find out the reason for their merry lives. Bruno pretends to share with him an imaginary secret and weaves the fiction that they are members of a society founded by the necromancer Michael Scott which

---

[22] For this mythographic motif, see Dante, *Paradiso*, VIII, 1–9.

assembles twice a month and by magic practices enjoys the pleasures of banquets, music, and midnight revels.

Simon, like Calandrino earlier, is unable to decipher the transparent lie and is wistfully seduced by it. He believes that the world of appearances pulsates with occult life, that a mythic bond exists between appearances and the beyond. Eager to experience those imaginary pleasures, he begs to join what Bruno defines as a "paradiso a vedere" (paradise itself, p. 748), so that he might enjoy the most beautiful woman in the world.[23] In this sense, the story comically conjures the motif of the Saturnalia, the golden age of revelry where restraints are abolished and one's fantasies are realized.[24] When finally the night appointed for the meeting arrives, Simon is instructed to wear his most sumptuous robe and go to the cemetery of Santa Maria Novella. Of course, neither otherworldly prodigies nor erotic fulfillments take place.

The tale actually turns into a masque, a literal carnival which, as its etymology suggests, is the ironic counterpoint of the erotic expectations.[25] While Simon waits in fear, Buffalmacco disguised as a bear and wearing the mask of a devil

[23] The comical role of parasites that Bruno and Buffalmacco play in the story is imaginatively yoked to the role of "corsari," (p. 749), those who steal the property that belongs to others. In this sense the two friends fulfill Calandrino's own desires. More than that, Boccaccio is lining up Calandrino, Bruno and Buffalmacco, and the pirates (for which see II, 10, and the discussion in the next chapter) as figures that disrupt, in fact or in thought, the economic order. Socially they may well be "useless" or outright harmful, but they are *interesting*, in the full sense of the word, from an imaginative viewpoint.

[24] See, for one, Macrobius, *Saturnalia*, ed. Iacobus Willis (Leipzig: Teubner Verlagsgesallschaft, 1970), I, vii, 37ff., p. 34. Cf. also A. Lovejoy and G. Boas, *Primitivism and Related Ideas*, especially pp. 65ff.

[25] Paolo Toschi, *Le origini del teatro italiano* (Turin: Edizioni scientifiche Einaudi, 1955). Toschi focuses on the motif of the carnival and in passing alludes (p. 173) to this story of Boccaccio as a "document" proving the use of demonic masks in the late Middle Ages. Cf. also Mikhail Bakhtin, *Rabelais and His World*, trans. Helen Iswolsky (Cambridge, Mass.: The M.I.T. Press, 1965). The literary connection between representation and masking is explored by Angus Fletcher, *The Transcendental Masque: An Essay on Milton's Comus* (Ithaca: Cornell University Press, 1971), pp. 8–68.

comes to take the physician to share in the delights of the magic paradise but, after a few moments, throws him into a ditch of excrement. Bruno and Buffalmacco are hardly able to contain their laughter at their own trick. The morning after, with their bodies painted to simulate tortures received on account of Simon's cowardice, they visit him to complain for the troubles he has caused them. Fearful of becoming a public laughing stock, the doctor from that day forth pampers the two friends more than ever before.

Simon's fall into the mire marks a symbolic degradation, the manipulation by which he is defined as an inferior to the two tricksters. Above and beyond this apparent pretext, the degradation implies that laughter is linked with a fall from Paradise. But for Boccaccio the fall has no theological focus: Paradise is an illusory misnomer and what is really lost by the fall is Hell.

The novella, I submit, features a deliberate Dantesque design, as if Boccaccio were directly involved in a parody of Dante's Hell. The allusion to Michael Scott is an overt recall of *Inferno* xx, the canto of contorted shades where divination and necromancy are expiated;[26] the ensuing description of the assembly's entertainment, "Costoro adunque servivano i predetti gentili uomini di certi loro innamoramenti e d'altre cosette liberamente; . . . poi . . . preserci di grandi e strette amistà con alcuni, più gentili che non gentili" (These two men freely assisted the above-mentioned nobles in certain love affairs and other little escapades of theirs . . . and afterwards they acquired a good number of intimate friends, without caring whether they were nobles or plebeians, p. 747) is a paraphrase of Iacopo della Lana's commentary on that canto.[27] The painted bodies of Bruno and Buffalmacco, simulating the tor-

[26] "Quell'altro che ne' fianchi è così poco, / Michele Scotto fu, che veramente / de le magiche frode seppe 'l gioco" (*Inferno* xx, 115–117).

[27] Iacopo della Lana's commentary reads: ". . . usando con gentili uomini e cavalieri, e mangiando come si usa tra essi in brigata a casa l'un dell'altro, quando venia la volta di lui d'apparecchiare" (Guido Biagi, *La Divina Commedia nella figurazione artistica e nel secolare commento: Inferno* [Turin: UTET, 1924], p. 507). Cf. Branca's note, *Decameron*, p. 1447.

tures, echo the description of the hypocrites as "gente dipinta" (painted people) in *Inferno* (XXIII, 58). And just as in Dante between the world of the sorcerers in *Inferno* XIX (the canto of *Simon magus*) and the world of the simulators there stands the so-called *commedia dei diavoli*, in Boccaccio's text we find its playful reenactment.

By staging the *commedia dei diavoli*, Dante primarily dramatizes the common medieval conception of Hell as the place of tricks and frauds. At the same time, he implies that laughter has a demonic property and is in touch with the dark powers. Like the Christian apologists, Tertullian, Cyprian and Boccaccio himself in the *Genealogy of the Gods*, Dante sees mimes and spectacles as arts of the devil, distracting man from his heavenward ascent.[28] He even goes further than this: the devils' comedy enacts a steady danger of spiritual degradation of self. Unsurprisingly the pilgrim, at this stage of the poem, is directly threatened by the devils. Commentators have tried to explain the impasse by resorting to raw autobiography, the suspicion that Dante in his own life may have been guilty of barratry.[29] In effect, the world of comedy is seen as black magic, a fradulent game in this area where "Michele Scotto, fu, che veramente / de le magiche frode seppe 'l gioco" (Michael Scott it was, who truly knew the game of magic frauds, *Inferno* XX, 116–117). Dante dismisses this ludic moment because it is an illusory instrument by which the world can be shaped and radically juxtaposes to it his own *Commedia*.[30]

[28] Tertullian, *De spectaculis, CSEL*, XX (pars. I), pp. 1–29; Cyprian, *De spectaculis, PL* 4, cols. 799–788. Boccaccio, *Genealogia deorum gentilium libri*, ed. Vincenzo Romano, 2 vols. (Bari: Laterza, 1951), XIV, 14, p. 724.

[29] This seductive hypothesis, by no means to be entirely discarded, was eloquently put forward by Luigi Pirandello, "Il canto *XXI* dell'*Inferno*," in *Letture Dantesche: Inferno*, ed. Giovanni Getto (Florence: Sansoni, 1955), pp. 395–414.

[30] There is in Dante's *Pardiso* what I call a theology of play, which deploys motifs such as the music of the spheres, the new Jerusalem as both a garden and an amphitheater (*Paradiso* XXX, 108ff.), songs, actors' craft, dance of the stars (which John Freccero, in a different context, has studied, see his "*Paradiso* X: The Dance of the Stars," *Dante Studies*, 86 [1968], pp. 85–111). In *Paradiso*

What for Dante is an experience of moral terror, Boccaccio displaces into sheer buffoonery. Part of the fun, no doubt, lies in the fact that Boccaccio, a serious commentator of *Inferno*, is here involved in a deliberate misreading of it. Historically it will be left to Pico and the Hermetic tradition to reverse altogether Dante's perspective and regain magic as a high wisdom, the imaginative realm of man's autonomy whereby the possibilities of angelic perfection or descent into matter are made available to him.[31]

For Boccaccio, Simon literally falls into matter in what seems to be an overt mockery of spiritual falls. In this context there is a further detail that deserves comment: the front wall of Simon's hospital bears the emblem of Lucifer.[32] By the detail, Boccaccio casts the physician as an ineffectual sorcerer and portrays medicine as a practice of black magic.[33] At the same time he exposes the lunacy in his belief both in the uncanny marvels of the Saturnalia and in mysterious bonds between symbolic representation and hidden essences.

Nor are the tricksters molders of worlds: to fashion themselves is simply a travesty, the wearing of a mask to make fun of, and gain ascendancy over, the gullible Simon. In the *Genealogy of the Gods*, Boccaccio still vindicates the value of the poet as a creature who forges and wields the illusion of new

---

this *theologia ludens*, of Neoplatonic origin, is the point of convergence of theology and esthetics, a question which deserves an ample investigation.

[31] Giovanni Pico della Mirandola, *De hominis dignitate, Heptaplus, De ente et uno e scritti vari*, ed. E. Garin (Florence: Vallecchi, 1942). Cf. E. Garin, *Medioevo e rinascimento* (Bari: Laterza, 1954), pp. 150–191. Particularly cogent is Frances A. Yates, *Giordano Bruno and the Hermetic Tradition* (Chicago: University of Chicago Press, 1964), pp. 44–168. See also D. P. Walker, *Spiritual and Demonic Magic from Ficino to Campanella* (London: Warburg Institute, 1958). The Christian attack on magic was formulated by St. Augustine, among others. Cf. *The City of God*, VIII, 18, 19, 26; IX, 1.

[32] "Egli è troppo gran segreto quello che voi volete sapere, e è cosa da disfarmi e da cacciarmi del mondo, anzi da farmi mettere in bocca del lucifero da San Gallo, se altri il risapesse: . . ." (*Decameron*, p. 746).

[33] Lynn Thorndike, *A History of Magic and Experimental Science*, I (New York: The Macmillan Co., 1923), pp. 566–615. Cf. also A. J. Festugiere, *Hermétisme et mystique païenne* (Paris: Aubier, 1967), pp. 141–180.

worlds. But in this story the imagination, the power by which man is the chameleon, is parodied. Bruno and Buffalmacco are the wizards who conjure the other world, who bring fictions into life and change life into fiction; but the process is contracted into play, a frivolous exercise which has renounced any claim to be vital.

By so doing, Boccaccio silences Dante's tragic sense of laughter in Hell and is far removed from Pico's belief in myth-making through the arcana of magic. In a sense, he purifies the ground, as it were, of the supernatural and valorizes the world of play and *beffe*. The masque is the hub of play and we must look closely at it. For both Bruno and Buffalmacco, the mask is the sign of their superiority, the means of unmasking Simon's own self-deceit. By wearing the mask and simulating tortures they appear, however, as actors. Isidore of Seville gives a definition of the hypocrite which is cogent to our point: hypocrisy, he writes, is the practice of actors who paint themselves in order to deceive.[34] If Simon's appearance is false and hides an essential vacuity, Buffalmacco's impersonation of the devil is a pure fiction, a figure of substitution for nothing. As he wears the mask, he slips into Simon's very world of false appearance; more paradoxically, as he manages to frighten Simon he vindicates his belief that the world of appearance veils occult realities. Not one of them steps out of the bounds of illusion.

The young people of the *brigata*, gratified by the story, laugh at Simon just as they laughed at Calandrino and empathize with the tricksters. We surely understand why the physician is the object of laughter. After all, the introduction to the *Decameron* makes explicit the point that the art of Hippocrates is superfluous, has no restorative power from the threat of death.[35] The masque, which is significantly acted out in the

---

[34] "Hypocrita Graeco sermone in Latino simulator interpretatur . . . Nomen autem hypocritae tractum est ab specie eorum qui in spectaculis contecta facie incedunt, distinguentes vultum caeruleo minioque colore distincta . . ." (Isidore of Seville, *Etym.*, X, H, 118–120.

[35] See chapter 1 on this polemical view of medicine.

cemetery—the place of death—can hardly conquer death and is, in this sense, equally redundant. Yet, it seems to be a necessary alternative to mad visionaries, a style of mediocrity by which the tricksters always gain a superiority and the storytellers find temporary relief from their anxieties.

But can the game really be such a comforting fiction? Can we really make the world our own at the expense of fools or believe that nobody is ever laughing at us? We must turn back to the second day of the *Decameron* to find some possible answers to these questions.

The thematic burden of the day is the world of Fortune, which, in the introduction to the third story, appears as the Intelligence of God, the rational order that subtends and presides over the chaos of the fallen world of change.[36] This view of Fortune as the providential agency governing the economy of the world recalls explicitly, as has often been remarked, Dante's digression in the canto of the avaricious and prodigals. Dante's discourse casts human rationality as a precarious construct, beset on the one hand by the unintelligibility of Pluto, the god of wealth, and on the other by Fortune's providential but inscrutable designs. The sinners who in their lives transgressed the economy of exchange by overvaluing or dissipating common goods now ironically exchange insults and move in a gloomy circle that parodies the perfect circularity of Fortune's wheel. From man's temporal standpoint, Fortune's movement does not follow any discernible plan: man, however, can still conquer Fortune by the exercise of virtue and by the acknowledgment that she reigns over the things of the world and that there is nothing which really belongs to us.[37]

Boccaccio's extensive rephrasing of Dante's view of For-

[36] See chapter 3, n. 9. See also *Inferno* VII, 61–69. Cf. Vincenzo Cioffari, *The Conception of Fortune and Fate in the Works of Dante* (Cambridge, Mass.: Dante Society, 1940). More generally, see Howard R. Patch, *The Goddess Fortuna in Medieval Literature* (Cambridge, Mass.: Harvard University Press, 1927).

[37] "Valorose donne, quanto più si parla de' fatti della fortuna, tanto più, a chi vuole le sue cose ben riguardare, ne resta a poter dire: e di cio' niuno dee aver maraviglia, se discretamente pensa che tutte le cose, le quali noi sciocca-mente nostre chiamiamo, sieno nelle sue mani, . . ." (*Decameron*, II, 3, p. 108).

tune is comically altered later on in the day when the adventures of Andreuccio da Perugia (II, 5) are recounted. This story, in fact, is a parody of the spiritual allegory of man's confrontation with, and binding of, Fortune. Andreuccio, as the etymology of the name implies, is the little man caught in the world of change.[38] He is a merchant, a horse dealer who on a Monday (a detail that suggests that his destiny is linked to the phases of the moon and that he belongs to the sublunary world of change and corruption) appears in the marketplace of Naples to strike his deals.[39] While he uncautiously shows off his money, he is seen by Fiordalisi, a woman who, in flagrant inversion of her name, is a prostitute. She invites him to her house in Malpertugio, which means, in Boccaccio's own etymologizing, a place of ill affair. Andreuccio has no *virtue* and actually mistakes his manhood for *virility*. He accepts her invitation only to have his erotic fantasies deluded. Fiordalisi tells him that she is his natural sister, entertains him for the whole evening in a room which suggests the garden of love, and finally robs him of his money.[40] Only when Andreuccio has fallen into the excrement does he seem to realize that he has been tricked.

As he is fallen, he is involved in what is a transparent parody of the spiritual dark night: the city of Naples is a ghostly labyrinth from which there seems to be no exit. Andreuccio falls once again into a well where he cleanses himself. As he is betrayed by his accomplices, he comes forth as *homo sibi relictus*. Finally, with the two thieves he goes to the church to steal the ring off the archbishop who has been buried that day. The church, far from being the place of moral regeneration, is literally transformed into a den of thieves. Yet here he finds his

[38] "Andreas . . . sermone autem Graeco a viro virilis appellatur" (Isidore, *Etym.*, VII, ix, 11).

[39] ". . . dove giunto una domenica sera in sul vespro, dall'oste suo informato la seguente mattina fu in sul Mercato, . . ." (*Decameron*, II, 5, p. 126). Carlo Muscetta, *Giovanni Boccaccio* (Bari: Laterza, 1972), p. 196, mistakenly believes the story takes place on Sunday night.

[40] "Ella appresso, . . . con lui nella sua camera se n'entro', la quale di rose, di fiori d'aranci e d'altri odori tutta oliva" (*Decameron*, p. 128).

conversion, a figurative death and resurrection comically inverted. He steals the ring and gets caught in the crypt; but then, by an unexpected reversal of the wheel of Fortune and an acquired virtue to exploit the coincidence, he gets out of the crypt, gaining both a new lease on life and the archbishop's ring.

The name of the archbishop, we are told, is Filippo, literally a lover of horses. By this etymological resonance and the fact that the ring is worth more than the florins he lost, the movement of the story both mimes the circulation of Fortune and suggests that there is a gain for Andreuccio.[41] Whereas for Dante, Fortune is conquered by not clinging to earthly goods, Boccaccio inverts Dante's moral paradigm by showing how the very opposite takes place. These reversals are not simply techniques of Boccaccio's art; they are, as we shall now see, the very core of the story.

Rather than being the order of a providential agency, the world is the empire of *alea*, a veritable *regio dissimilitudinis* where things are not ever what they seem to be.[42] This view of

[41] The point is stressed by Giovanni Getto, *Vita di forme e forme di vita nel Decameron* (Turin: Petrini, 1958), pp. 78–94. See also Aldo Rossi, "La combinatoria decameroniana: Andreuccio," *Strumenti critici*, 7 (1973), pp. 1–51. For a view that emphasizes the symmetrical correspondences in the *Decameron*, see Tzvetan Todorov, *Grammaire du Decameron* (The Hague and Paris: Mouton, 1969). Of interest are also Gregory Lucente, "The Fortunate Fall of Andreuccio da Perugia," *Forum Italicum*, 10 (1976), pp. 323–344; Millicent J. Marcus, *An Allegory of Form: Literary Self-Consciousness in the Decameron* (Saratoga, Calif.: Anma Libri, 1979), pp. 27–43; Karl-Ludwig Selig, "Boccaccio's *Decamerone* and The Subversion of Literary Reality (*Dec.* II / 5)," *Italien und die Romania in Humanismus und Renaissance*, eds. K. W. Hemper and E. Straub (Weisbaden: Steiner, 1983), pp. 265–269. More generally on the motif of circularity, see Teodolinda Barolini, "The Wheel of the *Decameron*," *Romance Philology*, 36 (1983), pp. 521–538.

[42] Pierre Courcelle, *Les Confessions de Saint Augustin dans la tradition litteraire* (Paris: Etudes Augustiniennes, 1963), especially pp. 278–288 and pp. 623–640 where Courcelle gives abundant evidence for the occurrence of the *topos*. See also F. Chatillon, "Regio dissimilitudinis," in *Mélanges E. Podechard* (Lyon: Facultés Catholiques, 1945), pp. 85–102. The notion that the fallen world governed by Fortune is a *regio dissimilitudinis* is implied by Boethius, *Consolation of Philosophy*, II, m. 3, 13–18.

Fortune sustains the ambiguities, constant inversions, falls and reversals of the novella: three times does Andreuccio fall and rise; by the extensive use of etymologies, Boccaccio seems to suggest that there are names which are "proper," stable receptacles of a univocal sense and identity. But the names appear as deceptive masks: Fiordalisi, regardless of her name, is a prostitute; Andreuccio's own name wavers between virtue and virility. More generally, he possesses, loses, and regains; there is a sister who turns out not to be a sister; the city of Naples is ironically twisted into a disorienting space where all directions are confused.

This land of unlikeness is triggered by Andreuccio's vainglory, concupiscence of the eyes, and concupiscence of the flesh.[43] But as this conventional moral scheme is hinted at, it is quickly discarded. In this perspective, allegory—voided of its moral structure and parodied—is the poetics of dissemblance, for it represents a condition whereby things are not what they mean.[44] By parodying the allegory, Boccaccio seems to be on the side of Bruno and Buffalmacco in showing that the gap between the semblance of things and their meaning can never be bridged.

The only order in such a world of dissemblance and instability is the regularity of Fortune's shifts. If the marketplace is the metaphor of traffic, the space where goods are brought to be exchanged and assessed at their proper value, the wheel of Fortune mocks the merchant's efforts. It is Fortune who is the true trickster of the world. For Dante she is the distant spectator of the "corta buffa" (brief mockery, *Infermo* VII, 61) who "beata si gode" (rejoices in her bliss, 96); for Boethius she

---

[43] The classical text for these temptations is 1 John 2:16 which urges man to give up "concupiscentia carnis, concupiscentia oculi et superbia vitae." In patristic exegesis the three sins are variously interpreted as gluttony, sexual pleausres, pursuit of riches and vainglory. For a literary application of the motif to the medieval English literature see Donald R. Howard, *The Three Temptations: Medieval Man in Search of the World* (Princeton: Princeton University Press, 1966).

[44] This is a standard definition of allegory as "alieniloqui. Aliud enim sonat, et aliud intelligitur" (Isidore, *Etym.*, I, xxxvii, 22).

behaves dissemblingly like a play actor, "sic illa ludit . . . hunc continuum ludum ludimus." She teases man's power to dispose of goods and assigns them in a constant and irrational exchange.[45] In this sense, she enacts Calandrino's very madness in his changing one order of reality for another and in his desire to rob the bank, the place where exchange occurs. This view of Fortune tells us that human mastery, gain and hierarchy— that which is embodied by the *beffa*—are always provisional and contingent, just as the identity between the proper name of Filippo and its sense for Andreuccio is sheer chance, an ironic undercutting of any notion of providentiality.

When Andreuccio's adventure ends happily, the *brigata* laughs, pleasantly relieved at the last twist and turn of the wheel of Fortune. But in spite of the happy ending of the story, there is no real closure: the steady rotation of the wheel asserts the open-endedness of events. Andreuccio wins, but we are asked to extend the trajectory and realize that his fall may happen all over again because even as he is at the top of the wheel, he is always on its shifty curve. What is more, the virtue by which he wins over chance is an act of thievery: the ruby into which his money was metamorphosed may have permanence, but ironically, because of its permanence, it is the more coveted and its possession ever endangered by other thieves.

Both Andreuccio's constant predicament and the *brigata's* relief disclose the central oddness of the games of laughter— the comical tendency, that is, to mistake provisional appearances for the whole reality. This ambiguity informs the novella genre in the *Decameron*. The novella is a deliberate fragment, a cross section of a totality which, if it exists at all, can never be fully grasped. Boccaccio repeatedly tries to impose on his kaleidoscopic range of stories a unified design and cohe-

---

[45] Boethius' text reads: "Thus doth she play, to make her power more known, / Showing her slaves a marvel, when man's state / Is in one hour both downcast and fortunate" (*The Consolation of Philosophy*, trans. H. F. Steward [Cambridge, Mass.: Harvard University Press, 1968], II, m.1, p. 179.)

sion: the frame, the thematic movement of the text from the chaos of the plague to the difficult order in Griselda's tale, the transitional passages, the topics by which stories are duly placed within given fields of signification, the symbolic numbers of totality (ten days and one hundred novelle). All are expedients which suggest how the sequence can be constructed as a unified totality.

Much like Petrarch's *Canzoniere*, the *Decameron* aspires to be a whole of parts but, at the same time, declares the impossibility of its being arranged as a total and coherent pattern. In the *Canzoniere*, the principle of repetition—as each poem begins anew, it inexorably ends up echoing what has already been said—shows that totality is an illusory mirage.[46] Nonetheless, the *Canzoniere* has had, and continues to have, readers who are taken in by the esthetic simulation of order; the *Decameron*, I might add, has had exactly the same destiny. Auerbach's close analysis of a passage of a tale, for instance, depends on the assumption that each part reflects the totality and by the synecdoche one knows a fragment and, thus, one can grasp the whole. In a real sense, Auerbach is like the *brigata* in the garden which seizes on the provisional and the partial and wistfully extends it to cover the whole.

Wistfulness is the heart of laughter. It betrays the desire for sense and relief which governs the life of the characters and, for that matter, of the critics. For Boccaccio the metaphor of totality, the project of both Calandrino and Simone, is madness and hence unspeakable. Dissolving their pretenses and borrowing from them there is the world of *beffe*, the play which discloses the illusoriness of the metaphor and which has laughter as its proper response.

In the wake of Aristotle, Thomas Aquinas and Dante speak of laughter as precisely the activity proper to man. "Pratum ridet," as an exchange of properties, is a metaphor to describe the coming of spring. "Homo ridet," instead, has a proper

---

[46] Giuseppe Mazzotta, "The *Canzoniere* and the Language of the Self," *Studies in Philology*, 75 (1978), pp. 271–296.

sense, for laughter is man's distinctive and inalienable quality.[47] Boccaccio shows both how laughter is a hollow mask which deceives, blinds us to what we lose, and how it is produced by a mask behind which the tricksters try to appropriate the world and, like the *brigata*, enjoy it.

The *Decameron* constantly moves between the dream of utopia and the pleasure of the representation: laughter is the precarious point where these polarities intersect and at the same time pull apart. This constant movement discloses laughter as the domain of the imaginary which seeks pretexts and occasions to become "real" and is always a put-on. The rhetorical name for this movement is catachresis, the figure of a borrowed property, the elusive borderland of madness where all efforts at sense are defied.

[47] Thomas Aquinas, *In Epistolam ad Galatas*, IV, lectio 7, in *Opera omnia*, ed. S. E. Frette (Paris: L. Vives, 1889), XXI, 230. For Aristotle, see *Parts of Animals*, trans. A. L. Peck (Cambridge, Mass.: Harvard University Press, 1961), III, 10, p. 281. For Dante see the discussion of Love as if it ". . . fosse una cosa per sé, e non solamente sustanzia intelligente, . . . le quali cose paiono essere proprie de l'uomo, e spezialmente essere risibile" (*Vita nuova*, ed. Fredi Chiappelli [Milan: Mursia, 1973] chap. 25. This is in the context of the metaphoricity of Love.

THE LAW
AND ITS TRANSGRESSIONS

With the exception of a few biographical references to Boccaccio's enrollment in the study of the law and to his contacts with Cino da Pistoia, there is not so much to be found on the question of the law in recent scholarship on the *Decameron* or even on the whole corpus of Boccaccio's work.[1] Yet throughout the *Decameron* there is a concern with the law and the judicial practice that is so extensive as to appear, on close inspection, nothing less than a central category of the narrative. By law here I do not mean the several scattered references to the "laws of youth," or to the "powers and laws of love," or even to the tyrant as a figure who arbitrarily departs from the injunctions of the law. These metaphors, which have been explored in some detail in previous chapters, are deployed in the *Decameron* side by side with a literal, even technical, frame of the law. One could point out, for instance, that in addition to well-

---

[1] Factual remarks on the links between Boccaccio and Cino da Pistoia can be found in Vittore Branca, "L'incontro napoletano con Cino da Pistoia," *Studi sul Boccaccio*, 5 (1969), pp. 1–12; see also P. G. Ricci, "La pretesa immatricolazione del Boccaccio nell'arte dei giudici e notai," *Studi sul Boccaccio*, 3 (1965), pp. 18–24 and "Dominus Johannes Boccaccius," *Studi sul Boccaccio*, 6 (1971), pp. 1–10. These contributions never probe the relationship between law and literature. The textual presence of Cino in Boccaccio's poetry has been studied by A. Balduino, "Cino da Pistoia, Boccaccio e i poeti minori del Trecento," in *Atti dei Convegni Lincei. 18. Colloquio Cino da Pistoia* (Rome: Accademia dei Lincei, 1976), pp. 33–85. The juridical culture of Cino da Pistoia, and his polemic against Accursius, has been treated by Gennaro Maria Monti, *Cino da Pistoia Giurista* (Città di Castello: Il Solco, 1924).

known statements about lawlessness in the city of Florence at the time of the plague, the first tale evokes the figure of a notary public, Ser Ciappelletto, who is engaged in a systematic forgery of legal deeds, in thievery and gambling; that other stories picture courtroom scenes where litigants settle their disputes, judges in their judgment seats administer justice and are exposed as fools or lechers, laws are variously amended or broken. In brief, the law court is both the arena where social and moral values are sanctioned and the theatrical space where sundry happenings are staged. These are the issues of the law which Boccaccio marshals in a number of novelle and which I shall examine in this chapter.

To be sure, it would be foolhardy to expect from the *Decameron* the sort of analytic overview of the principles and operations of the law that punctuate, say, the fourth book of John of Salisbury's *Policraticus*, where the provisions of the *Corpus juris* and those of *Deuteronomy* are combined with the aim of producing an elaborate theory of statecraft.[2] Even less can one expect to find something like Dante's iconography of justice, that is, either his steady musing on God's implacable tribunal as well as the crisis of canon and civil laws, or the rigor with which the poet judges the deepest secrets of the sinners' hearts. Still, as I shall argue here, Boccaccio goes to the core of legal thought, to the source of legal and moral authority, which both theologians and canonists posit as the *Lex naturae*. He even dramatizes tensions in the concept of the law, which simultaneously appears as both an ethical and rhetorical issue. In other words, he fully confronts and gauges the distance between law and literature, but also senses that the two cannot be framed as simply separate provinces of knowledge.

That Boccaccio had given considerable thought to the question of possible boundaries between law and poetry is quite evident from the lengthy fourth chapter of book XIV of the *Genealogy of the Gentile Gods*. In what is a scathing attack against

---

[2] John of Salisbury, *Policraticus*, ed. C.C.I. Webb (Oxford: Clarendon Press, 1909), bk. IV, 4, pp. 244ff.

jurists, which rivals in intensity the one in *The Fates of Illustrious Men*,[3] Boccaccio establishes a polarity between jurists and poets. The lawyers ". . . properly and essentially . . . have no business with poets, nor poets with them. Poets sing their songs in retirement; lawyers wrangle noisily in the courts amid the crowd and bustle of the market. Poets long for glory and high fame; lawyers for gold. Poets delight in the stillness and solitude of the country; lawyers in office buildings, courts and the clamor of litigants. Poets are friends of peace; lawyers of cases and trials. But if they will not listen to my plea, let them at any rate give ear to the authority of Solon, himself a most learned lawyer, who, when he had finished his tables, forsook the law for poetry, and who would have proved another Homer, if he had lived."[4]

This exalted vision of poetry at the expense of the law generally repeats, as later humanists such as Salutati, Bruni, Poggio and Valla will do, the sharp accusations that Petrarch hurled at the legal profession.[5] In a letter written in 1340 to a Genoese youth who had sought advice about a career as a jurist, Petrarch recounts the years he spent studying law at Montpellier and Bologna. He then evokes the world of lawyers as one of engagements in contracts and wills, without any

---

[3] "They (the lawyers) are like jackasses in robes. The problems they do not understand they ignore. Shamefully they try, if they can, to corrupt the law and they apply all their efforts to deprive it of its simplicity and sanctity so that they can spread an unwelcome discord among people. . . . Anyone who through fraud becomes wealthy, they proclaim a father of the law and a pillar of the court. They revere him as a high priest of truth, archive of jurisprudence" (*The Fates of Illustrious Men*, trans. L. Brewer Hall [New York: Frederick Ungar Publishing Co., 1965], pp. 95–96).

[4] *Boccaccio on Poetry*, trans. Osgood, p. 32.

[5] See, for instance, on this issue Coluccio Salutati, *De nobilitate legum et medicinae. De verecundia*, ed. E. Garin (Florence: Vallecchi, 1947); for the heated debate in the wake of Salutati's position, see Eugenio Garin, *L'umanesimo italiano* (Bari: Laterza, 1965), especially pp. 42–46. More generally, see Biagio Brugi, *Per la storia della giurisprudenza e delle università italiane. Nuovi saggi*, (Turin: UTET, 1921); see also Myron P. Gilmore, *Humanists and Jurists: Six Studies in the Renaissance* (Cambridge: The Belknap Press of Harvard University Press, 1963).

thought for "the study of the arts and origins and literature, which would be of greatest practical use for their profession."[6]

Like Petrarch, in a tradition that goes back to Vincent of Beauvais, Bernard of Clairvaux and St. Ambrose, Boccaccio indicts lawyers for their avarice and for making wealth the standard by which the value of the arts can be measured.[7] The chief source of their error is the false assumption that the real bonds of commerce and profit alone matter: their obsession with gain leads them to root the practice of the law in empirical realities (heredity, equity of payments, divorces) whereas poetry, like philosophy and theology, has no dealings with things that perish, but draws the minds of men into the "discovery of strange wonders."[8] In short, within the compass of the two activities there seems to be an unbridgeable gap between fact and value, private interests and gratuitous speculation. More precisely, whereas the law is characterized by a principle of referentiality and practical interest in the general business of life, literature is not directly tied to concrete concerns of everyday experience.

The bitter and unrelenting critique of the jurists' conduct and convictions gains momentum, paradoxically, through the implied recognition of the common ground law and literature share. Thus, if for Petrarch the study of literature and origins is useful to lawyers, for Boccaccio law is itself a degraded form of literature. Almost in response to Accursius' gloss on *Digest*

[6] The letter was written to Marco Portonario of Genoa; it is dated by E. H. Wilkins, *Petrarch's Correspondence* (Padua: Editrice Antenore, 1960) between 1355 and 1359. A convenient summary of the letter is to be found in *Letters from Petrarch*, trans. Morris Bishop (Bloomington and London: Indiana University Press, 1966), pp. 166–170.

[7] Vincent of Beauvais, *Speculum Morale* (Douai: Belleri, 1624; rep. 1964–65), VII, 13, cites authorities from Bernard to Jacques of Vitry to Augustine to Ambrose on avarice of lawyers.

[8] The passage reads: "But, though my opponents may not be aware of it, Poetry devotes herself to something greater, for while she dwells in heaven, and mingles with the divine counsels, she moves the minds of a few men from on high to a yearning for the eternal, lifting them by her loveliness to high revery, drawing them away into the discovery of strange wonders, and pouring forth most exquisite discourse from her exalted mind" (*Boccaccio on Poetry*, trans. Osgood, p. 24).

I, i, where law is defined as "vera philosophia," because, one infers, it yokes abstract knowledge to the contingent realities of life, Boccaccio casts lawyers as crude rhetoricians.[9] Their verbal exhibitionism, their personal ornaments (they are recognizable, we are told at the start of the chapter, by "rhetorical" traits such as the golden buckles of their togas, their impressive gait and fluency of speech), their skill in mere memory of what is written (and memory is, as is known, a central feature of rhetorical *inventio*), and the final point that Solon forsook law in favor of poetry, are all elements that betray Boccaccio's anxious sense of the perilous closeness between the spheres of poetry and law.

Within this context it may well be that Boccaccio's harshness of tone (which in truth is part of the traditional vocabulary against lawyers' vain ostentation) is calculated to offset the jurists' arrogant view of law's superiority to literature. Their claim rests on the opinion that law, not literature, is the foundation of public transactions and social order because it "holds tight rein on the evil forces that pervert society." At any rate the proximity between law and literature, conceptualized by rhetorical treatises, happens to be a historical fact of Italian culture. From the outset, literature was practiced by men of law such as Pier delle Vigne, Brunetto Latini, Bonagiunta, Iacopo da Lentini, Cino da Pistoia and others.[10] More fundamentally

[9] "Lawyers, in their practice of law, are skilled in mere memory of what is written, and dispense the decisions and rulings of legislators literally, but without intelligence" (*Boccaccio on Poetry*, p. 25). The link between law and rhetoric is, of course, a commonplace of any rhetorical treatise such as Cicero's *De inventione*. Accursius' gloss reads: "civilis sapientia vera philosophia dicitur, id est amor sapientiae." Accursius' *Glossa Ordinaria* to the *Digest* is contained in the *Corpus Iuris Civilis* (vols. I–III) (Venice, 1584). For the relationship between law and wisdom one should also recall Cicero. Stressing the importance of philosophy for determining the ends of man, he argues that "legal subjects are no doubt more popular, but philosophy is unquestionably richer in interest" (*De finibus bonorum et malorum*, trans. H. Rackham [Cambridge: Harvard University Press, 1967], I, iv–v, p. 15).

[10] There are several background studies to this historical issue, but there is no updated literary analysis of the question of the law in literature. See A. Viscardi, *Le origini* (Milan: Vallardi, 1939). A sharper view of the importance of legal studies in the development of Italiam Humanism is taken by Roberto

what joins law and literature is a theory of nature. It was Dante's insight to place in *Inferno* XV, the canto where the violence against the transcendent, objective order of nature is punished, the so-called "cherci e litterati grandi," such as Brunetto Latini, a rhetorician and notary public, Priscian, the grammarian, and Francesco d'Accorso, a jurist.[11]

Much more explicitly than he does in the *Genealogy*, Boccaccio in the *Decameron* brings to the foreground the notion that law and justice depend primarily upon a conception of nature. In the Introduction to the *Decameron*, after the account of the failure of medicine to cure and contain the infection, the text shifts to a description of the collapse of the social order and the failure of legal institutions.

> *E in tanta afflizione e miseria della nostra città era la reverenda auttorità delle leggi, così divine come umane, quasi caduta e dissoluta tutta per li ministri e essecutori di quelle, li quali sì come gli altri uomini, erano tutti o morti o infermi o sì di famiglie rimasi stremi, che ufficio alcuno non poteano fare; per la qual cosa era a ciascuno licito quanto a grado gli era d'adoperare.*[12]

In the face of so much affliction and misery, all respect for the authority of both divine and human laws had virtually broken down and dissolved. For like everybody else, those ministers and executors of the laws were either dead or ill or were left with so few subordinates that they were unable to discharge any of their duties. Hence it was lawful for everyone to behave as one pleased. (p. 13)

Weiss, *The Dawn of Humanism in Italy* (London: H. K. Lewis & Co., 1947), pp. 5–7 particularly. See also B. L. Ullman, "Some Aspects of the Origin of Italian Humanism," *Philological Quarterly*, 20 (1941), pp. 212–223.

[11] In the *Esposizioni sopra la Comedia di Dante*, ed. G. Padoan in *Tutte le opere di Giovanni Boccaccio*, VI (Milan: Mondadori, 1965), Boccaccio points out in his commentary on *Inferno* XV that Brunetto, an expert in the liberal arts and philosophy, was mainly a notary (p. 669); see also his remarks on Priscian and F. D'Accorsio on pp. 679–680.

[12] How the world of nature subtends this section of the Introduction is extensively argued in chapter 1 above.

In a general way, the textual movement from medicine to laws is part of a coherent and traditional metaphoric relationship between the two arts: the aim of medicine is the care of the body, the law's is the care of the soul.[13] Or, to paraphrase Plato, who in the *Republic* states that justice is the health of the soul, the observance of the laws guarantees the health of the body politic. Further, the conceptual link between law and medicine depends on the fact that both entail a correct moral conduct and are arts of nature in that both assume the natural order and harmony of creation.

More specifically, the passage just quoted, which fully acknowledges the sovereign power of the law for the stability of the city, conveys the essence of the law as the bond of political life. For if Isidore of Seville surmises that *lex* (law) is derived from *legere* (to read) because it is written[14] (in this, one might add, Isidore follows Cicero's hint in the *Nature of the Gods*, where the simultaneous origin of law and writing is attributed to the myth of Mercury),[15] St. Thomas Aquinas suggests a different etymology. Arguing that law is a rule whereby man is induced to act or is restrained from acting, he goes on to remark that *lex* (law) is derived from *ligare* (to bind) because it

[13] My point is that medicine is usually counted as one of the mechanical or adulterate sciences, the sciences such as fabric making, armament, commerce, agriculture, hunting, medicine and theatrics (the sciences that in the main figure in the *Decameron*). "Of these, three pertain to [the] external cover of nature, by which she protects herself from harms, and four to internal, by which she feeds and nourishes herself" (Hugh of St. Victor, *Didascalicon*, trans. J. Taylor [New York: Columbia University Press, 1968], II, 20, p. 74). Law, on the other hand, is thought of as part of the liberal arts, rhetoric, and "they require minds which are liberal, that is liberated and practiced . . ." (*Didascalicon*, p. 75).

[14] "Nam lex a legendo vocata, quia scripta est" (Isidore of Seville, *Etym.*, V, iii, 15).

[15] "This is the Mercury who is said to have slain Argus and for this reason to have fled to Egypt and given laws and the art of writing to the Egyptians. This is the Mercury whom the Egyptians call Thoth, and they give this name in their calendar to the first month of the year" (Cicero, *The Nature of the Gods*, trans. Horace C. P. McGregor [New York: Penguin Books, 1978], III, 55–56, p. 216).

binds one to act.[16] From this perspective it is clear that Boccaccio's phrase, "... era la ... auttorità delle leggi ... dissoluta," which literally describes the disintegration of the legal order, accords with St. Thomas' formulation. "Dissoluta," etymologically from *dis-solvere*, plays out the notion of political crisis as the tearing of the social fabric at its seams, because of the repeal of law's authority. The very meaning of "auttorità," it might be pointed out, a term that belongs to the judicial vocabulary and refers to the absolute foundation of legal sanctions, further bolsters this understanding of the law. One of the senses of authority is explained by Dante, for instance, exactly as the act of *tying* words together.[17]

The fall of the city as the crisis of the law is placed by Boccaccio within a sharply moral context. The sentence, "era a ciascuno licito quanto a grado gli era d'adoperare," echoes Dante's line, "che libito fe licito in sua legge" (she made lust lawful in her law) from *Inferno* v, 56, where it refers to Semiramis, the legendary queen of Babylon, who legalized incest. When pleasure becomes the law we witness, according to Dante, the tragic power of man's law to pervert nature's rule. Dante's line in Boccaccio's passage suggests, more than the unnaturalness of the law, its unnatural eclipse in the city. But the echo also works as an oblique strategy to dramatize the au-

---

[16] *Summa Theologiae*, Ia IIae, 90, art, I. The English text, in the Blackfriars edition (New York: McGraw-Hill, 1964) reads: "Law is a kind of direction or measure for human activity through which a person is led to do something or held back. The word comes from *ligando*, because it is binding on how we should act" (p. 7). St. Thomas is actually discussing the resonances of the word "obligation."

[17] "E dunque da sapere che 'autoridate' non è altro che 'atto d'autore.' Questo vocabulo, cioè 'autore,' sanza quella terza lettera C, può discendere da due principii: l'uno si è d'uno verbo molto lasciato da l'uso in gramatica, che significa tanto quanto 'legare parole,' cioè 'auieo.' E che ben guarda lui, ne la sua prima voce apertamente vedrà che elli stesso lo dimostra, che solo di legame di parole è fatto, cioè di sole cinque vocali, che sono anima e legame d'ogni parole, e composto d'esse per modo volubile, a figurare imagini di legame" (*Convivio*, eds. G. Busnelli e G. Vandelli, 2nd ed., ed. A. E. Quaglio, 2 vols. [Florence: Le Monnier, 1968], IV, vi, 3–5.

thority of nature as an intrinsically rational and benevolent entity in the pursuit of a virtuous life.

The impulse to escape from the chaos of the infected city to the garden is voiced by Pampinea precisely as an effort to restore, within the confines of the harmonious natural landscape, the moral order to nature. Fully aware that all laws, including those of obedience in monasteries where nuns choose to live lasciviously, have been violated, Pampinea appeals to what she calls "natural ragione," the natural rights of man.

> *"Donne mie care, voi potete, così come io, molte volte avere udito che a niuna persona fa ingiuria chi onestamente usa la sua ragione. Natural ragione è, di ciascuno che ci nasce, la sua vita quanto può aiutare e conservare e difendere: e concedesi questo tanto, che alcuna volta è già addivenuto che, per guardare quella, senza colpa alcuna si sono uccisi degli uomini. E se questo concedono le leggi, nelle sollecitudini delle quali è il ben vivere d'ogni mortale, quanto maggiormente, senza offesa d'alcuno, è a noi e a qualunque altro onesto alla conservazione della nostra vita prendere quegli rimedii che noi possiamo? . . ."*

Dear ladies, you will often have heard it affirmed, as I have, that no man does injustice to another in exercising his legal rights. Every person born in this world has a natural right to sustain, preserve and defend his own life to the best of his ability—a right so freely acknowledged that men have sometimes killed others in self-defense, and no blame whatever has attached to their actions. Now, if this is permitted by the laws, upon whose prompt application all mortal creatures depend for their well-being, how can it possibly be wrong, seeing that it harms no one, for us or anybody else to do all in our power to preserve our lives? . . .   (p. 20)

The phrase, "natural ragione," translates *ius naturale* or natural law, a law which, as St. Paul says (Romans 2:14) is graven in the human heart, and, as medieval jurists believe, is implanted by nature and is common to all nations. The primary

content of the natural law, which by and large designates those
things to which man has a natural inclination and are naturally
apprehended by reason, had been most clearly articulated by
St. Thomas Aquinas.[18] In a passage that probes whether the
natural law contains several precepts or only one, Thomas
states that the first inclination of man, because of the nature it
shares with every other substance, is the preservation of his
own being and whatever is a means of preserving human life,
and of warding off its obstacles, belongs to natural law.[19] This
ethical principle is central to Pampinea's concern that the *brigata* pursue what is lawful, "onesto alla conservazione della
nostra vita." The attribute, "onesto," one can add, places the
statement even more forcefully within the problematics of the
natural law: "honestum," says Cicero, is at one with virtue
and virtue is "animi habitus naturae modo atque rationi consentaneus."[20]

---

[18] Isidore of Seville, *Etym.*, v, iv, 25, writes: "Ius autem naturale est, aut civile, aut gentium. Ius naturale est commune omnium nationum, et quod
ubique instinctu naturae, non constitutine aliqua habetur; ut viri et feminae
coniunctio, liberorum successio et educatio, communis omnium possessio, e
omnium una libertas, adquisitio eorum quae caelo, terra marique capiuntur."
See also Tertullian, *PL* 2, col. 83; Ambrose, *PL* 16, col. 1251. For St. Thomas
see *Summa theologiae*, Ia IIae, 94, art. 2. See Philippe Delhaye, *Permanence du
droit naturel. Analecta mediaevalia namurcensia*, 10 (Louvain: Nauwelaerts,
1960). Cf. also O. Lottin, *Le Droit naturel chez S. Thomas d'Aquin et ses prédé-
cesseurs*, 2nd ed. (Bruges: C. Beyaert, 1931); M.-D. Chenu, *La Théologie au
douzième siècle* (Paris: Vrin, 1957); Brian Tierney, "*Natura id est deus*: A Case of
Juristic Pantheism?," *Journal of the History of Ideas*, 24 (1963), pp. 307–322; Joseph Fuchs, S.J., *Natural Law: A Theological Investigation*, trans. H. Reckter
and J. A. Dowling (Dublin: Gill and Son, 1965). For further bibliography and
an intelligent study of the principles contained in the *Decretum*, i.i.1, and pa-
tristics, see Michael W. Twomey, *The Anatomy of Sin: Violations of Kynde and
Trawe in Cleanness*, Cornell Dissertation, 1979.

[19] *Summa theologiae*, Ia IIae, 94, art. 2.

[20] Cicero, *De inventione*, II, 53. "A spiritual habit which conforms to the
habit of nature and reason." The translation is from *De inventione*, trans.
H. M. Hubbel (Cambridge: Harvard University Press, 1976), p. 327. In the
same chapter Cicero adds: "The law of nature is that which is not born of
opinion, but implanted in us by a kind of innate instinct: it includes religion,
duty, gratitude, revenge, reverence and truth" (trans. Hubbel, p. 329).

This section of Boccaccio's text says nothing about other principles that conventionally go under the heading of the natural law. Aquinas, in full agreement with Gratian's *Decretum*, for instance, recognizes that there is in man a natural inclination to those things (the inclination is natural because, taught by nature, it is common to all animals), such as sexual intercourse and the caring and education of offspring.[21] The issue of sexuality is raised by Boccaccio, however, in other parts of the *Decameron* exactly within the context of the law of nature. There are a few novelle that I would like to examine from this perspective. The first is the tale of Paganino da Monaco (II, 10), which is told by Dioneo.

The story, which focuses on the personal experiences of a judge, Riccardo di Chinzica, is preambled by Dioneo's statement that he intends to show the foolishness of Bernabò related in the preceding novella. This avowed intention practically obscures what turns out to be the dramatic center of the tale, the question of whether or not the moral operations of nature are clear and accessible to man, and whether the order of nature is as unequivocal as Pampinea's speech in the Introduction implies. It is almost given as an afterthought, yet twice in the preamble does Dioneo explicitly refer to the question of nature: he is going to talk, he says, of the foolishness of those who, "se più che la natura possenti estimando" (overestimating themselves more powerful than nature), attempt with specious reasoning to bring others to the point where they themselves are, "non patendolo la natura di chi è tirato" (while the nature of those who are forced to adjust can't bear it).

This abstract affirmation of a rift within the idea of nature is consistently borne out by the thematic design of the story, which at the beginning seems nothing more than a variation of

[21] See note 18 above. The commentaries of Gratian's *Decretum*, which are contained in the *Corpus iuris canonici*, 3 vols. (Turin, 1588), emphasize the biblical injunction, "crescite et multiplicamini" of Genesis 1:28 as the justification for sexual intercourse. On this see J. T. Noonan, Jr., *Contraception: A History of Its Treatment by the Catholic Theologians and Canonists* (New York: Mentor Omega Book, 1967).

comedy's stock situation: the marriage between an enormously erudite but sexually weak old man with a lusty and beautiful young woman, Bartolomea. But if this starts by being a comedy, it is a troubled one at the end.

Marriage, or as commentators such as Gratian and Hugutio of Pisa refer to it, "uiri et feminae coniunctio," is a centerpiece of the ethics of natural law.[22] What is crucial to the enactment of this law, however, is the "copula carnalis" (copulation), and in his reluctance or inability to comply with this condition, the judge, who is an interpreter of the law, is its chief violator. Nonetheless there is considerable humor in his efforts to circumvent Bartolomea's possible advances. Finally aware that his forces cannot be up to the task, he elaborates a calendar of feasts, which span practically the whole year, during which man and woman should abstain from sexual union. Thoroughly a man of law, Riccardo resorts also to astronomy, the laws of the stars, and other geometric calculations in order to conjure up what would seem to be a world of natural order. Clearly, the judge thinks of the world as a creation securely based on foundations of order and constraints, with universal norms God has written in heaven. His mingling of astronomy and liturgy suggests this much. There is considerable irony in his belief that a significant bond exists between two absolutely unrelated terms such as the laws of the cosmos and his own sexuality.

---

[22] "Ut uivi et femine coniunctio. Est ius naturale, id est effectus eius, scilicet ab eo descendit, ut in lege contineatur, ff. de iure naturali . . . Sed ad quod ius naturale spectat hec coniunctio? Ad rationem qui dictat homini ut matrimonialiter copuleretur femine uel causa sobolis uel causa incontinentie. . . . Mihi tamen uidetur quod intellegatur de coniunctione carnali matrimoniali, non fornicaria, cum ex iure naturali peccatum non possit esse; et hec est coniunctio de iure naturali quod dicitur instinctus nature et de eo quod dicitur ratio." These reflections by Hugutio on Gratian are quoted in Lottin, *Le Droit naturel chez S. Thomas d'Aquin*, pp. 110–111. For the question of adultery as violation of natural law, see the entries by R. Parayre and B. Dolhagary in the *Dictionnaire de théologie catholique*, eds. A. Vacant and E. Mangenot, "Adultère," I (Paris: Letouzey, 1909), pp. 464–468, and "Fornication," VI, i (Paris: Letouzey, 1915), pp. 600–611. The standard text is I Corinthians 6:13–20.

This interest in astrology on the part of a judge seems to allude comically to a long debate on its value.[23] Astrology, at least the natural form as distinguished from the superstitious one, is generally tolerated in medical practices, because of the belief that stars do influence our bodily complexions, as Hugh of St. Victor puts it, "like health, illness, storm, calm, productivity, and unproductivity, which vary with the mutual alignments of the astral bodies' . . ."[24] But the so-called judicial astrology, which was a sort of divinatory art, the belief that the planets, "by their conjunctions, or by being in this or that domicile," in the words of Alexander Neckam, decide things here below by some inevitable law of necessity, was severely dismissed.[25] Ironically, there is no hint that the judge preserves any faith in the stars when settling courtroom disputes, but he shows himself to have it when appeasing his wife's sexual demands.

In *De officiis* Cicero puts astronomy, law, geometry and dialectic together as arts which, as he says with pleasing alliteration, "veri investigatione versantur."[26] These arts for the judge are not tools of philosophical investigation: they are, at best, elements of his alibi to cover up his inadequacies and repress his wife's desire. In fact, at the start he has no knowledge of his own nature or that of his wife, and is fearful that somebody else might enjoy her.

The fear turns out to be a self-fulfilling prophecy. One day in the summer Riccardo arranges to go fishing and has his wife go along to watch from another boat. While absorbed in what

[23] A still valuable recent summary on astrology is T. O. Wedel, *The Medieval Attitude Toward Astrology. Yale Studies in English*, 60 (1928, rep. 1968).

[24] *Didascalicon*, II, 10, p. 68.

[25] Alexander Neckham, *De naturis rerum*, ed. Thomas Wright, Rolls Series, 34 (London, 1863), I, 8, pp. 39–40.

[26] The whole text reads: "All these professions are occupied with the search after truth; but to be drawn by study away from the active life is contrary to moral duty" (*De officiis*, trans. Walter Miller [Cambridge: Harvard University Press, 1968], I, 19, p. 21). The classification is standard in the Middle Ages. See, for instance, Isidore of Seville, *Etym.*, I, ii, 3: ". . . astronomia, quae continet legem astrorum." See also Hugh of St. Victor, *Didascalicon*, II, 6.

he is doing they have drifted far out to sea when the small galley of a pirate, Paganino da Mare, comes on the scene. Catching sight of the woman, Paganino disregards all other concerns and takes her aboard his galley. Before they reach Monaco the pirate gives the woman so much sexual pleasure that "il giudice e le sue leggi" (the judge and his laws) quickly fade from her memory. The galley, not the bark, is a veritable *navis amoris*,[27] over a sea which, from the husband's viewpoint, is a place for his innocent recreations and the emblem of nature's regularities, while from the pirate's viewpoint it is the emblem of unbounded desire and formless energy.[28] Within the confines of this story, both woman and pirate, who together and for different reasons stand in an obvious contrast to the judge—the woman's sexuality antagonizes her against her husband, the pirate's plundering is the transgression of all laws—seem to be in touch with nature's secrets and power.

This is not to suggest, the overt symmetries in the novella's construction notwithstanding (young-old, pirate-judge, law-lawlessness, etc.), that the story figures simply some static opposition between a myth of illusory order and the reality of desire's boundlessness. This is certainly the case, but what the novella also maps out is Boccaccio's insight that the two worlds—that of the judge and that of his wife and Paganino—though both based on nature, are mutually exclusive. The judge's laws, exemplified by his naive belief in the order of nature and bucolic pastimes by the sea, violate the woman's natural desires, while what to the judge is the pirate's lawlessness turns out to be the woman's law. The discrepancy within these forms of desire is at one with the discrepancy in the understanding of nature: in effect, nature, as the authoritative origin of the law, appears to be the locus of contradictory values.

[27] For this *topos*, known as the *nef de joie et de déport*, see, for instance, "Guido, i' vorrei che tu e Lapo ed io / fossimo presi per incantamento, / e messi in un vasel ch'ad ogni vento / per mare andasse al voler vostro e mio, . . ." Quoted from Dante, *Rime*, ed. Gianfranco Contini (Turin: Einaudi, 1965), p. 35.

[28] The imaginative link between sea and passion is exemplified by *Inferno* v, 28–30.

The outcome of the judge's experience bears this out. We are told that on finding out that Bartolomea lives in Monaco in the pirate's household, Riccardo sails there willing to pay a ransom for her freedom. But the wife, in their interview, at first pretends not to recognize him; later she admits that because he was always busy observing too many feasts, whereas with Paganino "work goes on all the time," she will not return to Pisa with him. The judge's last effort at persuasion is to remind his wife that she is living in mortal sin (a charge which in her reply she ironically twists into "peccato mortaio"—pestle sin), that she is a pirate's strumpet and that her immoderate appetite is unseemly.

The power of her desire is such that Riccardo, defeated, returns home, where he goes mad. At his death, Bartolomea and Paganino get married and, thus, reenter the world of the law. The happy ending for the woman cannot lessen, however, the old man's grief. His madness may be the just price he must pay (and he is a character who knows that there is always a price to be paid, as his offer of ransom shows) for his original foolishness. It may even be a response to what he perceives as the madness of desire. As it shatters the pattern of law and reason, his madness also shows how precarious is the foundation of judgment in the court of desire.

Not all the magistrates in the *Decameron* understand the abstract laws of the stars and expect human sexuality to conform to them, as does Riccardo di Chinzica. Riccardo's experience is recalled by Dioneo himself in another story he is about to tell (IV, 10), but only as a way of establishing a link between the judge and a physician, Mazzeo della Montagna. Mazzeo is also a philosopher of nature,[29] yet, for all his detailed knowledge of the body's anatomical structure, he is not much acquainted with his own wife's body. In an overt contrast to Mazzeo-Riccardo, there appears at the end of the novella a judge whose

---

[29] The tale of Mazzeo della Montagna, which takes place in Salerno, symmetrically balances the tale of Tancredi, Prince of Salerno, at the beginning of the fourth day. For the sense in which Mazzeo is a philosopher of nature see chapter 1 above.

role is to decide whether Ruggieri, the wife's lover who has been arrested during the night, should be incriminated as a thief. To save Ruggieri, Mazzeo's wife contrives to have her maid appear in front of the judge to testify that Ruggieri was her lover. This judge, unlike Riccardo, lies with the maid even before listening to what she has to say; nor does the maid, who knows how to get a better hearing, object to his request. The outcome of the contrivance is that the judge accepts the tall story the maid tells and, greatly entertained by the narrative, sets Ruggieri free.

This flagrant abuse of office in no way becomes the object of moral indignation in the tale. Nonetheless the movement of the story does endorse our sense that we are confronted with the representation of a split between a theory of nature and sexual practice. In the story of Riccardo the contradictions are lodged at the heart of the natural law; in the story of Mazzeo, this surgeon understands the mechanics of the body, but is blind to his wife's sexuality, while the magistrate, who is indifferent to questions of justice, uses his office for his sexual gratification and, in effect, is on the side of the woman's sexual transgression.

This judge's misconduct is not unique in the *Decameron*. The novella of Andreuola (IV, 6) begins by featuring a secret love affair between the young woman and Gabriotto, a man of low estate.[30] During one of their trysts Gabriotto suddenly dies, and Andreuola, who was carrying the body to his house so that he may be buried by his kinsfolk, is discovered by some law officers and taken to the chief magistrate's. In spite of the physicians' report, which actually confirms Andreuola's account that Gabriotto had died a natural death, the magistrate promises to set her free only if she yields to his pleasures. Andreuola refuses and the magistrate at first attempts to take her by force and, later, fearing that she might accuse him and im-

---

[30] The tale is a case of the commoner loving a woman of the high nobility, which Andreas Capellanus treats in his *The Art of Courtly Love*, trans. Parry, pp. 53ff.

pressed by her resoluteness, publicly confesses his wrongdoing and asks to marry her.

The law court is far from being always the place of deceit. Emilia's tale (III, 7) contains Tedaldo's moralistic reflections on the inequities in the administration of the law, what he calls ". . . la cieca severità delle leggi e de' rettori, li quali assai volte, quasi solleciti investigatori delli errori, incrudelendo fanno il falso provare, e sé ministri dicono della giustizia e di Dio, dove sono della iniquità e del diavolo essecutori" (. . . the blind severity of the law and magistrates, who often, as if they were zealously investigating errors, have recourse to cruelty in order to have lies accepted as proven fact, and call themselves ministers of justice and of God, whereas they are executors of the devil and his iniquities, p. 292). In his desire to shed light on Aldobrandino's innocence and regain Ermellina's love, Tedaldo even instructs the magistrate that his role is to uncover the truth so that ". . . coloro non portin le pene che non hanno il peccato commesso" (punishment may not be inflicted on those who have not committed the crime). At the same time the dangerousness of the law emerges full-fledged: it distorts the literal facts and may erect lies into truth.

Another novella (VI, 7) focuses more directly on the law court as the locus where moral values are ratified. Like the tenth story of the second day, discussed earlier, this one also deals with the theme of the *mal mariée*, but the plot takes a different turn. Filostrato recounts the experience of a woman, Madonna Filippa, who was discovered one night by her husband in her own bedchamber in the arms of her lover. The husband resists the impulse to kill his wife for fear of legal consequences, but remembering the existence of a city statute which requires that every woman caught in adultery by her husband be burned alive, whether she was with a lover or simply doing it for money, he decides to take the case to court.

Clearly the husband views the law as a weapon of his domination, but as the narrative unfolds, we see how deluded his vision is. Filippa, for one, against the advice of her friends and relatives, resolves to answer the summons, confess the truth, and die a courageous death, rather than be forced to live in exile for defying the court. As a consequence of her choice the story moves to, and reaches its development in, the courtroom where a compassionate judge asks the woman whether the complaints lodged against her by her busband are true. Filippa's defense is that she never violated her contract with her husband, for he was always entitled to and granted the full exercise of his marital privileges. When the husband agrees with this statement, she adds that if he has taken of her as much as he needed, then, she asks, ". . . io che doveva fare o debbo di quel che gli avanza? debbolo io gittare a' cani? non è egli molto meglio servirne un gentile uomo che più che sé m'ama, che lasciarlo perdere o guastare?" (What am I to do with the surplus? Throw it to the dogs? Is it not far better that I should present it to a gentleman who loves me more dearly than himself, rather than allow it to turn bad or go to waste? p. 558). The argument tops the most skillful juridic pleading and succeeds in having the chief magistrate amend the harsh statute.

But Filippa's argument succeeds because of two related strategies she deploys. One is to shift and redefine the question of justice. The expectation was that she would be punished for her guilt in terms of what is called, since Aristotle's *Ethics*, retributive justice, which prescribes that the punishment to be meted out should fit the crime. But Filippa shifts the issue to one of distributive justice, which concerns itself with the way material goods can be divided among those who have a share in society.[31] As Filippa treats her sexuality as an economy of goods to be liberally apportioned, she implies that no loss has

[31] In distributive justice, Aristotle argues, fairness is achieved through geometrical proportion. A person receives all the more of the common goods according to proportion between things and persons. In retributive justice, instead, the justice which is known as ruled by the principle of reparatory equality, the eye for the eye, etc., there is an equality between crime and punishment. See Aristotle, *Nichomachean Ethics*, trans. Martin Ostwald, The Library of Liberal Arts (Indianapolis-New York: Bobbs-Merrill Co., 1962), v, 2–5, pp. 115–128.

been inflicted on her husband and, in effect, that she is no law-breaker.

Her other strategy is to challenge the very legality of the law. Just as marriage is a *sacramentum magnum*, instituted by God even before man's fall,[32] so is adultery a breach of divine positive law sanctioned in Deuteronomy as well as the natural law.[33] Aquinas and Gratian agree in viewing adultery along with theft and the slaying of the innocent as acts against the natural law. Filippa does not argue with this principle and even shoulders the burden of her guilt. But her point is that laws should have the consent of those who are affected by them. When the punishment contemplated by the statute was passed, she adds, no woman gave her consent to it, "per le quali cose meritamente malvagia si può chiamare" (it can, therefore, be described a wicked law).

The upshot of her reasoning is that the statute is amended so that in the future it will apply only to those wives who took payment for being unfaithful to their husbands. Filippa, in short, manages to turn her trial into a judgment of the law that should have judged her and forces its revision. The change her argument causes implies that laws are arbitrary conventions and that there is no necessary and immutable relation between facts and values or, as the sophists put it, between *nomos* and *phusis*. It also implies that the system of justice, far from being a fixed moral structure as it is, say, in the law of *contrapasso* which organizes Dante's *Inferno*, is part of the rhetorical art of persuasion. In the novella of Madonna Filippa, more specifically, the magistrate was already favorably disposed toward her and felt compassion on seeing that she was beautiful, impeccably well-bred and magnanimous, "secondo che le sue parole testimoniavano" (as her words bore witness).

---

[32] The phrase, of course, is from St. Paul, *Letter to the Ephesians* 5:32, which states that marriage is a sacrament, "Sacramentum hoc magnum est; ego autem dico in Christo et ecclesia." The statement typologically fulfills the injunction of Genesis 1:28.

[33] Deuteronomy 22:22.

But it is her judicial oratory (one of the three standard divisions, along with the deliberative and the epideictic, as is well known, of rhetoric)[34] that moves the people of Prato, who have flocked to the court, to absolve her from wrongdoing and acknowledge that the woman is right. The general verdict absolving her also recognizes that she did "dir bene" (speak well). The phrase recalls the introduction to the novella in which Filostrato announces to his listeners that "bella cosa è in ogni parte saper ben parlare" (it is a good thing to have the capacity to say the right things in the right circumstances). The two phrases echo the conventional definitions of rhetoric in texts that range from Isidore of Seville, who calls it a science "bene dicendi," to Brunetto Latini, who states that rhetoric concerns "bone parleure."[35] As Filippa, by the power of her legal plea, wins her case, we confront how ethics and rhetoric are interchangeable categories in the court of law.

From the point of view of its explicit rhetorical focus, the novella extends the theme of the day, which turns upon those who with a "leggiadro motto'" (some verbal pleasantry) or by a prompt retort or maneuver have avoided danger, discomfiture or ridicule. Even Frate Cipolla's sermon from the pulpit at the end of the day (VI, 10) is a humorous distortion of the rhetoric of the *ars praedicandi*.[36] More pointedly, the introduction to this sixth day deals with a parodic version of a *question d'amour* in the court of love.[37] While Dioneo and Lauretta are

[34] "Aristotle, on the other hand, who did much to improve and adorn this art, thought that the function of the orator was concerned with three classes of subjects, the epideictic, the deliberative, and the judicial" (*De inventione*, trans. Hubbel, I, v, 7, pp. 15–17).

[35] "Rhetorica est bene dicendi scientia in civilibus quaestionibus, ad persuadendum iusta et bona" (*Etym.*, II, i; for Brunetto Latini, see his *Li Livres dou tresor*, ed. Francis J. Carmody [Berkeley and Los Angeles: University of California Press, 1948], III, i, p. 317).

[36] See chapter 2, above, n. 22. For a general overview of the traditions of preaching, see Harry Caplan, *Of Eloquence. Studies in Ancient and Medieval Rhetoric* (Ithaca: Cornell University Press, 1970), pp. 79–92.

[37] A probing of the issue in an entirely different context is Victoria Kirkham, "Reckoning with Boccaccio's *questioni d'amore*," *Modern Language Notes*, 89 (1974), pp. 47–59. For a larger theoretical statement, which is particularly

singing of Troilus and Criseyde, they hear the servants fighting in the kitchen. Two of them, Tindaro and Licisca, are having an argument, and the queen calls on Dioneo, the storyteller who ironically stands always outside of any law, to act as a judge in the debate. The scene is a playful reenactment of the *iudicia Amoris* in Andreas Capellanus' *De arte honeste amandi*.[38] The verdict Dioneo is asked to pass is whether or not young women go to their husbands virgins, and Dioneo rules in favor of Licisca, against Tindaro, that women are not so foolish as to waste their opportunities while waiting for their fathers to marry them off.

Dioneo's "sentenzia" effectively acknowledges his own *carpe diem* ethics. His decision also pokes fun at the legal procedure which the text deploys in that it sanctions the reality of sexual license, not laws, between men and women. To find Dioneo on the side of transgression is certainly not surprising. At the very outset of the *Decameron*, as we know, Boccaccio represents his storytellers engaged in elaborate and elegant rituals of legislating, of establishing their own contractual rules as to how to govern and conduct themselves. They even make allowance, at the end of the first day of storytelling, for Dioneo's refusal to submit to the general law and for his claim to infringe at will upon their agreements.[39] So powerful is the

---

suggestive because it explores the interaction of legal and rhetorical registers, see Warren Ginsberg, *The Cast of Character. The Representation of Personality in Ancient and Medieval Literature* (Toronto: University of Toronto Press, 1983), esp. pp. 98–133.

[38] "The various decisions in love cases" are treated in *The Art of Courtly Love*, trans. Parry, II, vii., pp. 167ff; see also Ginsberg, *The Cast of Character*, p. 99.

[39] ". . . Dioneo solamente, tutti gli altri tacendo già, disse: 'Madonna, come tutti questi altri hanno detto, così dico io sommamente esser piacevole e commendabile l'ordine dato da voi. Ma di spezial grazia vi cheggio un dono, il quale voglio che mi sia confermato per infino a tanto che la nostra compagnia durerà, il quale è questo: che io a questa legge non sia costretto di dover dire novella seconda la proposta data, se io non vorrò, ma qual più di dire mi piacerà. E acciò che alcun non creda che io questa grazia voglia sì come uomo che delle novelle non abbia alle mani, infino da ora son contento d'esser sempre l'ultimo che ragioni' " (*Decameron*, p. 89).

lure of transgression on Dioneo's imagination that, as has been shown in chapter 6, on the day he is king he takes Licisca's hint and assigns for discussion the topic of transgression within the marriage contract.

Dioneo's playful transgressions are in part an extension of his sense of the eclipse of the laws in the world: "Or non sapete voi che, per la perversità di questa stagione, li giudici hanno lasciato i tribunali? le leggi, così le divine come le umane, tacciono? e ampia licenzia per conservar la vita è conceduta a ciascuno?" (Are you not aware that because of the wickedness of the times, the judges have deserted the courts, the laws of God and man are in abeyance, and everyone is given ample license to preserve one's life as best one can? p. 576). Storytelling, Dioneo is suggesting to his company of young men and women, is such a license, the imaginative freedom, while marking time and keeping alive, to be able to talk about the scabrous subject he is proposing. Yet, for all his association with "licenzia," Dioneo turns into a lawmaker, anxious that the topic he has prescribed for the seventh day be not violated just as he has violated the other topics: "Senza che voi mi fareste un bello onore, essendo io stato ubidente a tutti, e ora, avendomi vostro re fatto, mi voleste la legge porre in mano, e di quello non dire che io avessi imposto" (You would do me real honor if, having elected me your king and lawgiver, you were not to speak on the subject I prescribe, especially since I have been obedient to all of you, pp. 576–77). The gentle self-mockery, in effect, calls attention to Dioneo's awareness of his dual impulse to encompass both the law and its subversion. Beyond this, there is Boccaccio's own awareness of the *Decameron* as a text with its own rules and conventions, and its power to supplant and challenge established conventions. It is because of this steady double focus of what we call the esthetic imagination, to be at the same time law and transgression of the law, that the confrontation between literature and the world of the law and magistrates can never quite be an easy one.

There are two novelle that will shed some light on Boccaccio's sense of the relationship between law and what summar-

ily can be called the world of art. The first is the novella of
Martellino (II, I), a buffoon, who, with two other professional
actors, earns a living making the rounds of the various courts
and entertaining audiences with impersonations. They arrive
in Treviso on a day when a German, Arrigo, had died in odor
of sanctity and all the sick people were crowding in the church
in the hope of being cured by contact with the saint's body.

The story's point of departure, in effect, is the presentation
of the tradition of supernatural healing. There were throughout the Middle Ages two distinct types of medicine.[40] One was
the Galenic-empirical branch, which depended on the study of
nature and which was practiced by physicians through the pre-
scription of drugs, dietary controls, life-styles and surgical in-
terventions—all the skills of medieval science. The other—
known as supernatural healing—deployed relics of saints,
amulets, charms or visitations to shrines as the means of re-
storing health. This miraculous healing, which implies the
presence of a vital power in what is supposedly a lifeless relic
or a corpse, depends on the assumption of an organic link between disease and sin. The position of the novella of Martellino in the text, I might add, immediately following the story
of Maestro Alberto (I, 10) dramatizes the two medical traditions, for Alberto, as has been shown earlier, is the physician-
philosopher who himself is in the throes of the love disease.

More to our concern, in order for Martellino to make his
way through the crowd to the place in the church where Arrigo's body is lying, he disguises himself as a paralytic. The
dissemblance is so perfect and the simulated contortion of the
limbs so spectacular that he, propped up by his two friends,
easily arrives at the corpse. Martellino's performance, while all
eyes are fixed upon him, is flawless: after lying motionless

---

[40] For the development of supernatural healing, which features imagina-
tively in Boccaccio as well as Chaucer's *Canterbury Tales*, with its pilgrims
going to the shrine of the martyr, see Loren C. Mackinney, *Early Medieval
Medicine, with Special Reference to France and Chartres* (Baltimore: The Johns
Hopkins Press, 1937). For the rise of a rational medical art, see Owsei
Temkin, *Galenism* (Ithaca: Cornell University Press, 1973).

across the saint's body, he begins to straighten out, one at a time, each of his limbs, thus miming the dramatic suspense and astonishment at the miracle. By his histrionics, Martellino, the consummate actor, in effect, improvises a miracle play, a "laude," literally, in honor of a saint.[41] As he transforms what to the crowd is a religious event into a theatrical piece, he obliquely denounces the illusoriness of the belief in supernatural healing and mocks, as well, the gullibility of the people. His act, predictably, appears as blasphemy when a Florentine bystander recognizes him and marvels aloud at his knack for disguise.

Fearing for Martellino's safety, his two friends contrive to have some law officers remove him from the clutches of the mob and haul him to the magistrate's place on trumped-up charges that he has stolen their purse. The appearance of the judge in the narrative, the references that follow his harsh means of managing the law and the violence of the punishment he threatens to inflict on Martellino are balanced by the experience of Riccardo di Chinzica at the other end of the day. The presence of this antithetical symmetry between the two magistrates in the same narrative unit of the second day suggests that no univocal, fixed value can be attached to the various figures of the law in the *Decameron*. In the case of Riccardo, his conflict with wife and pirate is both a measure of law's impotence (in every sense) and a dramatic counter to the mixture of knowledge and blindness which makes up his character. In the novella of Martellino the conflict between magistrate and artist comes forth as the confrontation of two distinct sets of value and power.

If Martellino, by virtue of his profession, antagonizes the mob, the judge, on the contrary, subscribes to the mob's false complaints that Martellino is a thief and tries hard to extort a confession from him. That the distance between judge and jester is wide appears from the detail that Martellino "rispon-

---

[41] For a delineation of the genre, see F. Torraca, *Il teatro italiano nei secoli XIII, XIV, XV* (Livorno: Vigo, 1884).

dea motteggiando," answers jocularly, when the judge inter-
rogates him. The people in the church, upset by the fact that
Martellino has made fools of them by pretending to be a cripple, seize him and beat him; with exact symmetry, the judge,
upset by Martellino's facetious behavior, has him tortured. In
both cases, Martellino's irreverence—his transgression—elic-
its violence. An inference forces itself on us as we observe the
common violent response of both judge and mob. The administration of the law seems to stand in relation to nature as
supernatural healing does to empirical medical practice: in
short, they both appear to be sheer fictions without any bearing on the world of nature. More specifically, the law is the
embodiment of communal values (here both spiritual and material, as if beliefs and purse have the same claims). As such,
the law can only attempt to control and constrain the violations of the jester's anarchic imaginative freedom, the emblem
of which is Martellino's extraterritoriality, his being a Florentine in Treviso. By the same token, the artist's transgressions
unavoidably depend on the existence of norms, which the
judge guarantees, so that a strange complicity can be said to
bind men of law and of art. Similarly the novella that features
Giotto and the jurist Messer Forese da Rabatta (VI, 5) probes in
many ways a version of this complicity.

   The story begins with the assertion of Nature's wondrous
powers: like Fortune, the other providential agency, Nature
conceals her gifts to men.[42] The praise of Nature's generosity
introduces the encomium of Giotto's art; his painting is not a

---

[42] "Carissime donne, egli avviene spesso che, sì come la fortuna sotto vili
arti alcuna volta grandissimi tesori di vertù nasconde, come poco avanti per
Pampinea fu mostrato, così ancora sotto turpissime forme d'uomini si truo-
vano maravigliosi ingegni dalla natura essere stati riposti" (*Decameron*, VI, 5,
p. 550). See also Pampinea's remarks in V, 2, p. 538: ". . . E certo io maladi-
cerei e la natura parimenti e la fortuna, se io non conoscessi la natura esser dis-
cretissima e la fortuna aver mille occhi, come che gli sciocchi lei cieca figurino.
. . . E così le due ministre del mondo spesso le lor cose più care nascondono
sotto l'ombra delle arti reputate più vili, acciò che di quelle alle necessità traen-
dole, più chiaro appaia il loro splendore." For the motif of blindfolded fortune
see chapter 5, n. 35.

flat, faithful mimesis of the physical world; it vies, rather, with Nature's own creativity.[43] The tribute, it should be remarked, reverses Dante's assessment. In *Purgatorio* XI (94–96) Giotto's fame is said to have obscured Cimabue's, but the homage, voiced as it is in the moral context of pride, turns against itself in a recognition of the vanity of esthetic achievements. The word "umiltà" (modesty) Boccaccio uses for Giotto seems calculated to intimate the distance between Dante's and Boccaccio's perspectives. In dramatic terms, the praise of Giotto's art functions primarily as a way of underscoring the legendary ugliness of his physical appearance. It also hints, since Nature is God's art—as we gather from the story that immediately follows, where God's art is said to be painting[44]—that Giotto's artifices are in touch with the essence of Nature.

Giotto's excellence is parallel to the distinction Messer Forese da Rabatta enjoyed as a jurist, and his appearance is just as ugly. The two are caught in a sudden storm and look unkempt and disreputable. Messer Forese, who had been listening to Giotto's stories, turns to him and remarks that if a stranger,

[43] ". . . Giotto, ebbe uno ingegno di tanta eccellenzia, che niuna cosa dà la natura, madre di tutte le cose e operatrice col continuo girare de' cieli, che egli con lo stile e con la penna o col pennello non dipignesse sì simile, anzi più tosto d'essa paresse, in tanto che molte volte nelle cose da lui fatte si truova che il visivo senso degli uomini vi prese errore, quello credendo esser vero che era dipinto" (*Decameron*, VI, 5, p. 550). For Giotto, see also *Boccaccio on Poetry*, XIV, vi.

[44] "Voi dovete sapere che i Baronci furon fatti da Domenedio al tempo che Egli aveva cominciato d'apparare a dipignere, ma gli altri uomini furon fatti poscia che Domenedio seppe dipignere" (*Decameron*, VI, 6, pp. 554–555). Obviously in jest, the lines enact the famous *topos* of Deus Pictor, an example of which occurs in *Paradiso* XVIII, 109–111: "Quei che dipinge lì, non ha chi 'l guidi; / ma esso guida, e da lui si rammenta / quella virtù ch'è forma per li nidi." See also the analogy between painting and writing in the *Conclusione dell'autore*: "Sanza che alla mia penna non dee essere meno d'auttorità conceduta che sia al pennello del dipintore . . ." (*Decameron*, p. 960). For a semiotic understanding of the questions of law and poetry, see Eugene Vance, "Augustine's *Confessions* and the Poetics of the Law" *Modern Language Notes*, 93 (1978), pp. 618–634. For further investigation, see the volume by John A. Alford, *Literature and Law in the Middle Ages: A Bibliography of Scholarship* (New York: Garland Pub., 1984).

who had never seen Giotto before, were to meet him now, he would never believe he was the greatest painter in the world. Giotto quickly replies that the stranger would believe it if, after taking a look at Messer Forese, he would believe the jurist knew his abc. The retort enacts a sort of poetic justice, in that the judge has been paid in kind: judged by his appearance, which is his measure, he is an illiterate. The charge is vicious since the law is that which is written. Retrospectively we can understand the value of the ostensible digression on Giotto's esthetics: his painting, which is the art of creating illusory appearances that can deceive the eye, but which also aims at giving more than visual delight, discloses the jurist's literal vision. Messer Forese, and in this he is an exemplary man of law, is too tied to the world of *evidence*: Giotto, the maker of appearances, knows their inscrutability and illusoriness. Undoubtedly a hierarchy is established between the world of art and that of the law in favor of art: the two worlds, however, are both drawn within the make-believe of appearances. There is an exaggerated, comical distortion of Messer Forese's bondage to what the eyes can detect in the story of Maso del Saggio (VIII, 5), the point of which, as suggested in the preceding chapter, is to expose what the jurist's cultivation of appearances can become: dissemblance and fakery.

It is through this metaphor of appearance that we can attempt to grasp Boccaccio's sense of the law. In the case of the *Divine Comedy*, the poet is nothing less than a "legislator of mankind," as the Romantic formulation has it. In the *Decameron*, Boccaccio views the law as the system whereby the undetermined generality of statutes and codes, indeed their metaphysical principles of nature, can be applied to particular, concrete situations and individuals. But he also shows that abstract principles of Nature are not univocal designations, that there is a gap between principles and the realities to which these principles refer, that the process of linking the two is best described as a rhetorical manipulation, and that, finally, the fictions of the law are never in touch with the complexities of nature as much as art is. To say that the law is caught in the web of literature is also to say what Boccaccio conveys with extraordinary clarity: however wanting the esthetic imagination finds the literal-minded practice and definitions of the law, and viciously satirizes it, the world of art (literature, painting, theatrical forms) for all its constitutive elusiveness which transgresses definitions, aspires to be the law. In this sense law and literature are two specular forms always caught in a process of substitutions, but always unlike each other.

THE VIRTUES:
ETHICS AND RHETORIC

The foregoing chapters have argued that there are no simple moral affirmations to be found in the *Decameron*, but they have also shown the overt and frequent presence of what could be called an ethical lexicon throughout the text. I have focused, let me recall briefly, on questions of justice and natural law, on various claims about the worth of man, references to vices and virtues and on the interplay between political despotism and love's tyranny. I have also examined stilnovistic and utilitarian values as well as the textual exposés of moral hypocrisies in their sundry disguises. So extensive are these concerns that it is necessary to tackle head on the issue of Boccaccio's morality in the *Decameron*. What are Boccaccio's reasons for deploying this moral vocabulary? Is it to be explained in terms of his ironic vision, as a way of dramatizing his perception of a gap between moral ideals and the bleak world of actualities? More than that, is the moral aspect of his language just a part of Boccaccio's representation of reality, but one that has no substantial value of its own? Or is it possible to conceive that Boccaccio the narrator actually ridicules institutions or abstractions which he, as a moralist, endorses? In other words, is the morality part of the irony or is the irony part of his morality, a way of living in and accepting the limitations of our imperfect world?

These questions are in no way new within the scholarly debates on the *Decameron* and are even banal, as a matter of fact, when viewed within the larger province of literary studies.[1]

---

[1] A text that confronts these issues is Paul De Man, *Allegories of Reading*. *Fig-*

From De Sanctis right down to our own days critics have directly or indirectly addressed them and have aligned themselves on opposite sides of the fence. It is as if the readers have
been asked, like Hercules at the *bivium* where he had to make
his choice between *virtus* and *voluptas*, to make up their minds
as to whether the *Decameron* is or is not a moral text. Some
have denied that Boccaccio's concern is anything but the im-
peratives and constraints of art; others, predictably, insist on
the text's ethical finality.[2] This finality has been variously described, but it is often called a social finality, the recognition of
a necessary reconstruction of the social world after its crumbling under the effect of the plague.[3]

These opposite views must be challenged, not so much because they may be wrong as because the formulation of the
problem in both cases takes for granted and neglects what is,
in effect, the core of the issue. The claim about the morality or
amorality of the *Decameron* cannot be sustained unless one is
willing to confront its problematics of virtue and pleasure.
Pleasure is paramount in the narrative: its point of departure is
"piacere" and the "piacevoli ragionamenti d'alcuno amico e le

ural Language in Rousseau, Nietzsche, Rilke, and Proust* (New Haven: Yale University Press, 1979).

   [2] Umberto Bosco, *Il Decameron: saggio* (Catanzaro: Brazia, 1929); Giovanni
Getto, *Vita di forme e forme di vita* (Turin: Petrini, 1958); Benedetto Croce, *Poesia popolare e poesia d'arte*, 5th ed. (Bari: Laterza, 1967); Attilio Momigliano,
ed., *Il Decameron*, ed. E. Sanguineti (Turin: Petrini, 1972); Thomas G. Bergin,
Boccaccio (New York: The Viking Press, 1981), esp. pp. 286–336 for a review
of scholarly positions. In a variety of forms these are some of the critical contributions insisting on the esthetic finality of the *Decameron*.

   [3] Joan Ferrante, "The Frame Characters of the *Decameron*: A Progression of
Virtues," *Romance Philology*, 19 (1965), pp. 212–226; Janet Levarie Smarr,
"Symmetry and Balance in the *Decameron*," *Mediaevalia*, 2 (1976), pp. 159–
187; Millicent Joy Marcus, *An Allegory of Form. Literary Self-Consciousness in
the Decameron* (Saratoga: Anma Libri, 1979); Joy H. Potter, *Five Frames for the
Decameron* (Princeton: Princeton University Press, 1982). A sustained study of
the "social and esthetic" dimensions of the *Decameron* is Marga Cottino-Jones,
Order from Chaos (Washington: University Press of America, 1982). See also
the more historically minded argument by Giorgio Padoan, "Mondo aristocratico e mondo comunale nell'ideologia e nell'arte di Giovanni Boccaccio" in
Il Boccaccio Le Muse il Parnaso e L'Arno (Florence: Olschki, 1978), pp. 1–91.

sue laudevoli consolazioni" (the pleasant conversation of some friends and their welcome comfort, p. 3); the storytellers leave the physical and moral ruins of the city to go to the garden to seek "piacere" (p. 23); the stories themselves are meant to give "diletto" as well as useful advice to the women of leisure. Pleasure, in short, is one of the main metaphors for the text and it is through this category that we are forced to raise the issue of the moral value of the *Decameron*.

Is the pleasure the work conveys merely esthetic or is it also a moral good, what in ethics is called a virtue? Can this pleasure ever become the foundation on which social life is to be constructed? If so, what specific moral scheme does Boccaccio respond to or does he adopt? And how exactly can the imaginative play of utopia, which the storytellers experience in their retreat, be translated into practical terms? Whose pleasure is going to be the law?

These are admittedly difficult questions and their importance can be gauged as soon as they are allowed to resonate against the most general background of moral speculation. A commonplace in the Christian dispensation, for instance, envisions pleasure as the crown of life, the reward to be received when the day's work is done.[4] The sabbath is the day when joy is apportioned. Appropriately, it is in the Garden of Eden that Dante, after his difficult ascent, will take his own pleasure as his guide.[5] In the Aristotelean scheme of values pleasure is, like health, a virtue, but it is not the supreme good. Against Eudoxus, who asserts that pleasure is the good, Aristotle maintains in his *Ethics* that the true character of pleasure is to complete an activity, and it is the type of activity one is engaged in that can determine the moral value of pleasure.[6] Since Nature,

[4] This motif, which depends on the notion of the day of rest at the end of the week of Creation in Genesis, is explored by Renato Poggioli, "The Oaten Flute," *Harvard Library Bulletin*, 11 (1957), pp. 147–184. See also Michael O'Loughlin, *The Garlands of Repose: The Literary Celebration of Civic and Retired Leisure* (Chicago: University of Chicago Press, 1978).

[5] " 'Tratto t'ho qui con ingegno e con arte; / lo tuo piacere omai prendi per duce; / fuor se' de l'erte vie, fuor se' de l'arte" (*Purgatorio* XXVII, 130–132).

[6] The exposition of Eudoxus' views is in *Nichomachean Ethics*, x, 2; the na-

to paraphrase Cicero's remarks in his *De officiis*, has not brought us into the world to behave as if we were created "ad ludum et iocum"—for play and jest, but rather for earnest pursuits, the enjoyments that derive from thought are superior to those that come from the senses.[7]

To map the place the *Decameron* occupies in this complex debate we should from the very start clear the ground of some possible misunderstandings. It should thus be said that in the Introduction to the *Decameron* pleasure is not viewed as a reckless, self-indulgent gratification. The crude hedonism of those who are given to gratifying the belly and, during the plague, move from one tavern to another is discarded, just as the licentious excesses of others are denounced as shameful. The standards of conduct the storytellers impose on themselves are, from this viewpoint, exemplary. Even Dioneo, the libertine whose own pleasure ends up being everybody else's law (with the obvious implication that behind every libertine there looms the shadow of the despot), even Dioneo asks the women of the *brigata* "a sollazzare e a ridere e a cantare con meco insieme vi disponete" (to be willing to amuse themselves and laugh and sing along with me, p. 27) but makes allowance for their "dignità"—their decorum and observance of bounds—in their entertainment. That propriety may the more

---

ture of pleasure is defined as follows: "Pleasure completes the activity not as a characteristic completes an activity by being already inherent in it, but as a completeness that superimposes itself upon it, like the bloom of youth in those who are in their prime" (*Nichomachean Ethics*, x, 4). The translation is by Martin Ostwald, The Library of Liberal Arts (Indianapolis-New York: The Bobbs-Merrill, 1962), pp. 281–282.

[7] The whole passage reads: "For Nature has not brought us into the world to act as if it were created for play or jest, but rather for earnestness and for some more serious and important pursuits. We may, of course, indulge in sport and jest, but in the same way as we enjoy sleep or other relaxations, and only when we have satisfied the claims of our earnest, serious tasks. Further than that, the manner of jesting itself ought not to be extravagant or immoderate, but refined and witty" (*De officiis*, trans. Walter Miller [Cambridge: Harvard University Press, 1968], I, 103, p. 105). The pleasures of contemplation are treated eloquently by Aristotle, *Nichomachean Ethics*, x, 7–8, pp. 288–295 in Ostwald's translation.

easily be secured, Pampinea opposes the very possibility that the calls of pleasure be given unlimited license and insists on "modo"—order and measure (p. 27)—as the norm to be followed. Accordingly, the storytellers establish rules whereby there is an even flow of honorable delight in their daily transactions. The paradigm for their reasonable agreement is the contract to exchange stories, to have each of them provide for and share in their common pastimes.

As if aware of the asocial quality of pleasure and its potential destructiveness, on account of its exclusivism and inherent self-centeredness, Boccaccio stresses in his Proem the bond and virtue of reciprocity as the principle inspiring the *Decameron*. The initial *sententia*, "Umana cosa è avere compassione degli afflitti" (It is human to take pity on those who are in distress), which is a conventional device of exordium in medieval rhetoric, comes forth with the force of a moral aphorism.[8] As such, it announces what can be construed as a fundamental moral norm in the conduct of human life. This compassion for the suffering of others is identified in the second paragraph of the Proem as a virtue of gratitude: "E per ciò che la gratitudine, secondo che io credo, trall'altre virtù è sommamente de commendare e il contrario da biasimare, per non parere ingrato ho meco stesso proposto di volere, in quel poco che per me si può, in cambio di ciò che io ricevetti, . . ." (And since I believe that gratitude, of all the virtues, is most highly to be commended and its contrary condemned, so that I may not appear ungrateful, I have decided to make restitution, as best I can, for what I have received. . . , p. 4).

In formal terms the statement echoes the definition of epideictic rhetoric, the technique by which either censure or, as here, praise is conferred.[9] The object of this subdivision of rhetoric is *honestas*, what is honorable or more generally, as Cicero has it in *De inventione*, virtue understood as a habit of

---

[8] See the equivalent "The lyf so short, the craft so long to lerne," from Chaucer's *The Parliament of Fowls*.

[9] "Demonstrativum est quod tribuitur in alicuius certae personae laudem aut vituperationem; . . ." (*De inventione*, I, 7).

mind in harmony with reason and the order of nature.[10] The word, "virtù," recurs with high frequency throughout the *Decameron* and although it is used loosely (it can designate courage, excellence of character, bodily health, the inner, talismanic as it were, power of objects, etc.), it always carries a positive overtone. What Boccaccio means by the word in this stretch of the text is simply to qualify gratitude as a moral virtue.

The rationale why gratitude is conceived of as a moral virtue is available in a tradition of thought that ranges from Aristotle's *Ethics* to its medieval commentaries such as St. Thomas Aquinas' and, obliquely, Dante. One can recall, for instance, that Dante refers to ingratitude as a form of treachery in that it violates the equations of justice.[11] It is, however, in Aristotle and St. Thomas that one can find the precise philosophical ground for viewing gratitude in ethical terms. In book v of the *Nichomachean Ethics*, under the heading of justice, the Stagirite discusses reciprocity as justice's distinctive mark. The community is held together, we are told, by bonds of mutuality and the reciprocal return of what is due. But there cannot be an exact equality in the return or restoration of a service given. A requital is needed and this requital is the proper province of gratitude. "We should return our services," Aristotle writes, "to one who has done us a favor and another time take the initiative by doing him a favor."[12] Or, as St. Thomas sharply puts it, "Gratitude means that the beneficiary is under a moral obligation to bestow something gratis in return, something which exceeds the quantity of the favor received. This excess

[10] *De inventione*, II, 159: "Nam virtus est animi habitus naturae modo atque rationi consentaneus."

[11] ". . . onde, avvegne che ciascuna vertù sia amabile ne l'uomo, . . . la giustizia . . . è tanto amabile, che, si come dice lo Filosofo nel quinto de l'Etica, li suoi nimici l'amano, . . . e però vedemo che 'l suo contrario, cioè la ingiustizia, massimamente è odiata, sì come è tradimento, ingratitudine, falsitade, furto, rapina, inganno e loro simili" (*Convivio*, eds. G. Busnelli e G. Vandelli, 2nd ed., ed. A. E. Quaglio [Florence: Le Monnier, 1964], I, xii, 9–11). See also Cicero, *De officiis*, I, 47ff. and II, 20. Cf. *Inferno* XI, 61–63.

[12] *Nichomachean Ethics*, V, 5, p. 124 of Ostwald's translation.

is usually paid in money, which, thus, acts as a guarantee of future exchange."[13]

The reference to gratitude in the Proem is couched in the discrete language of commercial transactions (the text speaks of exchange, need, lending, usefulness, etc.), as if to stress that at stake there is an economy of emotions which double but also spoof, and are removed from, the sphere of material goods. It is no doubt possible to exercise a critical suspicion toward this claim of reciprocity and gratitude in a text such as the *Decameron*. The suspicion is legitimate in the light of the obsessive concerns with profit displayed by the most memorable figures who populate the amusing and somewhat perverse universe of the tales: merchants, prostitutes, thieves, cheats, squanderers, gamblers, etc. Chapter 2 has examined the ironic reversals that ensue from the split between the idyllic world of the storytellers and their imaginative constructions in the tales they tell. But the *Decameron* is not only a world of self-serving knaves, liars and fools. There seems to be, actually, a prolongation of the idealized moral world of the storytellers in the stories of the tenth day, and we must turn to them because the question of the *Decameron*'s morality hinges on the value of the *exempla* of liberality narrated under the rule of Panfilo.

Liberality, what Aristotle calls *eleutheriotes*, is a central moral virtue in the *Nichomachean Ethics* and is the mean between extravagant dissipation and stinginess.[14] Since technically it belongs to the orbit of the *bona temporalia*, the virtue tempers the selfish excesses which in the *Decameron* the mercantile ethos, with its focus on profit, favors. For liberality, in the words of Dante's *Convivio*, is the moderator "del nostro dare a del nostro ricevere," while magnificence, generally viewed only as a pleonasm or a mere reinforcement of liberality in the announcement of the theme of the tenth day, is a virtue that moderates "le grandi spese."[15] At any rate, magnif-

[13] *Summa Theologiae*, IIa IIae, 106, art. 6. The translation is taken from T. C. O'Brien, Blackfriars (New York: McGraw-Hill, 1972).

[14] *Nichomachean Ethics*, IV, 1, Ostwald, pp. 83–89.

[15] *Convivio*, IV, xvii, 5.

icence, as Neifile says at the outset of the tenth day, is the light of all the other virtues, the way the sun is the ornament and beauty of the heavens.[16]

We should not be detained at this point (although, as will be seen, it is of great moment) by Neifile's language of ornamentation, which is the province of rhetoric, to describe a moral virtue. Her simile can be taken for now as the means to stress the beauty of magnificence, an approximate equivalent of the argument put forth in Dante's *Convivio* about the beauty of morality.[17] In either case esthetic attributes are made to serve or at least coincide with ethics. Nor can Boccaccio's open insistence on ethics come as a complete surprise. Boccaccio is not given to speculative, philosophical thinking, as Dante, say, is; there is, however, as argued throughout this study, a large and identifiable staging of philosophical concerns in the *Decameron*, and moral philosophy plays a special role. The reason is fairly obvious. So bound is this text to the concrete world of experience, so rooted are its characters in the realm of the variable and the contingent that ethics, that branch of philosophy which is concerned with the practical order of choices and values and which is conventionally defined as the "ars bene vivendi," is the appropriate discipline for probing the principles within which ideal social interactions can be envisioned.[18] Finally, Boccaccio's concern with liberality seals, as it were, the direction of his imaginative path. The occupation of philosophy is traditionally a *meditatio mortis*.[19] To reflect on ethics is to shift the assumptions of philosophy's finality and

[16] "Grandissima grazi, onorabili donne, reputar mi debbo che il nostro re me a tanta cosa, come è a raccontar della magnificenzia, m'abbia preposta: la quale, come il sole è di tutto il cielo bellezza e ornamento, e chiarezza e lume di ciascun'altra virtù" (*Decameron*, x, 1, p. 850).

[17] *Convivio*, iii, xv, 11.

[18] "Ethicam Socrates primus ad corrigendos conponendosque mores instituit, atque omnem studium eius ad bene vivendi disputationem perduxit, dividens eam in quattuor virtutibus animae, id est prudentiam, iustitiam, fortitudinem, temperantiam" (Isidore of Seville, *Etym.*, ii, xxiv, 5).

[19] ". . . Philosophia est ars artium et disciplina disciplinarum. Rursus: Philosophia est meditatio mortis, . . ." (*Etym.*, ii, xxiv, 9). The point of departure of Dante's *Convivio* is the seeking of consolation for Beatrice's death.

move, as the *Decameron* in fact seems to do, away from the
morbid absorption with mortality and the attitude generally
identified as *contemptus mundi* to an imaginative project for survival.

To find out how Boccaccio tests the consistency of the so-
cial-ethical values, as Brunetto Latini classifies them, we shall
look at two stories of the tenth day. The story of Nathan (x,
3) is primarily an exotic, oriental fantasy about the virtue of
liberality. From a strictly rhetorical perspective it can be said
that Boccaccio's narrative point of departure is the exploita-
tion of the technique to the *interpretatio nominum*. The etymology of Nathan, I would like to suggest, is "dans vel dantis."[20]
Nathan, accordingly, is a character who lives out the magic
power of his name in order, paradoxically, to make himself a
name by the systematic practice of generosity to those who
travel by the splendid palace he builds. This etymological figure is of no mere marginal value to the unfolding of the story:
in a context of material possessions lavishly given away, the
proper name—that which one inalienably owns and to the per-
petuation of which the protagonist subjects all he has—will
turn out to be, in this reading, the hub of the novella. For now,
let me stress how the importance of the name finds a thematic
extension in Nathan's concern with "fama," a word that punctuates the narrative and which is to be taken in its full etymological sense from *fari*, that which is spoken of.[21] Nathan
wants to translate his life into a legend. There is another virtue,

[20] "Nathan dedit, sive dantis" is the etymology given by Isidore of Seville,
Etym., VII, viii, 7. On etymology as a category of thought, see E. R. Curtius,
European Literature and the Latin Middle Ages, trans. W. R. Trask (New York
and Evanston: Harper & Row, 1963), pp. 495–500. On the figure of Nathan
and its etymological value, see the remarks by Gian Roberto Sarolli, *Prolego-
mena alla "Divina Commedia"* (Florence: Olschki, 1971), pp. 240–246.

[21] "Fama autem dicta quia fando, id est loquendo, pervagatur per traduces
linguarum et aurium serpens. Est autem nomen et bonarum rerum et ma-
larum" (Isidore, *Etym.*, v, xxvii, 26). See also the following: ". . . avvenne
che la sua fama agli orecchi pervenne d'un giovane chiamato Mitridanes, . . .
il quale . . . divenuto della sua fama . . . invidioso . . ." ". . . come della fama
di Natan udiva diminuimento della sua estimava . . ." (*Decameron*, x, 3, pp.
861–862).

magnanimity, that coupled with his liberality, will serve him well in his efforts. The text alludes to his magnanimity when we are told at the outset that he has "... animo grande e liberale e disideroso che fosse per opera conosciuto, ..." (lofty and generous mind, and eager to be known by the works he performs, p. 860).

Actually, if this were the *Divine Comedy*, Nathan's magnanimity would have gained him "onrata nominanza" (honored fame), as Dante calls the recognition granted the great spirits ("spiriti magni") who lived outside of the Christian dispensation (*Inferno* iv, 76ff.) and would be sitting not too far from the lonely Saladin, as another embodiment of the luminous earthly values sheltered, ironically, in the semiobscurity of Limbo.[22] But Boccaccio assigns a central place to what Dante puts in the noble castle at the threshold of the beyond. Nathan, in fact, is said to dwell at the midpoint of the crossroads of the West and East in what clearly is a symbolic reformulation and acknowledgment of the virtue of classical Humanism.

This virtue impels man to perform great deeds, or as Brunetto Latini and Bono Giamboni respectively put it—"faire les hautes choses" and "fare grandi cose"—and as such it is the very principle of the story's dramatic action.[23] Nathan gives himself completely to his "opera" and to his "fare," while Mithridanes' own plan to kill Nathan is itself an "impresa," a

---

[22] *Inferno* iv is inhabited by the figures of antiquity who have won "onrata nominanza" (l. 76). Ironically, in this area of poets and learned men, Dante also puts the infants ("infanti," l. 30)—a word that has to be understood in its etymological sense as those without language—a sharp counterpoint to the wisdom and poetic achievements of the other shades. It should be pointed out that the Saladin is among the "spirit magni"—"e solo, in parte, vidi 'l Saladino" (l. 129). I shall consider the story of the Saladin as told in x, 9. On this story see the fine reading by Franco Fido, "Il sorriso di Messer Torello," *Romance Philology*, 23 (1969), pp. 154–171; see also the remarks by Giorgio Cavallini, *La decima giornata del "Decameron"* (Rome: Bulzoni, 1980), pp. 147–174.

[23] Brunetto Latini, *Li Livres dou tresor*, ed. Francis J. Carmody (Berkeley and Los Angeles: University of California Press, 1948), II, xxiii, "De Magnanimité," p. 193. See also *Il Tesoro di Brunetto Latini volgarizzato da Bono Giamboni*, ed. P. Chabaille (Bologna: Romagnoli, 1880), III, p. 73.

counteraction to Nathan's noble deeds. At the same time, as a virtue opposed to pusillanimity, magnanimity accounts for Nathan's firmness in confronting Mithridanes' threat.

In this battle of virtues and vices, Nathan's virtues are not without dangers.[24] Almost in defiance of the more canonical views that make liberality the practice by which man may live without fear and in a reasonable expectation of a good end, Boccaccio shows how Nathan's liberality sparks Mithridanes' rivalry and homicidal compulsion. The urge to do away with Nathan certainly comes from his envious resentment at his own inability to equal the rival's renown. From this perspective the tale is a straightforward parable of a contrast between liberality and envy, and the contrast is also figured as one between the old and the young. The contrast is resolved when Mithridanes acknowledges his sin, envy, and, in a transparent punning with the etymology of the word, "invidia," he says he has now opened the eyes of his intellect to his error.[25] But the overt contrast between Nathan's virtue and Mithridanes' vices notwithstanding, the two characters are close from the start: the blind rage of the one originates from his desire to emulate the prestige of the other. There is a telling parallel between them: they both disguise their respective identities. Eventually, believing Nathan's disguise to be true, Mithridanes confides to the old man his plan by a ". . . lunga circuizion di parole" (a long circumlocution, p. 863). The phrase, I submit, translates the technical *circuitus verborum* and it qualifies Mithridanes' rhetoric of concealment which he, paradoxically, reveals to Nathan himself.[26] In effect, Mithridanes os-

---

[24] Even the story of Gualtieri and Griselda (x, 10) can be read in terms of a *psychomachia*. See chapter 4 above.

[25] ". . . a Idio, più al mio dover sollicito che io stesso, a quel punto che maggior bisogno è stato gli occhi m'ha aperto dello 'ntelletto, li quali misera invidia m'avea serrati." For the sense of the pun see the metaphoric equivalence between blindness and envy in *Purgatorio* XIII.

[26] This is a moment in the text when Mithridanes, who generally simulates his intent of killing Nathan, opens up to Nathan, who is concealing his true identity. The two principals are caught in the same moves, albeit for completely different reasons.

cillates between emulation and aggression and in this bind each impulse is like the other face of the same coin. But what about Nathan's generosity? Is it as entirely innocent a virtue as it seems?

Nathan is presented at the start as being "ricco senza comparazione" (p. 860)—so incomparably rich that the practice of liberality can easily place him above all things. In this sense he enacts the moral principle whereby the wealthy man, to avoid being a slave to his own money, must manage, in the formula of Brunetto Latini, ". . . sousmetre mes choses a moi, non pas moi a mes choses."[27] By placing himself above all things and giving them away, the virtue of liberality frees him. His freedom from things is so total that he can even go around disguised as the humblest servant of his own household. But his freedom enslaves all people to him and to the things he renounces. He is acknowledged as being at the apex of the hierarchy he establishes; by the same token, as the recipients get all Nathan does not value, they subject themselves to those very things. The structure of generosity always makes the virtue suspect. This perception about the ambiguous implications of the metaphor of giving is not an interpretation made possible only by the awareness of contemporary critical perspectives; it is, rather, a reflection explicitly voiced by moral authorities such as Bono Giamboni and Brunetto Latini, who states that "rechevoir don n'est autre chose ke vendre sa franchise; . . ."[28] In the system of values Nathan sets up, it is especially Mithridanes, Nathan's greatest rival, who is his greatest slave.

It is in the context of this insidious, subtle narcissism at the heart of the most altruistic virtue imaginable, liberality, that we can grasp the sense of the final section of the novella, which to commentators has seemed to be little more than an appendage to the brunt of the action. The triumph of virtue over vice is ostensibly sealed with Mithridanes' discovery that the humble servant assisting him in his murderous plans is Nathan in

---

[27] *Li tresors*, II, cxviii, 6, p. 300.

[28] *Li tresors*, II, lxxxxv, 10, p. 278; see also *Il Tesoro. Volgarizzato da Bono Giamboni*, III, p. 398: "Ricevere dono non è altro, che vendere sua franchezza."

disguise. The reconciliation that ensues climaxes with Nathan's offer to Mithridanes that they exchange roles: "Tu rimarrai, giovane come tu se', qui nella mia casa e avrai nome Natan, e io me n'andrò nella tua e farommi sempre chiamar Mitridanes" (You remain here in my house, young as you are, and assume the name of Nathan, while I go and live in yours and shall call myself Mithridanes, p. 867). The remark is primarily the logical outcome of Nathan's generosity, the unflinching giving away of his own very life to one who wants it. But there is also a sinister underside to it. For Nathan is engaged in a gesture of appropriation of the young rival-emulator to the continuity of the legend of his life and his name.

Paradoxically, then, by the end the parable of liberality edges toward making liberality appear open to the suspicion that it may also be a strategy for achieving the triumph of one's fame, for an unequivocal passion for the name possesses and transcends the minds of the two principals. In the *Divine Comedy* the magnanimous souls are awarded with "onrata nominanza"—a privilege that is at the same time the virtuous heathens' pain. Boccaccio, who ponders in this novella the value of the values, as it were, ambiguously celebrated in Dante's Limbo, hints how the practice of total liberality slides into a selfish, all-consuming desire for fame, how Nathan's liberality is a slave to his name's fame.

There is no doubt that for all its ambiguity liberality comes forth as a splendid virtue, one that reverses the values of the world (kings are intent on laying waste cities for the sake of their fame, says Nathan in his speech). Yet a cloud of unreality hovers over Filostrato's account. This unreality is suggested by the fact that the narrative takes place in a far-away mythical land, like many other stories of the tenth day. It is also hinted at in the preamble when we are told the origin of the tale: its source is the oral report of some Genoese merchants. The very phrase, ". . . se fede si può dare alle parole d'alcuni genovesi . . ." (if one is to believe the words of some Genoese, p. 860) reminds us that at stake is the question of the authority, in the sense of the authenticity of the source. One is also reminded of the long tradition, which stretches from Vergil's *Aeneid* to Dante's *Inferno*, about the Ligurians' fraudulence.[29] The point is not simply that one should outright disbelieve, however hyperbolic and equivocal, the *exemplum* of liberality; one is invited, on the contrary, to entertain the suspicion that one is reading a tale with a questionable truth value.

There is another story of the tenth day where ethical virtues are recalled and their impasse is dramatized. This is the novella of Tito and Gisippo (x, 8), which unfolds at the time of the Roman Empire when Augustus was emperor. The implication is that Boccaccio is probing a pre-Christian value system and, more precisely, the ordeals of a classical humanistic virtue (about which Christian thinkers were legitimately uneasy), friendship. In book VIII of Aristotle's *Ethics* friendship is acknowledged as a central moral virtue, an experience by which two partners in a friendship hold things in common and wish the same thing for one another.[30]

The friendship between Tito and Gisippo is nurtured from their boyhood when Tito, a Roman, is sent by his father to Athens to live in Gisippo's household so that together the two boys, for all their differences, may be taught to perpetuate their own parents' friendship and pursue the most complete agreement, as Laelius, in Cicero's *De amicitia*, says friends

[29] *Aeneid*, XI, 700 ff. ". . . And next she comes upon the warrior son of Aunus, who had ridden from the Appennines, one not the least of the Ligurians so long as fates allow him still to cheat." The translation is taken from *The Aeneid of Vergil*, trans. Allen Mandelbaum (New York: Bantam Books, 1972), p. 297. See also *Inferno* XXXIII, 151–153: "Ahi Genovesi, uomini diversi / d'ogni costume e pien d'ogne magagna, / perche non siete voi del mondo spersi?"

[30] "The perfect form of friendship is that between good men who are alike in excellence or virtue. For these friends wish alike for one another's good because they are good men, and they are good *per se* (that is, their goodness is something intrinsic, not incidental). Those who wish for their friends' good for their friends' sake are friends in the truest sense, . . ." (VIII, 2, Ostwald, p. 219). The *topos* of friendship in this story has been examined by Barry L. Weller, *The Other Self: Aspects of the Classical Rhetoric of Friendship in the Renaissance*, Yale Dissertation, 1974.

ought to do.[31] For Cicero the guide to friendship is nature. In this novella the act of friendship is not just a spontaneous natural experience, but is achieved through an exercise of education, what in antiquity was known as *paideia*, the discipline through which individuals shape their lives in pursuit of virtue. The boys' instruction is provided by Aristippus.[32] Who is Aristippus? Why does Boccaccio use this name?

Neither medieval scholars nor editors of the *Decameron* have told us much about this philosopher: the presence of his name in the novella is generally attributed to his having been the founder of the Cyrenaic school, and because he is believed to have lived in the fifth century B.C., it is correctly pointed out that it would be an anachronism to identify Tito's and Gisippo's tutor with the founder of that school.[33] There is, however, a substantial medieval tradition that consistently makes Aristippus the generalized emblem for an ethical hedonism, for the belief, that is, that only practical ethics offers a reliable pathway to the pursuit of a life of happiness and that happiness is dependent on pleasure.

The text that is likely to have been the storehouse of opinions on Aristippus is Cicero's *De finibus* in which repeatedly the philosopher's views are linked to those of Epicurus.[34] The

[31] "For friendship is nothing else than an accord in all things, human and divine, conjoined with mutual goodwill and affection . . ." (Cicero, *De amicitia*, trans. W. A. Falconer [Cambridge: Harvard University Press, 1964], vi, 20, p. 131).

[32] "Dal qual Tito nelle proprie case di lui fu allogato in compagnia d'un su figliuolo nominato Gisippo, e sotto la dottrina d'un filosofo, chiamato Aristippo, e Tito e Gisippo furon parimente da Cremete posti a imprendere" (*Decameron*, p. 901).

[33] "Nome evidentemente coniato su quello del celebre filosofo di Cirene vissuto nel IV sec. a. C." (Branca, *Decameron*, p. 1532).

[34] See, for instance, the following: "The Chief Good is pleasure, say you Epicureans. Well then, you must explain what pleasure is; otherwise it is impossible to make clear the subject under investigation. Had Epicurus cleared up the meaning of pleasure, he would not have fallen into such confusion. Either he would have upheld pleasure in the same sense as Aristippus, that is, an agreeable and delightful excitation of the sense . . ." (*De finibus*, trans.

same link is asserted by Lactantius who distinguished, however, between Epicurus' notion that the *summum bonum* is to be found "in voluptate animi" and Aristippus' conviction that the highest good is to be found "in voluptate corporis."[35] A fuller characterization of Aristippus' thought is available in St. Augustine's *City of God*.[36] After discussing the two schools of philosophy, the Italic and the Ionian, St. Augustine focuses on Socratic philosophy as the first to have directed its efforts to teaching principles for living a moral life. Socrates' handling of moral questions, St. Augustine tells us, allows his disciples to give diverse and contradictory opinions in defining the chief good. Whereas Antisthenes assigned the *summum bonum* to virtue, Aristippus assigned it to pleasure. Later in book xviii Aristippus and Antisthenes are once again mentioned together as an instance of the contradictions within the Socratic doctrine, and Aristippus is said to make the delight of the body the chief good, while Antisthenes places it in the virtue of the mind.[37] The idea that Aristippus stands for physical pleasures alone

---

H. Rackham [Cambridge: Harvard University Press, 1967], ii, 18, pp. 99–101). See also *De finibus*, ii, 34, 39, 41, etc. Particularly important is Cicero's discussion of friendship and Epicurus in i, 65.

[35] A survey of the various texts dealing with Aristippus and Cyrenaic thought is available in Gabriele Giannantoni, *I cirenaici. Raccolta delle fonti antiche, traduzione e studio introduttivo* (Florence: Sansoni, 1958). See also D. R. Dudley, *A History of Cynicism from Diogenes to the 6th Century A.D.* (London: Methuen, 1937). For Lactantius, see *Divinae institutiones* in *Corpus Scriptorum Ecclesiasticorum Latinorum (CSEL)*, xix, iii, 7, 7; cf. also iii, 8, 6 and iii, 15, 15.

[36] "Now, that which is called the final good is that at which, when one has arrived, he is blessed. But so diverse were the opinions held by those followers of Socrates concerning this final good, that . . . some placed the chief good in pleasure, as Aristippus, others in virtue as Antisthenes" (*The City of God*, trans. Marcus Dods [New York: The Modern Library, 1950], viii, 3, pp. 246–247).

[37] "Were not both Aristippus and Antisthenes there, two noble philosophers and both Socratic? yet they placed the chief end of life within bounds so diverse and contradictory, that the first made the delight of the body the chief good, while the other asserted that man was made happy mainly by the virtue of the mind" (*The City of God*, xviii, 41, p. 649).

reappears in a Church Father such as Eucherius, who writes that to make beautitude reside "in corporis voluptate" is to believe that "Deus venter est et gloria in pudendis eius."[38]

This alleged emphasis on the practical, material terms of happiness (devotion to wealth, luxury, enjoyment of the moment) accounts for the persuasion that Aristippus' teaching is ultimately a recognition that power alone counts. This particular aspect of what can be called the mythography of Aristippus is stressed by Valerius Maximus in his *Factorum et dictorum memorabilium*, a text which is conventionally taken to be the actual source of the novella of Tito and Gisippo.[39] Under the heading, "De abstinentia et continentia," Valerius juxtaposes the frugality of Dyogenes the Cynic and the hedonism of Aristippus, who flatters the tyrant of Syracuse, so that he may have room in the tyrant's palace.[40]

The novella does not provide any hint of the substance of Aristippus' doctrine: the two young men grow together in friendship, for friendship is the goal of philosophy, whereby friends, in good will, converse together. This harmonious relation between them lasts till Tito falls in love with Sofronia, the young woman Gisippo is expected to marry. In a dramatic context such as this, which overtly focuses on the education of two philosophers, it is difficult to ignore the resonance of the young woman's name. For Sofronia is akin to *sophrosyne*, which literally means soundness of mind. The term has also come to mean in Aristotle's *Ethics*, self-control and mastery in

[38] *Epistola Paraenetica, PL* 50, col. 724.

[39] The importance of Valerius Maximus for Boccaccio has long been the focus of critical attention: A. E. Quaglio, "Valerio Massimo e il *Filocolo* di Giovanni Boccaccio," *Cultura neolatina*, 20 (1960), pp. 45–77; M. T. Casella, "Il Valerio Massimo in volgare: dal Lancia al Boccaccio," *Italia medioevale e umanistica*, 6 (1963), pp. 49–136; by Casella see also "Nuovi argomenti per l'attribuzione del volgarizzamento di Valerio Massimo al Boccaccio," *Studi sul Boccaccio*, 10 (1978), pp. 109–121. The presence of Valerius Maximus in the story of Tito and Gisippo is suggested by Giorgio Padoan, "Sulla genesi e la pubblicazione del 'Decameron,' " in *Il Boccaccio Le Muse il Parnaso*, pp. 107–108.

[40] Valerius Maximus, *Factorum et dictorum memorabilium libri novem*, ed. C. Kempf (Stuttgart: Teubner, 1966), IV, iii, 4, p. 187.

dealing with the pleasures of the body.[41] But Boccaccio's tale is not an allegory of a quest for intellectual wisdom, and, ironically, Sofronia is a bodily beauty in the presence of which Tito loses his rational self-control. His love does not entail a direct espousal of Aristippus' likely hedonistic vision. Quite to the contrary, Tito's mind is a theater on the stage of which a genuine moral debate is played out. The terms of the *psychomachia* (the text explicitly refers to Tito's thoughts and ". . . la battaglia di quegli . . . ," p. 904) are the age-old contrast between *amor* and *amicitia*, passion and reason, pleasure and duty. Love's hegemony is undisputed and its anarchic power is said to shatter all restraints and order, incite incestuous passions and, a fortiori, violate the bonds of friendship (p. 903).

There is no doubt that the claims of reciprocity, which friendship fosters and which lie at the root of friendship, collapse under the pressure of an implacably exclusive passion. In reality, it is even possible to infer that the very reciprocity of friendship generates the various complications of the plot. As in the case of Guglielmo Guardastagno and Guglielmo Rossiglione (IV, 9), where the love for the same woman is the logical outcome of the mirrorlike identity of the two knights as well as its inevitable stumbling block, here too we see how Tito's love for Sofronia belongs to this ambiguous pattern of identity and difference. Tito's disclaimer in his soliloquy (". . . Io non l'amo perché ella sia di Gisippo, anzi l'amo che l'amerei di chiunque ella stata fosse . . .") (I do not love her because she is Gisippo's; were she anybody else's I would still love her, p. 903) betrays the suspicion, above and beyond Tito's denial, that theirs is a love triangle, wherein the woman is the passive focus of displacement of the two friends' rivalries: for Tito, this is a way of owning what Gisippo owns and, at the same time, of establishing the difference between themselves, but in his terms.

This fundamental self-centeredness of passion does not come to the tragic denouement that seals the destiny of the two

---

[41] Aristotle understands self-control as a mean in regard to pleasures: it deals with the pleasures of the body, but not with all of these (*Nichomachean Ethics*, III, 10).

Guglielmos. Tito and Gisippo, by contrast, are bent on denying what their actions dramatize. Thus, pleasure is not viewed
as a divisive experience that friendship can't accommodate,
and as Tito says, ". . . Ecco, Gisippo, io non so quale io mi dica
che io faccia più, o il mio piacere o il tuo, faccendo quello che
tu pregando mi di che tanto ti piace; . . ." (See here, Gisippo,
I do not know which it is I am doing, my pleasures or yours in
carrying out what you tell me would please you so much, p.
907). This private reconciliation of conflicting pleasures is belied by the dramatics of the novella: the arrangement the two
friends devise, to have Tito secretly replace Gisippo in Sofronia's bedroom and marry her without her knowledge, draws
attention to the absurdities of the scheme. Later, when Tito is
summoned back to Rome and the two friends' contrivance becomes public, Gisippo loses his social prestige and Tito must
defend himself from the charge of having injured, by his actions, the Greek families' ethos.

The story turns, at this point, into an overt rhetorical performance whereby Tito deploys all the weapons of his oratory
(flattery, self-praise, value of his lineage, Rome's mastery over
Athens—which is itself the worn-out motif of the two cities'
rivalry) both as a way of celebrating the sovereign virtue of
friendship and, ironically, his own superior worth. The irony
is compounded, as the myth of friendship is upheld, by the fact
that Tito now reverses his earlier statements about the su-
premacy of love. The clear implication of the reversal is that
Tito's assertions are rhetorical ratiocinations he crafts to place
his actions on a moral high ground. Seen from this perspective, the novella dramatizes not just the abiding value of
friendship, but also the sheer power of rhetoric to create values, to provide moral justifications that fit radically contrasting actions. It can be said, in this context, that the shadow of
Aristippus could not have loomed larger: the name, with all
the resonances it has in the history of medieval moral philosophy, obliquely discloses the reality of self-serving convictions and pleasures unwittingly breaking through the abstract
system of rational ethics.

More to the point, the power of rhetoric to establish moral

values comes particularly to focus when the dramatic action moves to the courtroom in Rome. We remember the unlikely series of events leading to this climactic scene: Gisippo—as Boccaccio says using commercial metaphor, ". . . da tutti poco a capital tenuto," (held generally in little esteem, p. 915)—is banished from Athens and comes to Rome where he is unjustly accused of murder. In the courtroom, Tito finally recognizes his friend and, to save him, accuses himself of the crime till the real murderer, in a fit of compassion, steps forth to confess his guilt. The general shedding of concealments and disguises that the text dramatizes seems in itself a rhetorical deception: the restoration of Gisippo's fortunes (he marries Tito's sister) confirms the point of the story, the overpowering, noble value of friendship; yet the theatricality of the finale draws the harmonious resolution of the two friends' ordeal within the confines of a probable self-delusion. The judge, for instance, falls under the spell of the friends' rhetoric of one's self-immolation for the other (which in itself carries the hint that rivalry inheres the supposed harmony of friendship, especially as one tries to prove oneself the better friend of the other) and condones the killer. This excess of pathos is a parody of a just judgment and as it blots out the violence of the killing, it casts light on the ambivalent edge of friendship; friendship is an ethical virtue that may harbor and conceal violence.

The moral ambivalence of these various virtues cannot lead us to the hasty conclusion that Boccaccio endorses in the *Decameron* an ethics of private pleasures, the sort of "Epicurean" values that Aristippus' name exemplifies, above and beyond the idealized practice of reciprocity and social order. What he does probe, here as well as everywhere else in the *Decameron*, is the fragility of all abstract assumptions, the shiftiness of principles and interests, the stubborn contradictions that dwell in the middle of our realities. Medieval encyclopedias, such as the *Trésor*, represent the world through neatly distinct categories of knowledge: ethics, rhetoric, politics, science. This purity and rigor of arrangement is exactly what the *Decameron*, which resembles an encyclopedic text, reshuffles. There is never an action that is absolutely disinterested and yet, what seems to be an economic pursuit under close inspection may turn out to hide within itself an esthetic disinterest; erotic passion may also be a political statement; ethics can be confused with rhetoric; the arts, such as medicine and law, vie with the world of play. Boccaccio's grasp of these confusions, of the unalterable contradictions which the various characters muddle through, is what makes him so firmly antisystematic. More than that, his sense that there are no unvarying rules or fixed moral absolutes leads him to elaborate *an art of the possible*, the sort of writing, such as the *Decameron*, which is of necessity a universe of relative, multiple perspectives and reversible metaphors, and in which literally everything can happen.

This kind of art cannot be prematurely reduced to a form of tragic irony, for irony is an intellectual weapon that establishes the hierarchy of the mind over the body; it is the trope of the mind that, detached, knows all along both the futility and inevitability of all efforts at making sense. Boccaccio's art can best be described in terms of humor, which is to be understood both as the genial recognition of fatuity and of the contingency of any formulation, and as the willingness to laugh with and at our efforts to keep in focus the disparate facets of our encounters, to know how to put aside the spirit of seriousness and, simply, to play. How does this ethical virtue of play become part of the social experience and where does Boccaccio find this notion?

There is no laughter, as the fathers of the Church well knew, in the Bible.[42] St. Augustine and St. Ambrose must have felt

---

[42] But there is laughter in the Church. Leaving aside the vision the Franciscans had of themselves as *ioculatores Domini*,—a motif that certainly accounts for the ease with which they figure as material for literary parodies and jests— one could recall the still valuable article on Church and laughter by E. R. Curtius, "Scherz und Ernst in mittelalterlicher Dichtung," *Romanische Forschungen*, 53 (1939), pp. 1–26. Even John of Salisbury admits that "Iocundum quidem est et ab honesto non recedit uirum probum quandoque modesta hilaritate mulceri, . . ." (*Policraticus*, C.C.I. Webb [Oxford: Clarendon Press,

comfortable with the biblical dismissal of the "assembly of jesters," if for no other reason than that this was an obvious point of contact with Roman *gravitas* or, at least, with Cicero's warnings about that "genus jocandi," which he calls "illibe-rale, petulans, flagitiosum, obscoenum."[43] But it was left to St. Thomas Aquinas to update and rethink the virtue of play which he found in the *Nichomachean Ethics* and which he calls, in due acknowledgment of Aristotle, *eutrapelia*.[44] The *eutrape-los* for Aristotle is literally "the one who turns well" and stands between the *bomolochos*, the vulgar buffoon who itches to have his jokes at all costs for the sake of a good meal and who never keeps within the bounds of decorum, and the *agroikos*, the boor who is of no use in playful conversation, who contributes nothing and takes offense at everything. The *eutrapelos* is the person who jests with good taste, and is witty and versatile, that is to say, full of good turns.

St. Thomas develops the Aristotelean text by making pleas-ure, the relaxation from worldly and intellectual cares, a nec-

---

1909], I, 8, p. 48). On this issue see especially Romano Guardini, *The Church and the Catholic and the Spirit of Liturgy* (New York: Sheed and Ward, 1935); David L. Miller, *Gods and Games: Toward a Theology of Play* (New York and Cleveland: The World Publishing Co., 1970); Hugo Rahner, *Man at Play*, trans. B. Battershaw and E. Quinn (New York: Herder and Herder, 1972).

[43] "Duplex omnino est iocandi genus, unum illiberale, petulans, flagi-tiosum, obscenum, alterum elegans, urbanum, ingeniosum, facetum. . . . Fa-cilis igitur est distinctio ingenui et illiberalis ioci. Alter est, si tempore fit, ut si remisso animo, gravissimo homine dignus, alter ne libero quidem, si rerum turpitudini adhibetur verborum obscenitas. . . . Suppeditant autem et campus noster et studia venandi honesta exempla ludendi" (*De officiis*, I, 104). The phrase "assembly of jesters" is from Jer. 15:17. St. Ambrose, commenting on Luke 6:25, "woe to you who laugh now, for you shall weep," dismisses ex-cessive fun, *PL* 33, col. 961. For St. Augustine, see *Super Joan.* 16, 14, *PL* 35, col. 1891.

[44] "Eutrapelia" is listed, along with "Affabilitate," as one of the virtues by Dante in *Convivio*. Discussing the moral virtues in Aristotle's *Ethics*, he enu-merates the eleven virtues starting with "fortezza," to "temperanza," "liber-alitate," "magnificenzia," "magnanimitade," ". . . Eutrapelia, la quale mod-era noi ne li sollazzi facendo, quelli usando debitamente" (IV, xvii, 6). An ex-tended discussion is by St. Thomas Aquinas, *Summa theologiae*, IIa IIae, 168, art. 2. See also Aristotle's *Ethics*, II, 8.

essary remedy for the soul's fatigue, for "the human spirit would snap were it never unbent."[45] The solaces of the soul are available to the *eutrapelos*, the person with a happy cast of mind that ". . . convertit aliqua dicta, vel facta in solatium."[46] Not even Ambrose, St. Thomas thinks, banished altogether jocularity from "conversatione humana," but only from theology.[47] Accordingly, neither the acting profession nor actors are in a state of sin, provided that their art is temperate, that is, they do not labor with indecent phrases and actions, and "play is not intruded into unfitting times and occasions."[48]

There is no doubt that the whole of the *Decameron* begins from this occasion of the "piacevoli ragionamenti d'alcuno amico e le sue laudevoli consolazioni" (the pleasant conversation of some friends and their welcome comfort, p. 3) Boccaccio has received and which he now gratefully offers for the relief of lovers' melancholy absorptions; and it is equally clear

[45] The text continues "Those words and deeds in which nothing is sought beyond the soul's pleasure are called playful or humorous, and it is necessary to make use of them at times for solace of soul. This is what Aristotle says, that in the social intercourse of this life a kind of rest is enjoyed in playing" (*Summa theologiae*, IIa IIae, 168, art. 2, Blackfriars' trans. pp. 217–219). In question 168 article 3 St. Thomas makes allowance for the acting profession: "Nor are actors in a state of sin provided their art is temperate, that is, they do not labour with indecent phrases and actions, and play is not intruded into unfitting times and occasions" (Blackfriars, p. 223).

[46] *Summa theologie*, IIa IIae, 1682, resp.: "Et ideo circa ludos potest esse aliqua virtus, quam Philosophus *eutrapeliam* nominat: et dicitur aliquis eutrapelus a bona conversione, quia scilicet bene convertit aliqua dicta, vel facta in solatium. Et inquantum per hanc virtutem homo refrenatur ab immoderantia ludorum sub modestia continetur."

[47] "Unde Ambrosius non excludit universaliter iocum a conversatione humana, sed a doctrina sacra: . . ." (*Summa theologiae*, IIa IIae, 168, 2, r. 1). Cf. Bono Giamboni's adaptation of Brunetto Latini's *Tresor*: "A tenere lo mezzo si è, che l'uomo sia piacevole in parlare e conversare ed in usare con le genti. . . . E questa conversazione è quasi somigliante all'amistà, ed evvi differenza in questo: che l'amistà conviene avere compassione ed umile coraggio, la conversazione no, però che l'uomo che non cognosce" (*Il Tesoro*, ed. Chabaille, III, p. 81). For Brunetto Latini's own text, cf. *Li Livres dou tresor*, ed. Carmody, II, xxv, p. 196. Cf. also *Convivio*, IV, xvii, 6, for the virtue of conversation which Dante calls "Affabilitade."

[48] *Summa theologiae*, IIa IIae, 168, 2, p. 223.

that the play in the garden is consistent with good manners so that one could say with Cicero that the light of a sound mind is cast on the storytellers' very fun. But it is particularly in the sixth day of the *Decameron*, which is under the rule of Elissa, that conversation, speaking well, either as "leggiadro motto" or as "pronta risposta," is celebrated in terms which recall St. Thomas' virtue of *eutrapelia*.

A convenient contrast to Boccaccio's concern with the "leggiadro motto" is the *Novellino* which is openly centered on "fiori di parlare" and "belle cortesie . . . be' riposi . . . belle valentie e doni, secondo che, per lo tempo passato, hanno fatto molti valenti uomini."[49] The patterns of this collection's imagination are crystallized in the parenthetical remark, "per lo tempo passato." For here there is a full display of an imaginative longing for the past, a past of heroes, social grace and polish of manner. The anaphoric epithet, "bei . . . belle," clearly announces that the aristocratic world, evoked by memory's conjurations, is one of esthetic grace, and the flowers of speech are its code of propriety. In this reverie of the idealized courtly conventions, to speak well is never a question of vocabulary or syntax and even less is it a question of confronting the secrets of style. The flowers of speech are coextensive with the moral virtues of noble deeds and gifts in a circuit of free exchange by exceptional characters.

The sixth day of the *Decameron*, by contrast, ushers in a narrative situation whereby speaking is primarily the place of encounter of different social classes. In the elegant setting of the Introduction, Dioneo and Lauretta are engaged in singing about Troilo and Criseida; in a comical counterpoint to this song, there is a "romore"—a word repeated four times—that comes from the kitchen. Tindaro and Licisca, as it happens, have been involved in a debate about women's sexuality and their families' repression. The humor in Licisca's account comes not

---

[49] I am using the edition of *Il Novellino*, ed. G. Favati (Genoa: Bozzi, 1970). On the collection, see S. Battaglia, "Premesse per una valutazione del *Novellino*," in *Giovanni Boccaccio e la riforma della narrativa* (Naples: Liguori, 1969), pp. 83–118.

from any breach of linguistic decorum, but from her effort to veil, under the guise of personification and metaphors of bloody warfare, a transparent sexual feat. In the story of Cisti (VI, 2), the Florentine baker who offers some wine to Messer Geri and refuses it later to him when one of Geri's servants brings a huge flask to be filled, taste is not the monopoly of courtiers or of characters of higher ranks. It is as if in this brief story the principle of style is both a moral and esthetic attitude, an experience in which propriety (in the double sense) and generosity mingle. This impression of social grace and wit comes forth in the novella of the Marchioness of Montferrat (I, 5) who through the subtleties of her social behavior puts down the king's improprieties.

The social value of speaking well, finally, is openly dramatized, as the scholarship on the *Decameron* has long acknowledged, in the novella of Madonna Oretta (VI, 1) in which the pleasures of storytelling, the talent to know how to turn a sentence, the subtle art of obliquity in the reprimand all come together.[50] The story, as is known, is told for the entertainment of Madonna Oretta while she and the teller are riding on a horse. Clearly a link is established between riding and storytelling: Madonna Oretta begs the knight to set her down because, she says, the horse trots jerkily—an affable, if blunt, rebuff of his poor performance. If this were a Platonic parable of virtue, the riding of the horse would inescapably be the metaphor for the soul's poise and steadiness, but in Boccaccio's handling, riding stands for esthetic control. There is a special resonance, I would like to add, that comes forth from the parallel deployment of the two metaphors of riding and storytelling and I take the resonance to be the emblem of what a conversation is. What is essential to a conversation is the viewpoint—not simply the joining of the two perspectives in

[50] Pamela Stewart, "La novella di Madonna Oretta e le due parti del *Decameron*," *Yearbook of Italian Studies* (1973–75), pp. 27–40; Franco Fido, "Boccaccio's *Ars narrandi* in the Sixth Day of the *Decameron*," in *Italian Literature: Roots and Branches*, eds. G. Rimanelli and K. J. Atchety (London and New Haven: Yale University Press, 1976), pp. 225–242.

agreement, but the bringing of different and independent viewpoints to bear on a common concern.

It may well be that this ethical virtue of playful conversation, which shapes the *Decameron* and the world of the *brigata*, foreshadows the ideals of "civile conversazione," which is at the same time the distinction and legacy of the Italian Humanists. One is encouraged to stress the link between the two historical periods by the evocation, on this sixth day of the *Decameron*, of the concreteness of the Florentine neighborhoods as the context within which the possibility of a social-esthetic harmony is celebrated.[51]

We cannot, however, fully endorse this idealized picture without risking a falsification of the complexities of this text. For this virtue of language, which in and of itself, all rhetorical treatises tell us, is the foundation of the city, is so contracted, so narrow in scope that one, effectively, confronts how polity turns into politeness, the fragmentation of ethics becomes a question of etiquette, the tensions of the city a matter of civility. These qualities, politeness, etiquette and civility, need not be thought only negatively as degraded ceremonies of social life. However precarious, they are formal acts which organize and express the conventions and practices of the community. Nonetheless, we cannot isolate the idyllic quality of this day without recalling how, both earlier and later in the text, we are told that surface values are deceptive, that the appearance of order may be illusory, that, in short, storytelling and pleasant

---

[51] But the doctrine behind this notion of conversation is Cicero's: "The power of speech in the attainment of propriety is great and its function is twofold: the first is oratory; the second, conversation. Oratory is the kind of discourse to be employed in pleadings in court and speeches in popular assemblies and in the senate; conversation should find its natural place in social gatherings, in informal discussions, and in intercourse with friends; it should also seek admission to dinners. . . . Conversation, then, in which the Socratics are the best models, should have these qualities. It should be easy and not in the least dogmatic; it should have the spice of wit. And the one who engages in conversation should not debar others from participating in it, as if he were entering upon a private monopoly; but, as in other things, so in a general conversation he should think it not unfair for each to have his turn . . ." (*De officiis*, I, 132–134, pp. 135–137).

exchanges may be rhetorical exercises and a mere ornamentation.

To say that playful conversation, like all other virtues, straddles ethics and rhetoric is to make a number of claims for the *Decameron*. The first claim is that in this equivocal position lies the extraordinary lucidity of Boccaccio's art. Unlike the grand designs of visionary poets, who unavoidably end up defeated, and against the untestable, deluded claims of rhetoricians, who make rhetoric the path to undertake in order to edify the state, Boccaccio's vision, rather, brings to mind the Sultan's bride, Scheherazade, in the *Arabian Nights*, who tells tales in order to postpone death and gain time.

A second claim is for Boccaccio's concomitant sense of reality. This position, put forth by Francesco De Sanctis, to be sure still holds, in a variety of sociological formulations, in the scholarship on the *Decameron*.[52] What this position means is that Boccaccio has constructed a world, in the elegant phrasing of Thomas Bergin, ". . . where individuals are motivated by hedonism, self-interest, and an honest respect for the forces of nature and the legitimate claims of human sentiments. Yet, for all that, it is a world that accepts conventional usages, condemns pretentiousness and arrogance, and has nothing against the practice of virtue so long as it doesn't interfere with the pursuit of happiness."[53]

The statement is unimpeachable and it accurately describes the movement from a certain aspect of Boccaccio's ideals of art to the ideals of life—ideals of wit, conviviality and tolerance. This move, which, as I have implied, was powerfully inaugurated by De Sanctis and has also been given currency by critics such as Getto and Muscetta, undoubtedly responds to one strand of Boccaccio's text.[54] As a matter of fact, for all the easy admissions that the meaning of the *Decameron* is yet un-

[52] Cesare De Michelis, "Rassegna Boccacciana-Dieci Anni Di Studi," *Lettere italiane*, 25 (1973), pp. 88–129. See also the remarks in the Introduction.

[53] Thomas G. Bergin, *Boccaccio* (New York: The Viking Press, 1981), p. 336.

[54] Giovanni Getto, *Vita di forme e forme di vita nel Decameron* (Turin: Petrini, 1958), pp. 188–282; see also Muscetta's summary: "Il 'convenevole' è il mo-

clear, critics unanimously accepted the notion that it shows how the pleasures of art and the pressures of living can be brought together.

But this view, however common, is not the whole story for it fails to account for the radical elusiveness that is the distinctive trait, paradoxically, of this most realistic of literary texts. This elusiveness comes from the fact, for instance, that the moral contradictions, which scholars have widely acknowledged, do not depend simply on Boccaccio's awareness that the complications of life are unassimilable to one unified scheme. The contradictions are present within each figure and each figure is always on the point of becoming other than itself. This elusiveness finds its textual embodiment in Boccaccio's fascination for figures—whores, thieves, buffoons, liars, fools—who have not a social but an *imaginative* value. This elusiveness, I will say at the risk of lapsing into the oxymoron of defining it, is the imagination—the thought of utopia, romances, and visionariness which are always deflated by Boccaccio's art, but which, in turn, topple our assumptions about reality, norms, laws, reason, virtues, the stuff that scholarship, from De Sanctis down, has taken to be the boundary of that art. The elusiveness is Boccaccio's irony, the perspective which gives a dark edge to his humor and which brings with it the disclosure that simulations, jests, the turns of the imagination, are not mere interludes in the business of life but the shadow of the play of the world.

This insight into play, as the ludic and the elusive, departs from the containment of play in Aristotle and St. Thomas but recalls, I would like to suggest, Dante's figuration. Dante, whose morality is so remote from the lure of hideous specta-

mento decisivo nell'uso della parola, la proprietà che da generica, fondamental e coronatrice legge dell'*ars dicendi*, diventa legge di recupero e di ricostruzione dell'integrità dell'uomo in quanto totalità eloquente pur nell'ambito della totalità sociale in cui sempre e realisticamente si colloca. Sicchè la novella è la necessaria forma storica di questa totalità conseguibile e appropriabile rapidamente, misura del contrasto tra gli individui ben circoscritto e definito nei particolari interessi e appetiti, nei beni della natura o nei beni della fortuna" (Carlo Muscetta, *Giovanni Boccaccio* [Bari: Laterza, 1972], p. 313).

cles that it often resembles that of the stern Christian apologists, such as Cyprian, Tertullian and St. Augustine, still elaborates in *Paradiso*, if I may allude to work that logically belongs elsewhere, a *theologia ludens* as he envisions the song of the blessed, the "triunfi," the dance of the heavens, and the spectacle of the stars wooing each other in God's vast theater.[55] In the *Decameron* the theology is absent or it is present as the object of laughter, but play is the category through which Boccaccio enjoins us to look at the world and at its suspected but also elusive secrets.

[55] In opposition to the "gioco" of Michael Scott, alluded to earlier in chapter 7, as well as the devils' fun, in *Paradiso* laughter is holy: "Non però qui si pente, ma si ride / non della colpa, ch'a mente non torna, / ma del valor ch'ordinò è provide" (*Paradiso* IX, 103–105). See also the explicit theme of the angelic sports: "Poscia ne' due penultimi tripudi / Principati e Arcangeli si girano; / l'ultimo è tutto d'angelici ludi" (*Paradiso* XXVIII, 124–126). The ramifications of the celestial *gaudium* are so complex that I can give only these few hints in the present context.

INDEX

Library of Congress Cataloging-in-Publication Data

MAZZOTTA, GIUSEPPE, 1942–
THE WORLD AT PLAY IN BOCCACCIO'S DECAMERON.

BIBLIOGRAPHY: P.
INCLUDES INDEX.
I. BOCCACCIO, GIOVANNI, 1313–1375. DECAMERONE.
I. TITLE.
PQ4287.M39 1986   853'.1   85–43299
ISBN 0–691–06677–9
(ALK. PAPER)